THE FUTU

100

—— 改變未來的 **100** 件事　**2023** 年全球百大趨勢 ——

+
WUNDERMAN THOMPSON

A REPORT BY WUNDERMAN THOMPSON INTELLIGENCE

書　　名 / 改變未來的100件事-2023年全球百大趨勢

作　　者 / Wunderman Thompson Intelligence

總 編 輯 / Emma Chiu

編　　輯 / Emily Safian-Demers

撰 稿 人 / Marie Stafford, Chen May Yee, John O'Sullivan,
Sarah Tilley, Carla Calandra, Jamie Hannah Shackleton,
Francesca Lewis

副 編 輯 / Hester Lacey, Katie Myers

設計總監 / Shazia Chaudhry

協作編輯 / Jill Chang 張玫,Rita Cheng 鄭冠瑄,Julie Hsueh 薛
郁翎,Joyce Lu 呂念潔,Raquel Hung 洪任葵,Cassie Chiang 姜
芷萱,Jessica Chien 簡邑儒,Ann Chen 陳嘉安,Joyce Lo 羅雅
菊,Alison Hung 洪藝珊,Cloud Kao 高幫旂,Robin Yang 楊鎮
謙,Easy Tsai 蔡昆莛,Leo Jian 簡重年,Meg Huang 黃馨儀,Ai
Hsiao 蕭嬡,Kevin Huang 黃靖凱,Timothy Yeh 葉則均,Hailey
Lin 林思瑩,Ben Hu 胡維班

翻譯 / Rye Lin 林庭如, Tina Hsieh 謝雨軒

出版者 / 香港商台灣偉門智威有限公司台灣分公司

地址 / 台北市南港區市民大道7段8號13F之五

電話 / (02)3766-1000

傳真 / (02)2788-0260

總經銷 / 時報文化出版企業股份有限公司

電話 / (02)2306-6842

地址 / 桃園市龜山區萬壽路2段351號

書籍編碼 / Z000153

出版日期 / 2023年03月

定價 / NTD 500

ISBN / 9789869899239

+ WUNDERMAN
THOMPSON
A REPORT BY WUNDERMAN THOMPSON INTELLIGENCE

序言

社區、創造力和色彩充滿活力地描繪了 2023 年，
因為去年的無限樂觀情緒轉變為對鼓舞和
玩耍的旺盛需求。

所有跡像都表明，由於經濟不穩定、政治不穩定和環境惡化持續存在，今年將是黯淡和混亂的一年。然而，面對持續的困難，人們決心表現出韌性、創新和快樂。Pantone 為其 2023 年度代表色 Viva Magenta 做出了明智的選擇，抓住了一種活潑的情緒：它是"非常規時間的非常規色調"（第 21 頁）。Joyconomy 今年正在興起，各品牌為所有年齡段的人提供無拘無束的遊戲（玩樂不分年齡，第 95 頁）和模仿扔五彩紙屑感覺的運動課程（快樂健身法，第 192 頁）—請加入我們（揮動雙臂大量）。

過去幾年的壓力強調優化思想和身體以賦予提升的自我能力（至尚真我，第 188 頁）。企業越來越多地以情商領先，並將心理健康作為其品牌使命的優先事項（精神皮膚學，第 124 頁和精神益生菌，第 190 頁）。整體健康方法在所有類別中都很明顯，因為人們希望在每個接觸點積極提高他們的健康，這表明每個品牌都需要成為健康品牌。科技的閃電般的步伐見證了從構建到生活元宇宙的演變。元宇宙正在探索生活的方方面面—從我們的數位身份（第 36 頁）到虛擬家庭的前景（虛擬照護者，第 26 頁），再到構建虛擬家庭（元宇宙宅一起，第 159 頁）。更重要的是，隨著去中心化時代以 Web3 的形式慢慢形成，元宇宙正在打開通往 3.0 未來的大門。邀請社區、創作者和品牌建立一個真正屬於每個人的

民主互聯網，為從所有權（新型態所有權，第 17 頁）到社區參與（加密會員俱樂部，第 166 頁）到零售（共同創作的雙贏模式，第 146 頁）的一切引入新的公式。

此外，人們要求品牌通過將可訪問性和包容性放在首位，利用其影響力改善社會。86% 的全球受訪者認為，為了支持弱勢群體，品牌需要與他們合作，而不僅僅是為他們服務。各種品牌已經在鼓勵多樣化的聲音（力挺多元背景的創作者，第 88 頁），並且越來越多的企業正在將包容性產品引入主流（大眾共融的品牌，第 93 頁）。

準備好迎接 100 個趨勢，這些趨勢提供了色彩、靈感和對即將展開的一年的深刻洞察。

Emma Chiu
偉門智威智庫全球總監
wundermanthompson.com/expertise/intelligence

序言

「新科技賦能」或「持續很久的大事件」都是形成趨勢的原因。今年的「Future 100改變未來的100件事」正是科技與反思的成果。

新冠疫情已持續了三年多，在許多國家都已解封之際，台灣也於2022年十月開放國門，並逐步調整「口罩政策」。回顧過去三年，口罩早已成為人們生活的標準配備，人與人的問候語也從「打疫苗沒？」變成「你中過了嗎？」似乎大家也就習以為常與病毒共存，對於疫情的恐慌也就漸漸消失，慢慢回到生活的正軌。

雖說人們對於疫情不再像過去那麼恐慌，不過疫情確確實實改變了人們的生活與價值信念。因為疫情，追求身心靈的放鬆、在乎工作與生活的平衡儼然成為一股大趨勢，尤其是 GenZ。年輕世代更展開了一股新的風潮，那就是「聚會不喝酒」，他們重視健康與永續。除此，我們也看到只為頂級富豪所推出的「排他性服務」突然暴增。對比服務富豪，也有另外一股「退而不休」，甚至是「不退不休」的趨勢正在成形。為什麼不退休？因為他們希望繼續保持與人、社會的連結跟財務的穩定。

而氣候變遷與環境保護仍然是全球性課題，沒有人可以置身事外。越來越多的人對於氣候變遷的議題感到焦慮，不過「氣候樂觀主義」正在成形，因為年輕世代相信對抗氣候變遷就必須保持樂觀，把焦慮化為行動力。甚至有新創公司主張「把地球設為公司的唯一股東」，因此盈餘全歸地球所用。

俄烏戰爭已延續了一週年，它對於全球的供應鏈與地緣政治的影響不言而喻，不過有旅行業者推出「烏克蘭戰爭旅遊團」，目的在「selling the negative」，讓參加者去體會烏克蘭人的「恐懼」，進而更加珍惜所擁有的美好。

或許現在談「元宇宙」這個詞感覺有點過氣，不過它的應用層面越來越廣。例如永續元宇宙、元宇宙提款機、元交通等創新思維與服務，加上各種沈浸式的科技，讓虛擬與現實的界線越來越模糊。

我想，「新科技賦能」或「持續很久的大事件」都是形成趨勢的原因，因為它影響著人們的生活與價值觀，進而形成趨勢浪潮。而這次 2023 年「Future 100 改變未來的 100 件事」的發行，正是科技與反思的成果。不過，不管環境有多挑戰，我們都可以用更樂觀的態度來擁抱未來！

鄧博文
台灣偉門智威 執行長

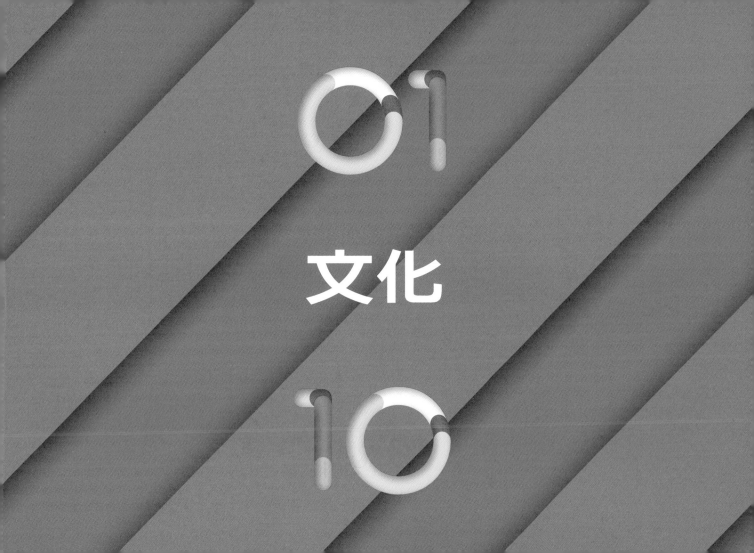

01
10

文化

01

新現實

元宇宙正在進化中。

元宇宙概念的發展，影響我們對於新興科技的想像，使其成為日常生活中無處不在、不可或缺的一部分，更模糊了虛實之間的界線，形塑出一個「新現實」。

DoorLabs 公司運用科技提升虛擬世界的易用性，探索如何利用「元宇宙裡的全新沉浸式科技，照顧並協助有特殊需求的人們，使其未來不再受限」，共同創辦人 Kunho Kim 向偉門智威智庫（Wunderman Thompson Intelligence）說道。

社會思辨設計師暨總監 Liam Young 則透過虛擬實境（VR）推廣社會運動。他向偉門智威智庫表示：「虛擬實境使我們從被動的觀眾轉為主動的公民。作為一個沉浸式世界的公民，和只能呆望螢幕的被動觀眾截然不同。」

蘋果公司執行長提姆・庫克（Tim Cook）預測擴增實境（AR）將成為人們日常生活不可或缺的一部分。庫克向荷蘭雜誌《Bright》表示：「未來回首，你會納悶現在的自己如何度過沒有擴增實境的生活。就像今天我們會納悶，我們這些過去沒有網路可用的人是怎麼長大的？擴增實境是足以改變一切、影響深遠的科技。」

為了迎接沉浸式科技時代的全面到來，科技巨頭相繼投入鉅額資金開發擴增實境與虛擬實境。根據《商業內幕》報導，Meta 於 2019 年至 2022 年 9 月 30 日間，已挹注 360 億美元在其元宇宙及虛擬實境部門 Reality Labs 當中。創投公司 Loup Funds 的分析師 Gene Munster 估計谷歌研發部門投資於擴增實境的資金約有 390 億美元。社交媒體公司 Snap 則全心投入擴增實境，在 2022 年第三季的財務報告中將投資擴增實境技術列為三大首要策略之一。

值得關注的原因：
數位時代的下個階段將會出現多元的沉浸式科技，使虛擬與現實世界的界線更加模糊，引領新現實的誕生。

O2

創作者社群

下一個數位社群世代將以創造力為核心。

創作者社群 Pools 為創作者及品牌提供建立自有加密貨幣社群的工具。「Pools 顛覆了我們看待和評價創作者的方式。」投資 Pools 的超模 Coco Rocha 向《Paper》雜誌表示。在 2022 年 10 月，該公司又推出「創作者世界」（Creator Worlds）做為創作者登陸數位生態系的速成工具。

2022 年 6 月，Pools 與 YSL 彩妝（YSL Beauté）合作，推出音樂人 Agathe Mougin 和 Kittens 的創作者代幣。擁有代幣的使用者能進入各個藝術家的 Pools 社群，解鎖客製內容和體驗、VIP 活動票券以及收聽藝術家的 Podcast 頻道，甚至享有進入 YSL 彩妝 Web3 平台的特權。

「好萊塢、華爾街和矽谷，這些傳統具有影響力的聚落較以往更加同質化，也造就以創作者和受眾為中心的新興市場。」Pools 將社交代幣視為「創作者和粉絲直接互動的新管道，可以透過現實生活與元宇宙中的體驗、產品、活動等媒介互動。」

Mona 是另一個孕育創作者社群的平台。2022 年 6 月，Mona 募資近 1,500 萬美元為創作者建立元宇宙平台，其執行長 Justin Melillo 向科技部落格 GamesBeat 說道：「Mona 是一群創作者為其他創作者建立的 Web3 元宇宙，是一個打造元宇宙世界的平台以及社群。」Melillo 建立 Mona 的目標是希望「把焦點放在創作者上，使元宇宙成為創作者成長茁壯的社交網絡。」2022 年 7 月，該平台成為 The Row 舉辦發表會的線上場地，The Row 是會員制的虛擬社群，以知名創作者設計的建築為其特色。

Adobe 也擴展了元宇宙的創造力。在 2022 年 10 月的 Adobe Max 大會中，該公司宣布其應用程式 Creative Cloud 將推出新的協作功能及人工智慧工具。Adobe 數位媒體事業總裁 David Wadhwani 表示：「我們持續提升協作功能，因為越來越多創作仰賴團隊合作，包含和其他創作者協作、或請客戶提供回饋等。」

值得關注的原因：

「我們將創作者和開發者視為元宇宙的支柱」，Melillo 表示。隨著數位參與從被動消費轉為主動創造（想要深入了解此轉變，請參考我們的報告《元宇宙創造新現實》，原文為 New Realities:Into the Metaverse and Beyond），品牌的角色也必須調整。創造力正在成為未來數位時代的身份象徵，而品牌也正在改變產品策略，以成為連結消費者與創作者之間的橋樑

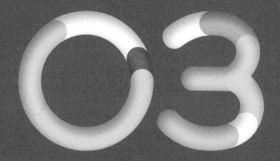

03

野化生態系

我們有可能讓自己的身心「重新野化」嗎？

我們有可能讓自己的思維及行為重新恢復荒野狀態嗎？2022 年 5 月《BBC》提出了這個問題，Lindsay Baker 在該報的專文中寫道：「我們能在大自然中找到驚喜與意義，不只是因為人類與自然本身有所連結，更是因為大自然帶給我們希望與再生。」

近期，遊戲玩家對提倡環保永續的電玩遊戲趨之若鶩。《源起重生》（Terra Nil）這款於 2023 年初推出的遊戲，引領玩家重建受氣候危機重創的生態系。在這款遊戲中，玩家重建城市的方式是要努力復育大自然，而非掠奪自然資源。這款遊戲的概念令人想起另一款遊戲《模擬城市》（SimCity）中城市的發展模式，但是翻轉其中的優先順序，將自然環境擺在高樓大廈與城市建設之前。

根據偉門智威智庫《元宇宙創造新現實》的報導，全球有 81% 的消費者會透過電玩消遣放鬆。在玩家透過螢幕和遊戲主機消除身心疲勞的同時，他們也更傾向在下班後選擇重新野化自然的休閒娛樂。

2022 年 5 月，戶外用品品牌 LL Bean 鼓勵顧客以生態療法取代逛街購物，不但將品牌的 Instagram 頁面換成「釣魚去（gone fishing）」的設計，更將社群媒體連結導向官網，在網頁中傳遞希望顧客及粉絲走進自然、放鬆身心的訊息。

值得關注的原因：
有永續發展意識的消費者開始關注擁抱自然的品牌，和他們一起邁向回歸自然與永續發展的新時代，同時重新省視自身習慣及生活，將心理健康及永續生活列為優先考量。

Timberborn game featuring "lumberpunk beavers," by Discord
member Cynical Entity, courtesy of Twitter

我們有可能
讓自己的思維及行為
重新恢復
荒野狀態嗎？

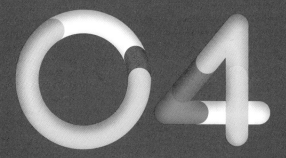

新型態所有權

新型態的數位架構催生出全新的所有權概念。

在即將來臨的 Web3 時代，使用者不僅能成為數位體驗的共同創作者，更能共同持有體驗的所有權。

在過去，如果使用者創作了某個圖像發布在 Instagram，該資產的所有權會歸屬於 Instagram。但像 Niche 這樣的平台則將掌控權交還給使用者。在該平台中，「會員就是所有權人。」Niche 的共同創辦人暨執行長 Chris Gulczynski 表示。

「傳統的社群媒體由單一企業掌控一切，並將所有資料鎖在伺服器內。」Niche 的共同創辦人兼技術長 Zaven Nahapetyan 告訴偉門智威智庫。「而去中心化的社群媒體平台，則是將資料交還給大眾，讓人們擁有自身資料的所有權，也能打包自己的資料。」

給予掌控權的做法也增加了 Niche 使用者的附加價值。Nahapetyan 表示，這讓人們「成為像公司股東一樣的所有權人。當他們的社群越引人注目、越獨一無二、得到越多媒體版面，他們手中所有權的價值也越高。」

Flyfish Club 正在實驗以非同質化代幣（NFT）為基礎的所有權概念。這間會員制餐廳預計於 2023 年開幕，並以 NFT 作為會員卡，會員可出借自己的 NFT 讓承租人獲得臨時會員資格。

"他們獲得所有權
及相關門路，
而非僅是租用
一項社交體驗"

David Rodolitz，
Flyfish Club的創辦人暨執行長

「NFT 已經改變了『會員權益』的本質。他們獲得所有權及相關資格，而非只是租用一項社交體驗。」Flyfish Club 的創辦人暨執行長 David Rodolitz 向偉門智威智庫說道。

NFT 作為一種所有權的數位憑證，也改變了使用者與數位媒體互動的方式。如同 Artifact Labs 的創辦人兼執行長劉可瑞（Gary Liu）對偉門智威智庫所說：「第一、二代網路（Web1、Web2）破壞了新聞業的商業模式，因為消息一旦發布在網路上，新聞載體本身便失去價值。然而，NFT 的出現改變了這項法則，讓數位媒體本身具有價值，造就新型的商業模式及更直接的互動關係。」

值得關注的原因：
人們的網路使用習慣正在發生重大轉變。去中心化讓數位平台變得更大眾化，打開通往新型態所有權的大門，提供品牌及消費者一種和數位產品、服務及內容互動的全新方式。

氣候樂觀主義

Z世代對氣候議題正逐漸從焦慮轉為樂觀。

根 據 2021 年 偉 門 智 威 智 庫 的《 再 生 崛 起 : 永 續 未 來 》
（Regeneration Rising: Sustainability Futures）報 告 中，有
66% 的 問 卷 受 訪 者 對 氣 候 變 遷 感 到 焦 慮，擔 心 會 影 響 到 他 們 的
生 活，而 Z 世 代 中 比 例 更 提 升 至 72%。為 了 緩 解 焦 慮 及 氣 候 變 遷
所 帶 來 的 影 響，Z 世 代 已 經 展 開 行 動。

偉 門 智 威 智 庫 收 集 的 另 一 份 資 料 顯 示，有 85% 的 受 訪 者 願 意 重
新 省 視 自 身 的 生 活 與 消 費 方 式，以 因 應 當 前 的 氣 候 變 遷 危 機，而
70% 的 人 更 願 意 為 此 作 出 大 幅 度 的 改 變。

《衛 報》也 針 對 許 多 Z 世 代 青 年 做 出 系 列 報 導。他 們 為 環 保 竭 盡
心 力，以 正 向 的 態 度 一 步 步 改 善 生 活 環 境。

2022 年 7 月，環 保 人 士 Zahra Biabani 創 立 了 第 一 個 以 永 續 時 尚
為 理 念 的 租 借 平 台 In the Loop，讓 像 她 一 樣 的 Z 世 代 能 有 更 多 機
會 接 觸 提 倡 永 續 的 品 牌。當 時 23 歲 的 她 在 訪 談 中 向《衛 報》表 示：
「氣 候 樂 觀 主 義 全 面 提 升 了 為 氣 候 問 題 尋 找 解 方 的 動 能，而 這 是
我 們 迫 切 需 要 面 對 的 挑 戰。」另 一 位 同 為 23 歲 的 受 訪 者 Thomas
Lawrence 則 創 辦 了 以 倫 理 價 值 為 本 的 銷 售 平 台 Good People
Inc，希 望 提 供 大 眾 在 各 大 網 路 零 售 平 台 之 外 的 另 一 種 選 擇。

在 美 國 路 易 斯 安 那 州，Franziska Trautmann 創 立 了 該 州 唯 一 的
玻 璃 回 收 工 廠 Glass Half Full，將 回 收 的 玻 璃 加 工 製 成 砂，修 復
路 易 斯 安 那 州 被 侵 蝕 的 海 岸 線。在 佛 羅 里 達，Caulin Donaldson
每 天 在 抖 音 平 台 上 發 布 淨 灘 照，截 至 2022 年 11 月，已 經 吸 引 近
160 萬 人 追 蹤。

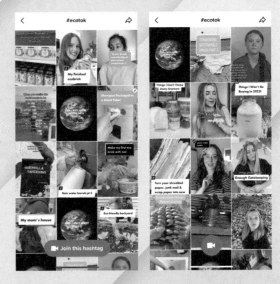

Caulin Donaldson 的 正 向 樂 觀 及 環 保 精 神 極 具 感 染 力，這 也 成
為 社 群 平 台 上 的 熱 門 趨 勢。至 2022 年 11 月 底，代 表 氣 候 變 遷
的 標 籤 #climatechange 觀 看 人 次 已 達 37 億、代 表 環 保 的 標 籤
#eco 有 21 億、代 表 抖 音 環 保 社 群 的 標 籤 #ecotok 則 有 近 7.74
億 的 觀 看 數。

值 得 關 注 的 原 因：
Z 世 代 正 採 取 有 效 行 動，讓 他 們 在 面 對 氣 候 變 遷 時 從 焦 慮 轉 為 正
向 思 考。因 應 消 費 者 的 氣 候 樂 觀 主 義，品 牌 也 需 要 在 環 境 議 題 上
改 採 正 向 積 極、鼓 勵 人 心 的 論 調。

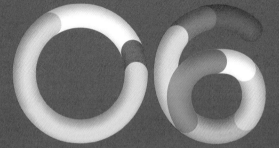

表現主義大進擊

2023是充滿朝氣、活力與能量的一年，
適合展現自我、賦予自己更多力量。

Pantone 宣布 2023 年度代表色為萬歲洋紅（Viva Magenta），這是一個大膽、充滿活力的顏色，該公司稱其為「在新世代打破傳統的色調」。當全球籠罩於經濟衰退、嚴重通膨，對氣候環境充滿不確定之際，Pantone 引領我們訴諸內心，找到力量、活力與希望。「洋紅色象徵勇敢無畏且樂觀正向，同時也是大膽、充滿智慧與兼容多元的顏色。」Pantone 執行董事 Leatrice Eiseman 表示。

美國油漆商班傑明摩爾（Benjamin Moore）選出的 2023 年度代表色──覆盆子紅（Raspberry Blush），也傳達相同氛圍。「過去我們熱愛低調柔和的色彩，但現在我們準備好要大膽一點，也渴望嘗試飽和度高的色調。」班傑明摩爾的色彩行銷暨研發總監 Andrea Magno 如此告訴《建築文摘》（Architectural Digest）。覆盆子紅生氣蓬勃的色調如同一份高調的宣告，散發出積極正向的訊息。Magno 認為：「它傳達了快樂的氛圍，我認為我們非常需要。」

各大奢華時尚品牌亦為伸展台添上鮮明色彩。根據《女裝日報》（WWD）的報導，巴黎時裝週「明亮大膽的用色散發著樂觀主義的氣息。」而尚 - 保羅 . 高堤耶（Jean Paul Gaultier）2022/2023 的秋冬系列則主打單一色調，以粉紅、紅色、藍色等大膽的色彩驚艷伸展台，展現「饒富趣味、頑皮搗蛋」的活潑氛圍，《女裝日報》的時裝編輯 Miles Socha 在其系列評論中如此寫道。

范倫鐵諾（Valentino）的 2022/2023 秋冬高級訂製系列也採用活潑的色彩，以皇家藍、螢光綠及亮麗橘等「彩虹色調」搭配大膽剪裁，其創意總監 Pierpaolo Piccioli 表示：「美，是堅忍不拔，而非逃避現實。」

值得關注的原因：
接下來的一年，會有股不受拘束、具影響力且強而有力的能量注入生活，在充滿不確定的時代中，賦予我們希望、喜悅與快樂。

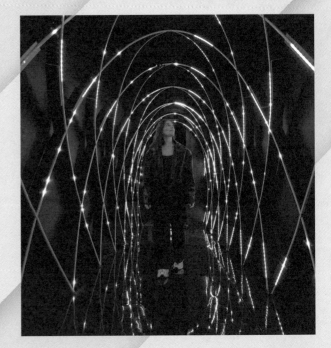

Pantone Color of the Year 2023, Viva Magenta. Courtesy of Huge

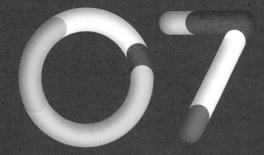

07

職人浪潮

對日常生活的不滿成為職人經濟復興的推力。

隨著工業經濟崩塌，專家預測一波新型經濟的興起——職人經濟。在 2022 年 7 月出版的《職人回歸》（Return of the Artisan）書中，人類學家 Grant McCracken 描繪了美國職人運動從不受注目到成為潮流的興起過程。受到後疫情時代經濟不景氣的影響，心灰意冷的僱員們捨棄朝九晚五的工作，投身起司製造、烘焙、珠寶設計等多元的手工藝領域。

職人生活賦予人們自主權及自由，而像 Etsy 這樣的設計商品販售平台也讓手工藝從副業到正職的接軌容易許多。McCracken 在《衛報》的訪談中預估，美國每三份新工作中就有兩份是由職人運動帶動的相關工作。

美國每三份新工作中
就有兩份是由職人運動
帶動的相關工作

《Vogue》在 2022 年 9 月的一篇文章中也指出，在疫情及疫後
階段出現了相當多由新手創作者成立的新興時尚品牌，如前行銷
專家 Delsy Gouw 便將對鉤針編織的興趣發展成全職事業，成
立品牌 Memorial Day。她向偉門智威智庫表示：「我喜歡這種工
作帶來的自由，喜歡在漫步街頭或踏入公園時靈感乍現，這是過
去在辦公室上班時做不到的事。」

而這波風潮並不侷限於美國。2022 年 7 月《雪梨晨鋒報》（The
Sydney Morning Herald）報導澳洲近期正出現一股工藝課程
的風潮，內容從製作刀具到陶作應有盡有。2021 年 11 月，Metro
Dynamics 為亞馬遜旗下平台 Amazon Handmade 所做的報告
中更顯示，截至 2020 年，手工藝相關事業已為英國經濟貢獻 48
億英鎊（58 億美元）。Amazon Handmade 當然也察覺到大眾
對手工藝的興趣逐漸提升的趨勢，因此正著手拍攝一系列影片，
紀錄手工藝賣家的商品製作過程。

值得關注的原因：
2 年前的微型創業家風潮開始進化成新型職人經濟，進而重新定
義工作與消費方式。

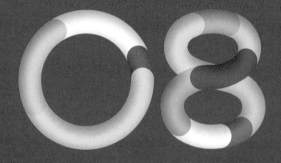

08
虛擬照護者

數位照護者對虛擬陪伴的需求
帶動數位照護平台的興起。

英國人工智慧（AI）專家 Catriona Campbell 預測元宇宙在 50
年內會出現虛擬孩童。她相信在 1990 年代熱衷於養電子雞的這
代消費者，會擁抱這類虛擬新生兒的科技，並預測未來這些虛擬
孩童將會長得像他們的「家長」，也能在數位居住環境中玩耍、互
動。在這個年輕人開始猶豫是否要成家立業的年代，虛擬兒童可
能會吸引他們成為數位照護者。

由 Tiny Rebel Games 創立的寵宇宙網路（Petaverse Network）
將在 2023 年初於以太坊推出他們第一代寵物貓。透過平台遊戲
化的 NFT 體驗和寵物建立情感，讓數位飼養關係具備真正的所
有權基礎。

3D 數位寵物狗研發公司 The Digital Pets Company 發行了由
AI 驅動的寵物狗 NFT，對現代愛好寵物的數位玩家而言，這可謂
寵物遊戲《任天狗狗》（Nintendogs）的進化版。飼主能透過多
元管道和他們的寵物狗互動、玩耍並加以照顧，包括虛擬實境
世界、混合與擴增實境平台，以及行動裝置及網頁版瀏覽器。

值得關注的原因：
在元宇宙及 Web3 的時代，人們開始組成數位家庭，「重組家庭」
一詞也被賦予全新意義。

Above: The Petaverse Network, courtesy of Twitter
Right: The Petaverse Network (both images)

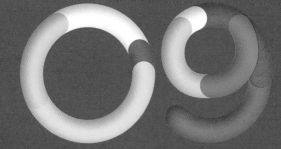

原住民工法與
自然共生

原住民工法為管理自然環境提供了再生之道。

+WUNDERMAN THOMPSON　Symbiocene, Julia Watson, Smith Mordak and Buro Happold, Mark Allan photography, Our Time on Earth 2022, Barbican Centre

原住民發展超過千年的工法能加強我們面對氣候變遷的因應能力，讓我們與自然共生，而非與之對抗。設計師與工程師正在重新評估將原住民工法應用於當前急迫議題的可能，包含洪旱災害管理、永續糧食生產模式、森林大火及碳封存技術等。

《共生》（The Symbiocene）一作為 2022 年倫敦巴比肯博物館（Barbican Museum）特展「我們在地球的日子」（Our Time on Earth）中展出的多媒體裝置作品。該作品帶領我們想像 2040 年的城市環境，以及我們運用原住民知識與科技後的未來景象。《共生》除了有多位原住民社群的代表投入創作，更和設計師 Julia Watson、工程公司 Buro Happold 的永續發展與物理總監 Smith Mordak 共同協力完成。

原住民社群展現了與自然共生的理念。印度東北部的山區部落卡西（Khasi）利用橡膠樹根搭建樹橋，藉此抵擋季風豪雨，並因此聞名；伊拉克南部的馬丹人（Ma'dan）則居住在漂浮於水上的茅屋村落中，與當地自然環境共存，為未來人類的水上發展提供實例。

能照護自然環境的再生創作也成為設計師日漸關注的焦點。2022 年 9 月在斯洛維尼亞首都盧布爾雅那（Ljubljana）舉辦的第 27 屆「斯洛維尼亞設計雙年展」（Bio 27），便以「超級常民」（Super Vernaculars）為題，檢視在面臨氣候變遷及生物多樣性議題的今日，如何透過回歸常民傳統及價值觀來因應；在 2023 年的威尼斯雙年展中，英國館將呈現離散族群的工藝文化在「非提取式」設計中扮演的角色；倫敦的中央聖馬丁藝術與設計學院（Central Saint Martins）也廣邀學子報讀第一屆再生設計碩士課程。

設計師 Julia Watson 在其 2019 年出版的書籍《原民智慧再進化》（Lo-Tek:Design by Radical Indigenism）中寫道：「設計師應致力於探索原住民哲學以重建新的知識體系，建立新的思考和對話，藉此促進永續發展及因應氣候變遷。」

值得關注的原因：

在地球面臨危機的此刻，原住民的長才迅速受到矚目。根據世界銀行的調查，原住民保護了現存 80% 的生物。借鏡他們的生活方式、工藝及技術，我們便能學習與大自然共生，創造永續再生的世代。

THE FUTURE 100 · 30

WUNDERMAN
THOMPSON

Lo-Tek: Design by Radical Indigenism by Julia Watson.
Living root bridge, India © Amos Chapple

10

新興戀愛型態

Z世代正重新定義戀愛關係的規則。

年輕世代有意地追尋短暫的伴侶關係，擁抱在「朋友」及「友達以上」的搖擺狀態。

《BBC》在 2022 年 9 月的專題報導中指出 Z 世代傾向擁抱感情中的灰色地帶，追尋隨性的交友關係及其伴隨的類承諾。密西根大學研究性別以及專攻這種「新興戀愛型態」的社會學教授 Elizabeth Armstrong 告訴《BBC》：「這種戀愛型態確實能解決人們對性、親密關係及陪伴的某種需求，且無須維持長期的關係。」

這種新興的戀愛方式也在社群媒體上掀起熱議。至 2022 年 11 月，抖音上標籤「現代戀情」（#situationship）的影片已累計超過 11 億觀看人次，而該名詞也出現在知名實境秀《戀愛島：英國篇》（Love Island UK）以及瑞典歌手 Snoh Aalegra 的歌曲〈現代戀情〉（Situationship）中。

《Vice》對戀愛顧問 Ben Goresky 及其身為伴侶諮商師的妻子 Sheleana Aiyana 進行專訪，並在訪談報導中揭露了這些關係之所以可行的要素。Goresky 表示：「你們必須非常清楚地傳達各自的需求，設定互動的規範及準則。」Aiyana 補充道：「不論有無承諾，溝通都很重要。」

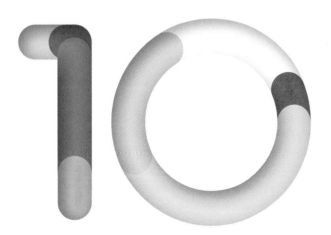

來自倫敦、27 歲的卡米向偉門智威智庫分享他對狀態戀情的定義。「友情和愛情的邊界是易變的。我認為多數人所謂的新興戀情最多只是朋友和炮友之間的模糊地帶。」他接著解釋為何這種關係在近年如此受歡迎：「現在的世界充滿不確定性，不論是自然環境或是政治情勢都是如此。在不確定未來是否安穩的情況下，你就比較不會走進傳統、專一的情感關係。」

值得關注的原因：
對年輕世代想約會的人而言，新興戀情是以坦誠溝通及彼此接納為基礎的正當關係。Z 世代勇於以健康的方式擁抱模糊地帶、以開放的心胸面對不斷變化的戀愛關係。

在不確定未來
是否安穩的情況下，
你就比較不會走進
傳統、專一的
情感關係。

Cami，gen Zer

科技&元宇宙

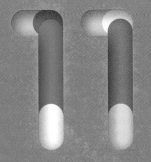

無障礙科技

企業開始重新打造數位環境，
以提高其無障礙性。

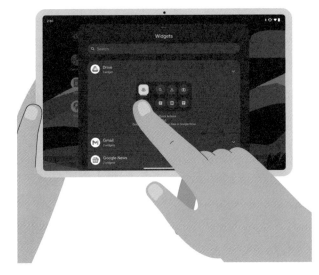

以無障礙與包容性設計不僅是現今發展趨勢，且還涵蓋了龐大的商機，在科技界尤為如此。據估計全球有超過 10 億名身心障礙人士，網路使用人口也超過 50 億人，這代表品牌若改進升級其裝置、平台與體驗的無障礙性將能享有龐大的商機。一如偉門智威全球共融設計總監 Josh Loebner 對偉門智威智庫所說：「包容性設計是比較優異的設計，且對身障人士或非身障人士來說，這些技術面的考量都有機會發揮絕佳功效。」

科技巨頭早已投入其中。2022 年 9 月，推特公告他們已全面推出新的替代文字工具，可幫助使用報讀軟體的人士盡情體驗平台上的圖像內容。Geogle 也在安卓裝置上推出大尺寸的小工具，藉此改善視力受損用戶的使用體驗。Instagram 將無障礙功能設為標準功能，自 2022 年 3 月起已開始根據影片內容自動生成說明文字，現在這也成為創作者介面的預設功能。

創新裝置亦對形塑無障礙的體驗有所助益，例如軟體公司 XRAI Glass 與製造商 Nreal 合作生產擴增實境眼鏡，並以語音辨識技術將語音訊息轉成文字來啟用產品。這款概念眼鏡使用擴增實境技術，即時將字幕投影在佩戴者的視線範圍中，讓聽障或者聽力受損的人士可以理解並參與對話。該產品以 Nreal 現有的設計為基礎，透過連接智慧型手機來實現語音輸入功能。

值得關注的原因：
無障礙設計不只存在於實體世界，在設計數位體驗或數位環境時，品牌也須思考如何以最佳做法來服務需求各異的觀眾。正如 Loebner 所言：「無障礙輔助科技能對邊緣族群伸出友善的雙手，邀請他們進入新的環境、社群和體驗並沈浸其中。」

12

數位身份

人們開始投射更多自我意志於虛擬國度之中。

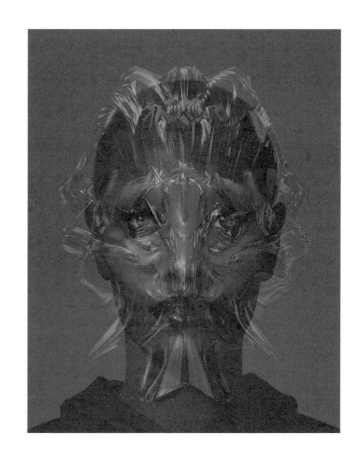

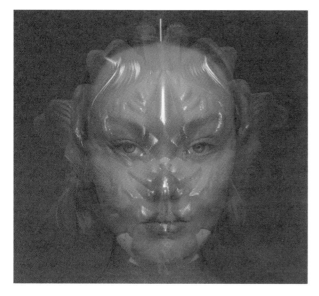

在元宇宙開始成形之際，使用者對他們的虛擬身份有何構想？根據偉門智威智庫的《元宇宙 - 創造新現實》報告顯示，在熟悉元宇宙概念的美國、英國及中國受訪人士當中，有 76% 的人希望他們的虛擬化身能彰顯他們在真實世界或線下世界無法展現出的獨特性格，51% 的人則覺得他們在元宇宙或數位世界當中更能做自己。

Liam Young 是社會思辨創造者，也是城市未來智庫 Tomorrows Thoughts Today 的共同創辦人，他預言未來線上和線下生活之間的差異將不復存在。他告訴偉門智威智庫：「我們使用『數位』、『實體』這樣的字眼，但我覺得這些詞彙都過時了。我們的生活在某種程度上都由數位世界延伸而出，我們在螢幕上看到的一切也對我們實際的生活有非常大的影響。若要說數位或實體世界能獨立存在，這種說法很有問題。」

身份設計師暨未來概念美妝師 Alex Box 同意上列說法，她的工作重點是要發揮創意，思考我們如何傳達自己的身份，並探索科技如何提升自我表達。「個人身份會橫跨實體與數位兩個世界，我將身份設計看作是元宇宙裡溝通、演繹多重自我的下一個重要步驟。」她對偉門智威智庫如此說道。

「我們在自己專屬的個人元宇宙裡，已經以多重身份生活很久了，在『社群媒體自我』、『職場自我』、『居家自我』、『專注當下的自我』等多重身份之間自由跑跳與穿梭。在我們進入 Web3 之際，想像未來身份的其中一種方式就是讓這些多重的自我獲得一種實體特性、面貌或元素，例如透過人工智慧的學習模式來自動生成一種屬於情緒或思考的『材質』。」

值得關注的原因：
在數位生活逐漸成熟之際，人們開始更深切地思考如何在虛擬世界當中保留或轉譯自己的身份特質。接下來表達身份的方式會越來越細緻，且能同時存在於實體與虛擬世界之中。

13

真實儀式

新一代的社群媒體開始將互動變成一種簽到儀式，
讓用戶得以細細品味生活。

近年來，社群媒體的運作都仰賴強大而精細的演算法，以增強黏著度的設計要求用戶要持續開啟、互動，但新一代的應用程式正在挑戰這種隨時都得上線的演算法，並轉而聚焦使用頻率降低但更能感受到正向回饋的程式設計。

這股新潮流由法國新創 BeReal 帶起，是 2022 年 8 月在美國、英國、澳洲的蘋果應用程式商店中，下載次數排行第一的社群軟體。BeReal 和多數社群媒體無止盡向下滑的設計理念不同，它的設計核心追尋簡單、真實的生活習慣，每天在某個隨機的時間點中，所有用戶都會收到上傳一組照片的要求，這組照片會由對外鏡頭與自拍鏡頭在那個當下所拍攝的兩張照片所組成。程式中沒有濾鏡，所以使用者分享的都是他們自己和周遭環境在當下最真實的樣貌，且只有他們的好友能看到這些照片。

許多既有的社群媒體平台都對 BeReal 的成功做出回應，他們的做法就是抄襲這項功能。抖音旗下的 TikTok Now 鼓勵用戶在未定的時間點內即時分享短片或照片，而據說 Instagram 內部也在測試類似的功能，並命名為「2 分鐘挑戰」（Candid Challenges）。相當成功的每日字謎遊戲 Wordle 和只允許單身用戶一週使用一天的交友軟體 Thursday，兩者也都是採取類似的邏輯思維。這些應用程式限制用戶的使用時間，而非大量佔據用戶的生活，這種使用模式讓用戶抱持更多期待，這也成為他們生活中有趣的日常儀式，讓他們能以更真實的方式和他人互動。

值得關注的原因：
追求真實的風潮與限制使用方式的應用程式崛起並更加進化，許多應用程式紛紛鼓勵用戶將每天的生活變成一種儀式。

14

良善元宇宙

品牌利用元宇宙來提升全球人道行動的規模。

元宇宙裡的數位消費提升了世界各地人道行動的支援力度。

人道組織「比特幣建造基金會」（Built With Bitcoin Foundation）將他們從 Built With NFT 計畫中獲得的所有利潤都投入非洲、亞洲、拉丁美洲的人道行動中，為接受其贊助的社群提供乾淨水源、建造學校、永續農耕及人道支援。該基金會以比特幣為運作基礎，其 NFT 作品來自受其贊助的社群，由當地的學生創作而成，並在比特幣生態系的 STXNFT 市場中完成鑄造。STXNFT 的創辦人 Jamil Dhanani 說道：「比特幣已經成為一股良善的力量，把經濟自由的概念帶給全球幾十億人。像是 Built With NFT 這樣的計畫就完美展示了這個理念，它不追求熱潮，而是期許能實現有意義的目標。」

品牌的數位商品不再只以娛樂為考量，現在也對實體世界有所助益。

2022 年 4 月，Epic Games 和 Xbox 宣布他們籌集了 1.44 億美元要支持烏克蘭的人道救援行動。Epic Games 在 3 月時承諾會捐出自公告日至 4 月 3 日前的所有遊戲內課金收益，而 Xbox 也採行類似做法，表示他們會捐出玩家在《要塞英雄》（Fortnite）這款遊戲中購買寶物時所支付的手續費。Epic Games 表示該筆款項會「捐贈給慈善團體『直接救濟』（Direct Relief）、聯合國兒童基金會、聯合國世界糧食計劃署、聯合國難民署與『世界中央廚房』（World Central Kitchen），支援他們的人道救濟行動，藉此幫助受烏克蘭戰爭影響的族群。」

烏克蘭也自行在推特上販售 NFT 作品，藉此為軍隊與居民籌募資金，「元歷史：戰爭博物館」（the Meta History: Museum of War）系列作品中，最開始的新作與攝影創作數量有 54 件，整個系列也記錄了俄羅斯入侵的事件經過。

值得關注的原因：
品牌的數位商品不再只以娛樂為考量，現在也對實體世界有所助益。企業若善加利用元宇宙彈性、快速、有國際號召力的特色，則可輕鬆地資助或支持社會公益，善用這種潛力即能讓元宇宙成為一股良善的社會力量。

品牌開始利用增加互動的工具來提升觀影體驗。

迪士尼的第一部擴增實境短片《記得》（暫譯自 Remembering）已於 2022 年 9 月上線，觀眾可以利用自己的 iOS 裝置掃描電影中的代碼，藉此獲得專為小螢幕設計的延伸體驗。迪士尼對科技媒體《TechCrunch》表示，這是第一個可以直接連結 Disney+ 平台內容的擴增實境應用程式，只要舒服地待在家中，就可以測試擴增實境提升觀影體驗與強化影像敘事的能力。

迪士尼的擴增實境手遊「英雄的漫威世界」（暫譯自 Marvel World of Heroes）將於 2023 年推出，玩家可以打造自己的超級英雄來打擊壞人，也可以在各自的裝置上和朋友組隊打怪。遊戲中會顯示每個玩家所在的實際環境與設置，就像「寶可夢 Go」的遊戲設定一樣。

在 2022 年 9 月高盛集團的會議上，美商藝電（Electronic Arts）執行長 Andrew Wilson 表示該公司計劃「投入更多心力與資金來打造內容」，並說藝電擁有「非常非常獨特與特別的機會來引領娛樂產業的未來」。由玩家所創造的內容佔了兩成，而他也對這些內容展現高度的信心，說有五成的玩家有使用到這些內容。

去年有新的實境節目上架到這些新型觀影平台上，那就是由動畫工作室 Invisible Universe 打造的作品《真實元宇宙》（The R3al Metaverse），裡面集結多個 NFT 角色，包含無聊猿遊艇俱樂部（Bored Ape Yacht Club）、Doodles、World of Women 和 Cool Cat 等。節目中的角色會突然現身於實體世界，粉絲可以與這些設有台詞的角色互動，讓這些角色帶領他們經歷劇情，並

15

擴增娛樂

擴增實境技術加速催生出全新的娛樂方程式。

得以藉此塑造實境秀的內容。觀眾只要擁有 NFT 製作人通行證（NFT Producer Pass），就能參與節目內容的製作，持有上述角色的 NFT 藏家也有機會以自己收藏的角色樣貌參與節目。

值得關注的原因：
擴增實境技術改變了玩家過往被動參與娛樂的模式，讓觀賞體驗多了一層互動的成分。

好社群 好心情

社群媒體動態牆開始變成振奮人心的場域。

應用程式設計師正在打造新的平台來提升正向思維。

在免費下載的應用程式排行中，蟬聯 2022 年數週下載冠軍的 Gas，是款關於極致讚美的應用程式。用戶須先完成指定的選擇題，其選項都是正向的內容，接著程式會將他們導引至讚美同學或同儕的頁面。這款應用程式以青少年為目標客群，要求用戶輸入其學校名稱，並發表讚許他人的言論，同時鼓勵用戶持續互相讚賞，創造樂觀正向、和樂融融的應用程式氛圍。

應用程式 Niche 則翻新社群媒體的概念，其內容不以用戶為導向，而是會歸屬於創作者所有。這款去中心化的 Web3 應用程式裡沒有用戶，只有會員。社群意識會因會員間共同的興趣及真誠的互動而提升，因為這裡的會員追求的不是按讚數或線上人氣，而是因為貼出正向、彼此有興趣的內容，而獲得的成就感。

Niche 的共同創辦人暨執行長 Christopher Gulczynski 告訴偉門智威智庫：「我們觀察到社群媒體規模越來越小、彼此關係越來越緊密，用戶會因共同的興趣、背景、身份而聚在一起。」另一位共同創辦人兼技術長 Zaven Nahapetyan 則談到社群媒體的未來，認為它們將會和線下的人際互動一樣，具有選擇權、掌控度和自主權。就像在現實生活中大家通常不會去看自己不想看的東西，所以 Niche 讓用戶可以和對自己的興趣發展有幫助的人多加互動。

值得關注的原因：
消費者開始在網路上追求正向互動模式和情感支持。新興社群媒體平台善用使用者心中對改變的渴望，轉而主打振奮人心的正向內容。

WUNDERMAN
THOMPSON

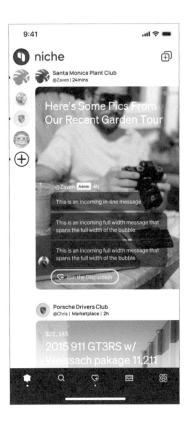

新興社群媒體平台
主打振奮人心的
正向內容。

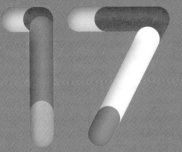

永續元宇宙

元宇宙的永續行動會以什麼形式出現呢？

品牌開始將永續行動延伸到數位平台上，讓該平台也成為其環保價值的一環，並藉此實現永續目標。根據偉門智威智庫的報告《元宇宙創造新現實》顯示，在了解元宇宙概念的受訪者中，71% 的人認為品牌應該思考元宇宙對環境的影響。

2022 年 9 月，以太坊將軟體全面升級，降低 99% 的碳排量。該公司把此次升級稱為「合併」（the merge），將驗證方式從工作量證明（proof of work）改為節能的權益證明（proof of stake，簡稱 PoS），使以太坊的用電量從 8.5 吉瓦（GW）有效地降低至少於 85 兆瓦（MW）。

有些數位平台則從源頭開始實踐綠色使命。泰卓鏈（Tezos）除了使用節能 PoS 共識機制，其 NFT 交易所需時間也比一般的區塊鏈更短，因此碳足跡更少也更環境友善。環保區塊鏈 EOSIO 提供碳中和的鑄幣機制，並使用節能的 PoS 演算法，不鼓勵礦工不間斷地挖礦。消費者若想選擇以永續為訴求的 NFT 交易市場，則可使用 Arbis.io，而選擇永續型的 NFT 藝廊，則可考慮 KodaDot。

根據偉門智威智庫的《再生崛起：永續未來》報告顯示，86% 的受訪者認為大企業應該參與解決更大規模的難題，如氣候變遷；88% 的人認為企業皆應以永續為發展目標；89% 的人則認為品牌應該採取更多措施來降低碳排放的影響。零售支付平台瑞波（Ripple）計畫在 2030 年前達成淨零排放的目標，該公司的多位高層皆為「加密氣候協定」（Crypto Climate Accord）

以及世界經濟論壇「加密貨幣永續倡議」（Crypto Impact and Sustainability Initiative）的共同發起人及活躍成員。

Gucci 除了開放以全球第一個大型的碳中和區塊鏈 - 瑞波帳本（XRP Ledger）的加密貨幣作為支付方式，也和碳中和數位收藏品創作平台 Superplastics 合作，打造自有的 NFT。Burberry 在 2022 年 6 月的派對活動 Blankos Block Party 上，推出第二款主打不需鑄造任何加密貨幣的 NFT 收藏品。

值得關注的原因：
無論企業是選用環保的區塊鏈，或是以綠色平台來平衡其碳足跡，現在都有諸多方案可讓他們利用更永續的方式進入元宇宙。

18

元宇宙華爾街

銀行正重新規劃數位金融服務。

消費者現在不只可以於網路世界中購買加密貨幣，還能使用傳統銀行服務。

2022 年 8 月，Decentraland 與 元 宇 宙 工 作 室 Metaverse Architects 和支付平台 Transak 聯手推出第一台元宇宙提款機。玩家可以像在現實世界一樣，從提款機提領金錢，並用來購買加密貨幣。而在 Decentraland 擁有資產的用戶，也可以在自己的虛擬小島放置一座專屬的提款機，方便領取加密貨幣。

摩根大通（JPMorgan）是第一個在元宇宙中建造服務大廳與辦公室的銀行，他們旗下的區塊鏈部門 Onyx 宣布此消息時，在闡述元宇宙能帶來商機的報告中提到「未來幾年，每個領域多少都會有元宇宙的元素滲透其中。」摩根大通同時也投資主打金融科技的支付平台 Tilla，其提供支付服務範圍涵蓋元宇宙中的遊戲、虛擬世界及行動裝置上的應用程式。該銀行告訴偉門智威智庫：「消費者投入越來越多時間在電玩遊戲，也希望擁有虛擬世界中物品的所有權，而目前已出現許多新型的獲利模式，我們當然也會需要適合的解決方案。」

2022 年 3 月，美國運通為其元宇宙中的虛擬市集與加密貨幣服務註冊商標，提供信用卡支付、提款機、金融業務和詐騙偵測服務，也為虛擬世界的客戶提供娛樂、旅遊和禮賓服務等選項。

自適應性數位銀行 Quontic 於虛擬辦公室中提供金融服務，並發行比特幣回饋至活存帳戶的簽帳卡，客戶也可享有現金回饋和高利率的報酬。數位銀行 Cogni 於 2022 年夏季購入一系列無聊猿遊艇俱樂部的 NFT 作品，透過發行無聊猿主題的簽帳卡，為未來的 Web3 用戶體驗鋪路。

消費者投入越來越多時間在電玩遊戲，也希望擁有虛擬世界中物品的所有權，而目前已出現許多新型的獲利模式

摩根大通

區塊鏈遊戲《沙盒》（The Sandbox）將成為多所大型金融機構的數位工作場域。匯豐銀行計畫在此成立數位辦公室；國匯商銀行（Siam Commercial Bank）將設立虛擬銀行總部，而星展銀行（DBS）也將於其中展開 DBS BetterWorld 計畫。另外，此種虛擬金融的互動經驗，也能讓消費者了解永續實踐的重要，並展現元宇宙如何成為一股良善的力量。

值得關注的原因：
銀行開始為消費者提供虛擬商務與諮詢、元宇宙金融、加密貨幣買賣等一站式服務，或許金融服務很快便會在數位世界普及了。

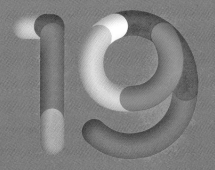

地圖實境

為何導航技術是未來 Web3 發展的關鍵呢？

某些頂尖的科技公司正投入一項看似非常基本的工作，那就是為實體世界繪製地圖。「我們觀察世界上最有影響力、最有價值，或者兩者兼具的科技公司，發現他們現在在做的事，是利用感測器和電腦視覺來繪製、查看與了解實體世界的樣貌。」Aglet 的執行長暨創辦人 Ryan Mullins 對偉門智威智庫如此表示，而他口中的科技公司正是特斯拉、蘋果、Instagram 和 Snapchat 等企業。

Meta、微軟、亞馬遜網路服務公司（Amazon Web Services）與荷蘭地圖公司 TomTom 於 2022 年 12 月攜手合作，開發具互通性的開放地圖資料。該計畫名為「序曲地圖基金會」（Overture Maps Foundation），此次合作的目的是要讓開放的地圖資料集可以跨程式、跨企業取得並能循環使用，藉此推動新產品的創新。

在 2023 年的美國消費電子用品展（CES）上，BMW 展示了 Here Technologies 這間提供自動化地圖繪製服務的公司所製作的 UniMap，讓使用者可以自行產製數位地圖與定位服務工具。

新興品牌也在瞄準這股成長中的風潮。同樣在 2023 年的美國消費電子用品展上，Loovic 推出穿戴式的導航裝置，且是佩戴在脖子上，讓使用者無需查看手機螢幕就可知道行進方向，也能幫助視力受損的人士強化空間感；同一場活動中，Ashirase 則推出附加於鞋子上的創新裝置，可透過語音助理（連接至手機）和導盲釘的輔助來為穿戴者指引方向。

為何要把重心放在地圖上呢？Mullins 解答道：「真正的革新不只在於地圖本身，而是在於使用者介面（UI）及網路互動所帶來的全新機會。地圖和電腦視覺的應用會帶出新的網路空間感，其中的實境體驗會以第一人稱的視角出現，不管是進行動作或和世界互動都是如此。」

值得關注的原因：
Mullins 將地圖繪製工作定位成「網路革命的最新發展階段」，將數位互動方式「從滑動網頁變成在不同地點之間移動」。Web3的重要性也不再只限於區塊鏈或加密貨幣領域，而是在於創造「以空間、地點為本的網路世界，且不只針對網頁和使用者，是連裡面的實境世界都能以機器可判讀的方式來設計。」

20

虛擬實境追愛

虛擬實境會是下個改變交友配對方式的主要推力嗎？

自 Tinder 大幅改寫線上約會的規則，至今已超過十年。現在元宇宙正引領著浪漫新紀元，虛擬世界開始成為尋找愛情的浪漫之地。

元宇宙交友的核心是以虛擬化身和他人互動，而 Nevermet 這款虛擬實境交友軟體，訂下嚴格的互動規則：不能放上大頭貼。在習慣以交友軟體上的照片評價他人的現今，雖然此舉堪稱大膽，但這也讓使用者得以利用不同的方式，探索與人交往的真諦。平台共同創辦人暨執行長 Cam Mullen 告訴偉門智威智庫：「Nevermet 是一款主打以個性配對為首的交友軟體，用戶必須先了解彼此的個性、契合度，接著才是對方的真實長相。」

了無新意的開場白、一成不變的約會地點，第一次約會往往欠缺驚喜的元素。然而，虛擬實境交友軟體 Flirtual，卻扭轉了此一現象，提供用戶只在虛擬實境才可能出現的驚艷約會。Flirtual 發表於 2022 年 3 月，其中的約會場地豐富多采，可以和鯊魚共游，也可欣賞黑洞奇景。

" 在虛擬實境中墜入情網比
其他數位媒介容易多了"

Anthony Tan，
Flirtual 共同創辦人暨執行長

借助虛擬實境的功能，Planet Theta 希望讓約會詐騙成為過去式。該應用程式主打革命性的身份驗證機制，其執行長 Chris Crew 向偉門智威智庫說明：「它可以判斷你的身份是否屬實，且準確度極高。因為它參考政府紀錄、線上資料庫、曾經外洩的資訊及其他來源，藉此查核姓名與電子信箱的配對是否正確。」

值得關注的原因：
往後元宇宙可能會成為第一次約會和戀愛萌芽的地點。Flirtual 的共同創辦人暨執行長 Anthony Tan 認為：「在虛擬實境中墜入情網比其他數位媒介容易多了。」虛擬實境成為建立親密關係的新興選項，同時也能解決目前線上交友平台或應用程式的某些缺點。

Above: Flirtual
Right: Planet Theta

旅遊＆觀光

21

30

21

深海觀光

遊客正勇於深入海底，追求極限歷險。

海洋之門（OceanGate Expeditions 美國海底勘探公司海洋之門，簡稱「海洋之門」）開始帶領遊客潛進未曾探訪的海底深處。該公司表示他們是「由一群致力於探索深海世界的探險家、科學家及製片人所組成的團隊。」2022 年，海洋之門帶領成員深入鐵達尼號（Titanic）船骸，成為首批進入其中的民間探險隊，成員需支付 25 萬美元的費用，才能潛至海平面下 4 公里的深海，一窺船隻遺骸。

對許多人而言，這趟深潛是夢寐以求的神聖旅程。銀行家 Renata Rojas 向《BBC》說道：「我並非百萬富翁，但我存了非常、非常久的錢，也犧牲了很多，只為了更靠近鐵達尼號」。

這些參加深海探索的遊客又稱為「任務專家」，他們必須符合規定的生理條件，包含基本肌力、平衡感、活動度及柔軟度。海洋之門提供的參考標準包括爬梯 2 公尺及舉重 9 公斤等。

該公司即將於 2023 年推出另一項深潛計畫，其執行長兼創辦人 Stockton Rush 預期市場需求將會上升。他向《BBC》說道：「未來有一天，人們將能以更低廉的費用頻繁地造訪外太空。同樣地，我認為深海世界也不再遙不可及」。

值得關注的原因：
近年來，科學家策畫的知性之旅逐漸興起，我們在《改變未來的 100 件事：2022 年全球百大趨勢》中亦有追蹤此一趨勢。一年後，旅遊業隨著解封潮持續回穩，人們開始尋求「一生一次」的旅遊經歷，更不惜深入未知、勇敢冒險！

21

怪異絕倫旅宿

隨著遊客開始追求獨一無二的住宿體驗，
古怪而美妙的旅宿也開始風行。

+ WUNDERMAN
THOMPSON　　Airbnb OMG! Fund

2023 年夏天到來之前，遊客就有機會住在智利的飄浮酪梨、美國的巨大花盆，甚至墨西哥綻放的粉色花朵中，且這些特色旅宿都只是 Airbnb「2022 標新立異房源基金」獲選名單中的幾個例子而已。

2022 年 10 月，Airbnb 投入一千萬美元，預計讓全球 100 個奇幻住宿體驗成真。這些旅宿計畫將公布於 Airbnb 網站的「標新立異類別」中，目前已放上獨特的短期住宿機會，包含改裝電影《天旋地轉》（Spice World）中原版辣妹巴士的英國房型，還有韓國的吉他造型房屋，應有盡有。

Airbnb 的投資計畫不僅彰顯了奇特旅宿有其市場，來自世界各地成千上萬的參賽計畫更展現了設計師、建築師及營造商的熱忱與創意。其中一位獲選者——來自墨西哥的 Pablo C，以科幻電影為發想來源，設計出蕈菇狀的太空梭旅宿，並表示「其理念是要設計出異於尋常、前所未聞，稀世美麗並令人印象深刻的作品。」

值得關注的原因：
遊客開始追尋新奇難忘且帶有古怪、趣味成分的住宿「驚艷」。

「其理念是要設計出異於尋常、前所未聞，稀世美麗並令人印象深刻的作品。」

Pablo C
Airbnb 標新立異房源基金獲選者

23

旅遊跟著溫度走！

持續上升的氣溫將促使遊客選擇
較涼快舒適的旅遊目的地。

氣候變遷對全球觀光業造成嚴重影響。2022 年夏季的高溫屢屢登上新聞頭條，甚至導致班機停飛及火車停駛。在高溫危機下，氣候涼爽的觀光景點挾其優勢，吸引想逃離居住地區酷暑不斷延長的遊客，而氣候炎熱的旅遊勝地則面臨遊客流失的難題。

2022 年 7 月，英國面臨熱浪來襲，推廣昔得蘭群島（Shetland Islands）的組織 Promote Shetland 在推特上發文，表示該群島「正式成為全英國最涼爽的地方。」昔得蘭群島坐落在北海中央地帶，夏季平均高溫約為攝氏 14 度。該推文希望吸引那些正在找尋氣溫合宜地點的遊客，以及從未將該群島納入夏日必訪景點的旅人。

未來，氣候變遷將成為
影響旅遊計畫的關鍵因素。

另一方面，美國舊金山也有機會吸引來自內陸城市、受高溫所苦的旅客。受益於靠海的地理位置，舊金山有涼爽的海風吹拂，夏季氣候宜人。舊金山旅遊協會（San Francisco Travel Association）執行長 Joe D' Alessandro 向《紐約時報》表示，他正「考慮以『來涼一夏』（Come cool down）的觀光口號行銷這個避暑勝地。」

對較熱的景點來說，最大的挑戰在於留住觀光客。倫敦市政府在 2022 年推出第三版的「涼爽空間」（Cool Spaces）地圖，標示出遊客及居民可避暑的室內外地點。

值得關注的原因：
未來，氣候變遷將成為影響旅遊計畫的關鍵因素。接下來幾年，隨著遊客對旅遊的想像逐漸改變，「暑假」一詞的意義也將有所不同。

24

元交通

汽車品牌正重新想像元宇宙中的交通方式。

汽車廠牌與製造商正開始在元宇宙內提供交通行動服務，如雷諾汽車（Renault Korea Motors）與遊戲平台《沙盒》（The Sandbox）合作，希望在元宇宙內為消費者提供虛擬駕車體驗。2022 年 9 月，雷諾汽車與該平台簽訂合約，將旗下汽車帶進虛擬世界，「結合汽車及其他數位資產，讓使用者在《沙盒》中得到全新體驗」，韓國沙盒的執行長 Cindy Lee 說道。

Volvo 於 2022 年夏季也在元宇宙推出了品牌最新款的電動車。WPP 廣告集團為概念化而誕生「富豪元宇宙」（Volvoverse）。印度 Volvo 汽車以該平台作為純電款 XC40（XC40 Recharge）的發表場地。在元宇宙中發表的行為，亦彰顯了富豪汽車看重永續價值的精神。「這次的元宇宙發表會也是我們永續行動的一環。相較於傳統發表會，在元宇宙進行發表所留下的碳足跡可說是微乎其微。」印度 Volvo 汽車總經理 Jyoti Malhotra 表示。

**MarketsandMarkets報告顯示，
對汽車工業而言，
元宇宙的市場商機預計會從
2022 年的19 億美元成長至
2030 年的165億美元。**

同樣在印度，現代汽車（Hyundai）於同年 8 月在遊戲平台 Roblox 上發表最新款休旅車。發表會中設有教育空間，如虛擬試駕、虛擬展廳及虛擬服務中心，同時也有社交遊戲單元，如迷你遊戲、拍貼機及尋寶遊戲等。

福特汽車為了前進元宇宙，為旗下品牌申請了 19 項商標，當中涵蓋虛擬汽車、卡車、廂型車、休旅車、服飾，以及正在計畫中的 NFT 交易平台。

值得關注的原因：
MarketsandMarkets 報告顯示，對汽車工業而言，元宇宙的市場商機預計會從 2022 年的 19 億美元成長至 2030 年的 165 億美元。汽車產業中勇於創新的領導品牌正重新思考元宇宙中的交通方式及傳統的顧客接觸點，希望從此波成長趨勢中獲利。

性健康靜修會所

新型養生會所正致力於推廣性健康。

2022 年，全球健康機構（Global Wellness Institute）預測 2025 年全球養生旅遊的商機將高達 1.3 兆美元，其中，性健康是成長最快的項目。在以養生為賣點的觀光商機中，親密關係與性愛知識課程的比例也逐漸增加。

住在墨西哥 St Regis Punta Mita 飯店的賓客現已能享受該飯店提供的最新服務─性健康靜修。這是該高檔飯店品牌首次推出的活動。過程中會由一位性專家帶領，讓參與者在私密的環境中探索心靈及牛理上的性慾，歡迎有伴侶或是單身的旅客參加。

坐落在紐約漢普頓的 Shou Sugi Ban House 為女賓客提供 90 分鐘的私人性工作坊。這個「性感戀人工作坊」（Sensual Lover workshop）每人收費 350 美元，目的是要「鼓勵賓客透過更親密的視角探索健康生活。」該飯店的創意總監 Jodie Webber 接受旅遊休閒雜誌《Travel and Leisure Southeast Asia》採訪時如此說道。此外，澳洲布里斯本的 W 飯店也有性學專家駐館，提供工作坊及靜修活動。

值得關注的原因：
消費者開始期待在旅遊過程中深度了解自己的身心靈，旅遊及飯店業便開始拓展性健康領域的養生服務。

26

全球三大熱門景點

摩洛哥是遠端工作者可負擔的新興發燒景點。
摩洛哥擁有溫和的氣候、豐富的歷史、沙漠與海灘，加上鄰近歐洲又有比歐洲更低的物價，因此開始吸引新的一批遠端工作者前來進駐。

2022 年，遠端工作及共居公司 Outsite 在摩洛哥的馬拉喀什巾買下一棟當地傳統庭園住宅。裡面的房間圍繞著中庭而建，建築內也有共同工作空間必備的共享廚房及辦公室，更有游泳池、土耳其浴及屋頂露臺供住客使用。2022 年 5 月，紐約證券交易所的上市公司 Selina 也在摩洛哥的阿加菲（Agafay）沙漠建造了豪華貝都因帳篷，成為該品牌在北非大規模擴展的第一站。即便摩洛哥尚未有數位游牧簽證，許多遠端工作者還是願意持 90 天的觀光簽證前來。

不再盲目迎合 Instagram 喜好，京都以精心策畫的小型旅遊吸引遊客回歸。
疫情前，京都的寺廟、花園、藝妓及美食文化每年吸引高達 900 萬遊客造訪，處處人潮洶湧，道路水洩不通。

現在京都已重新開放，並希望以小型的客製化行程帶給遊客有意義的深度體驗。三井財團旗下的京都奢華飯店 Hotel Thc Mitsui Kyoto 為房客提供二條城周邊的私人導覽服務，該城建於西元

1603 年，是江戶幕府初代將軍德川家康所建造的居所。丹麥大廚 René Redzepi 開設的餐廳 Noma 將在 2023 年春季於京都設立為期 10 週的快閃店，並以櫻花季期間的當地食材入菜。新創公司 Manabi Japan 將於 2023 年起，在京都市外圍舉辦小型導覽及參訪該語言中心的一日遊行程，客座講者分享的內容涵蓋能劇及藍染，希望能「幫助遊客深入了解日本文化」，其創辦人 Lucinda Ping Cowing 向偉門智威智庫如此說道。

坦尚尼亞迅速竄升成為獨遊者的旅遊首選。
過去以冒險旅程及家庭旅行聞名的坦尚尼亞，現在也吸引獨遊者前往。

坦尚尼亞有著許多世界之最。這裡有非洲最高峰—吉力馬札羅山、世界最大的完整火山口—恩戈羅恩戈羅火山口（Ngorongoro Crater）、地球上最重要的古人類遺址之一—奧杜威峽谷（Olduvai Gorge），還有以世界最大陣仗的牛羚、斑馬遷徙而聞名，同時擁有非洲最大規模獅群的塞倫蓋提國家公園（Serengeti National Park）。經營旅遊規畫網站 Fly with Queenie 的 Chanice Queenie Williams，在《華盛頓郵報》的訪談中描述了她在坦尚尼亞的獨旅，認為該地「相當適合獨遊者前往，特別是那些對獨自個人旅遊感到不自在的女性。」

27

城市靜地

飯店業者正在市中心設計豪華綠洲。

人們生活在城市中很難尋得一片靜謐，而飯店業者看準此商機，著手為此設立新據點。現在世界各地逐漸出現「城市靜地」，從提供賓客靜謐空間的飯店，到顧客能夠舒適地坐下放鬆、休息充電的餐廳，都讓人們能暫時逃離都市庸庸碌碌的生活，得到一份寧靜。

預計 2026 年開幕的比佛利山莊安縵飯店（Aman Beverley Hills）自詡為「傳奇城市裡的寧靜綠洲」。該度假別墅希望展現大自然之美，將加州的茂密森林與棕梠樹融入建築與造景中，讓住客在洛杉磯城市的喧囂中仍有一處安放身心之所。跨國飯店品牌安縵 2022 年已在紐約開設飯店，置身其中，旅客能從沉著和諧的設計中找回寧靜，與周圍的水泥叢林形成強烈對比。

歐洲也出現同樣的風潮，六善酒店（Six Senses）在羅馬新蓋了一座度假別墅，成為該品牌全球版圖中的最新力作，預計在 2023 年初開幕，屆時旅客步行便可抵達著名的特雷維噴泉（Trevi Fountain）。該別墅以古羅馬傳統洗浴文化為靈感，希望邀請旅客在水療池中探索洗浴之美，在喧擾的城市中修養生息；而旅客也能移步至頂樓寧靜的祕密花園，在裡頭放鬆身心。安縵及六善酒店都希望能讓旅客放鬆充電，在重回城市之際再次感到活力充沛。

希望幫助人們逃離城市喧囂的不只有飯店業者。位於墨爾本的 Au79 café 在繁忙的查斯頓購物中心（Chadstone Shopping Centre）中給予旅客一絲寧靜。這間咖啡店由室內設計工作室 Mim Design 操刀，室內的圓拱設計及吊掛盆栽營造出植物溫室的氛圍，成為顧客逛街疲憊時絕佳的休憩場所。

值得關注的原因：
未來豪奢旅遊必須兼顧兩大面向：與世隔絕般的寧靜和城市文化中的活力，以提供旅客絕佳的體驗。

27

The Tokyo Edition hotel, Toranomon. Photography by Nikolas Koenig

28

元宇宙旅遊

元宇宙的興起重新形塑了飯店觀光產業的未來。

隨著元宇宙興起，現實生活中的旅遊也逐漸融合虛擬世界的魔幻體驗，為旅遊一詞的定義掀起革命。

繼 2021 年在英國曼徹斯特開設首間實體飯店後，著重設計的飯店品牌 Leven 公布旗下第二間飯店將在 2022 年於虛擬實境平台 Decentraland 開幕。該飯店的專屬元宇宙 The Levenverse 將成為提供休閒娛樂、社交網絡及健康活動的數位空間，「藉由品牌合作、藝術、設計和行動，我們將旅客在現實世界的住宿經驗融入虛擬世界，希望不論在哪個世界中，旅客皆能有獨特的社交與遊戲體驗。」Leven 的共同創辦人兼 Wellbrook Hospitality 負責人 Timothy Griffin 告訴偉門智威智庫。

萬豪國際酒店集團（Marriott International）的旗下品牌 Moxy 飯店也搭上擴增實境風潮，在 2022 年 7 月推出「Moxy 宇宙，超越實境」（Moxy Universe, Play Beyond AR）的體驗，讓旅客能在 Moxy 宇宙創造自己的虛擬化身，透過一系列的擴增實境挑戰，將數位體驗融入實體飯店中。旅客創造的虛擬化身可以陪他們在

飯店酒吧喝一杯、陪他們回房間，甚至一起到健身房運動。上述體驗在亞太地區的 12 間 Moxy 飯店皆可享有服務，活動期間為 2022 年 7 月至 12 月。

奢華旅遊公司 Brown & Hudson 也開始為高淨值客戶提供元宇宙旅遊體驗，其中全新的元宇宙系列體驗之一——Capo，使用虛擬實境科技，讓客戶能重溫現實生活中的旅行回憶。攝影師會記錄客戶現實生活中的一舉一動，提供遊客除了照片外，更深入其境的回想管道。如此，他們便能重溫美好快樂的回憶，直至賦歸後仍能再次探索其中。

值得關注的原因：

隨著元宇宙觀光的興起，旅宿業者成為提供住宿及嚮導的角色。Leven 共同創辦人兼 Branco Capital 董事 Joshua Senior 預測「隨著元宇宙從科幻成為現實，任何受數位時代影響的產業都將感受到它的威力。而我們相信，富有創意的旅宿品牌有無限的成長潛力。」

旅遊秘境

為了吸引遊客來訪，過去禁止進入的景點
而今開始對世人開放。

過去幾年只允許外國遊客以非宗教理由入境的沙烏地阿拉伯，而今正投入鉅額資金發展觀光貿易，希望成為中東地區的觀光霸主。沙國向世界遊客分享先前不為人知的秘境，首度開放數座古老遺跡，比如異教古墓 Qasr al-Farid「孤獨城堡」，這似乎意味著該國過去嚴格的社會規範開始有所鬆綁。在 2022 年 9 月，該國政府更宣布要進一步簡化外國旅客申請入境簽證的流程，讓前往沙國旅遊變得更加便利。

除此之外，地底景點也逐漸開放。在羅馬，建於四世紀的康莫迪拉地下墓穴（Catacomb of Commodilla）等經過梵蒂岡宗座考古委員會修復完成後，預計於 2025 年首次對遊客開放。在倫敦，老舊的地鐵和隧道也將於時隔百年後的現在首度對外開放。倫敦交通博物館（London Transport Museum）的特展「不為人知的倫敦」（Hidden London）當中規劃了「牧者叢地鐵站」（Shepherd's Bush）導覽，這是該站自 1924 年以來首度公開露面。

值得關注的原因：
在過去數年，熱門觀光景點常以維護為由，試圖管制遊客數量或封閉歷史遺跡。然而，近期有越來越多旅遊勝地將過去禁止遊客進入的區域對外開放，吸引追求獨特體驗的遊客前去造訪。

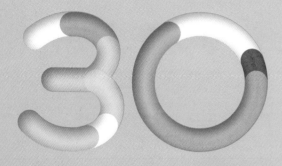

30

暗黑地帶

愛好歷史且具冒險犯難精神的旅客
開始探尋黑暗、沉重的景點。

暗黑旅遊和一般觀光不同，遊客不是前去沐浴陽光、休閒放鬆，而是造訪與死亡、戰爭及災難等事件有關的沉重場景，比如日本別稱「自殺森林」的青木原樹海、波蘭的奧斯威辛集中營，以及柬埔寨的殺戮戰場（Killing Fields），這些都是公認的暗黑旅遊景點。根據 Future Market Insights 於 2022 年 10 月的調查，暗黑旅遊的市場價值預估在 2032 年達到 365 億美元。

推廣烏克蘭觀光的團隊 Visit Ukraine 推出了許多導覽行程，如「基輔所向披靡」（Kyiv is unbeatable），該團隊表示這個導覽「非常受外國旅客歡迎」。自 9 月起，Visit Ukraine 便開始提供「去佔領」（deoccupied）及「已排雷」（demined）地區的城市導覽，地點涵蓋羅馬尼夫卡（Romanivka）、布查（Bucha）、伊爾平（Irpin）、戈斯托梅利（Hostomel）及博羅江卡（Borodyanka）等城市。「我們發現關心此事的人士有親眼見證戰事痕跡的需求。」該團隊的執行長 Anton Taranenko 如此說道。這些導覽不以營利為取向，並將所有收益捐獻給正受戰爭所苦的城市與人民。

Taranenko 向《CNN》解釋，他希望遊客除了見證戰爭的影響，也能從中體會烏克蘭人民果敢和寧死不屈的精神。

車諾比核災區在 2019 年 HBO 電視影集《核爆家園》(Chernobyl) 上映後，成為熱門旅遊景點。然而在 2020 年，隨著新冠肺炎（COVID-19）疫情爆發，旅遊人潮也隨之中斷。而今在旅遊業重新復甦後，根據訂房網站 Booking.com 的全球調查顯示，約有 73% 的遊客期待 2023 年能「跳脫舒適圈」，來場挑戰極限的旅行。

值得關注的原因：

暗黑旅遊的魅力在於它提供了不同的視角。「人們正嘗試理解黑暗的事物，嘗試理解死亡、垂死及暴力的現實狀況。富蘭克林與馬歇爾學院（Franklin & Marshall College）的行銷學教授 Jeffrey Podoshen 向《紐約時報》表示：「遊客藉由這類型的觀光行程來為人生做準備。」

73%的遊客期待 2023年能「跳脫舒適圈」，來場挑戰極限的旅行。

31

品牌&行銷

40

31

WEB3 品牌

各大領導品牌開始挑戰 Web3 新世界。

YSL 彩妝於 2022 年 6 月首度推出 Web3 與 NFT 企劃，希望打造全新的品牌忠誠度體驗。顧客只要持有 YSL 所發行的 NFT，就能進入 YSL 的虛擬精品世界全年暢遊，獲取加密貨幣並得到購買限定新品的管道等等。同月份 Prada 也推出第一個「時光膠囊」(Timecapsule) 系列 NFT 作品，讓持有者獨享相關體驗，自發布後該系列每月上架的新品皆全數售罄。Prada 的初期計畫也包含在 Discord 平台上創立「The Prada Crypted」社群，藉此拓展品牌的數位行銷範疇與社群規模。

Niche 是新型 Web3 社群平台，創辦宗旨是希望將資訊掌控權還給用戶，並為消費者、用戶及品牌創造成長機會。其共同創辦人 Zaven Nahapetyan 告訴偉門智威智庫，此一新平台「帶給消費者更多機會，這是傳統非屬去中心化的社群媒體所缺乏的。Niche 去中心化的本質可以讓用戶在平台上輕鬆交易創作內容。」

另一方面，餐飲品牌也充分把握這次機會。像是星巴克即將推出的 Web3 限定回饋機制，讓消費者可以收藏以咖啡為主題的 NFT 作品，這些代幣也會成為獲取獨家內容、會籍、參與活動的金鑰。而麥當勞的虛擬餐廳也將開始提供實體及數位商品外送服務，日前該品牌便為此一服務註冊商標，並將其應用於麥當勞及旗下品牌 McCafé 的服務範疇中。同時麥當勞也提及該企劃「是在線上經營一家提供外送服務的虛擬餐廳」，這代表將來麥當勞的粉絲可能有機會在網路國度中訂購虛擬的大麥克漢堡。

值得關注的原因：
Web3 趨勢勢不可擋，為因應此風潮，品牌紛紛著手打造全新的數位行銷策略。

Above top: YSL Beauté
Above: Starbucks

Web3 趨勢勢不可擋，
為因應此風潮，
品牌紛紛著手
打造全新的
數位行銷策略。

Soul Machines 以高度擬真且由 AI 驅動的數位人物來讓虛擬互動更加緊密而真實。「AI 或者廣義上所有自動產生的動畫都能加深品牌與消費者之間的連結,因為可以大規模地提供具同理心的擬人化服務。」Soul Machines 的副總裁 Shantenu Agarwal 對偉門智威智庫如此表示。該公司目前正為雀巢、Twitch 及世界衛生組織等客戶打造線上的客製化的顧客體驗。

Agarwal 解釋道:「我們發現許多品牌正利用這個新平台來重新規劃品牌形象,有些品牌瞭解數位工具可提供的幫助,讓他們能輕鬆打造出多種不同外貌與性格的虛擬角色。這等於是賦予品牌消費者選擇的權利,他們可以自由選擇想和誰對話、獲得哪一類的體驗,這是過去做不到的事情。」

元宇宙能提升 3D 虛擬世界中的互動體驗,而虛擬化身也因此增加了品牌的價值。在 2020 年 6 月於巴黎舉辦的指標性新創展 VivaTech 上,奢侈品集團 LVMH 推出數位品牌大使 Livi 來發表該集團的創新計畫。卡達航空(Qatar)推出元宇宙空服員 Sama 來為旗下平台 QVerse 中進入虛擬機艙的乘客提供指引。保養

32

虛擬品牌大使

品牌大使正在進行數位升級。

「我們的世界越來越數位化，
所以品牌也需要採取新的策略，
才更符合人性。」

電通集團

品牌 Dermalogica 打造了虛擬講師 Natalia，品牌全球執行長
Aurelian Lis 說道：「我們現在可以利用元宇宙技術來為數以百
萬計的顧客以及成千上萬的肌膚專家提供教育訓練，教導他們改
善膚況的做法。」

此外，品牌開始採用虛擬形象大使的這股趨勢，讓日本廣告商電
通集團（Dentsu）催生出專門創作虛擬角色的部門。電通表示：「我
們的世界越來越數位化，所以品牌也需要採取新的策略，才更符
合人性。」

值得關注的原因：
隨著元宇宙持續演進，在《改變未來的 100 件事：2022 年全球
百大趨勢》中談及的「升級版虛擬化身」，現在已成為品牌用來加
強顧客連結的工具。Agarwal 說：「品牌的未來在於加強連結，透
過這些沈浸式、互動型的體驗，甚至可能產生真切的互動關係。」

WUNDERMAN
THOMPSON　　QVerse by Qatar Airways

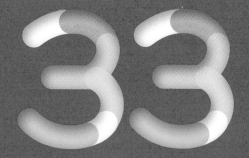

33

事關地球

我們的地球在企業董事會的利益關係獲得了
它應得的席位。

2022 年 9 月，創辦服飾品牌 Patagonia 的億萬富翁 Yvon Chouinard 將品牌贈與一家特別的信託公司，專門將品牌盈餘全數用在對抗氣候變遷造成的環境破壞上。Chouinard 的此番作為著實為企業的環境責任立下新的標竿。

該潮流戶外裝備品牌宣告：「現在我們唯一的股東就是地球，品牌所有獲利都會以永續年金的形式投入在拯救我們家園的任務上，也就是拯救地球。」

Patagonia 的此一做法攻佔媒體頭條，但卻與公開發行股票的上市企業大相徑庭。Chouinard 說：「與其成為上市企業，我們更想做的是成為有使命感的『上道企業』（going purpose）。與其掠奪自然資源，並將相關獲利轉移到投資人手中，我們更想把 Patagonia 的獲利拿來守護所有可以創造財富的自然資源。」

此舉和其他億萬富翁例如馬斯克（Elon Musk）、貝佐斯（Jeff Bezos）等截然不同，他們選擇把眼界放在拓展外太空殖民地的任務上。

Patagonia 的策略讓人目瞪口呆，卻又同時讓人毫不意外。這間設立於加州的企業過往長期捐贈 1% 的銷售額給環保團體，也以慷慨的員工福利著稱，提供職場托育服務及午後衝浪活動等。

同樣在 2022 年 9 月，總部位於愛丁堡的環保美妝企業 Faith in Nature 指派了維護大自然權益的「自然守護總監」一職，負責在董事會中為大自然發聲。在提倡環保的社會企業 Lawyers for Nature 擔任總監，同時兼任艾賽克斯大學法律學院（Essex Law School）講師的 Brontie Ansell 是第一位出任此職務的人士，她告訴《衛報》她的任務類似在法庭上代表兒童發聲的監護人。

Earth is now our only shareholder.

搭上永續潮流的企業還有英國高檔零售品牌 Selfridges，該品牌承諾在 2030 年前會讓 45% 的營業額來自於循環經濟活動，包含販售二手商品、提供租借服務、填裝商品、產品修復與回收再製等。

值得關注的原因：
儘管面對著連年的森林面積衰減、物種滅絕消失、極端氣候加劇等問題，多數企業所採取的永續行動仍如滄海一粟，並以股東對獲利的要求當作藉口。將地球視為股東則讓 Patagonia 等企業得以重擬董事會中的討論方向，並大幅提升企業永續行動的標準。

「現在我們唯一的股東就是地球，品牌所有獲利都會以永續年金的形式投入在拯救我們家園的任務上，也就是拯救地球。」

34

元宇宙走向包容性

品牌與創作者開始把多元包容的價值觀帶進元宇宙。

偉門智威智庫的《元宇宙創造新現實》報告中指出,聽過元宇宙的人,當中有 65% 的人認為它將會比真實世界更具包容力。現在,許多品牌開始投身相關倡議,希望實現這項承諾。

2022 年,世界經濟論壇與微軟、索尼、樂高、Meta 等企業共同發表一項倡議,希望聯手打造出「具道德意識且兼容多元的元宇宙」。

美妝品牌倩碧推出 NFT 概念「讓元宇宙更像我們」(Metaverse More Like Us),提倡元宇宙中的平等價值。倩碧與 Daz 3D 合作,打造出全球最具多元價值的虛擬化身系列之一「非同質化人物」(Non-Fungible People);倩碧還聘請三位彩妝師,他們皆為較被邊緣化的社群,共同為倩碧此次企劃創造招牌妝容,此組妝容也以數位形式同時發布於 Daz 3D 社群中。

雖然有些專案會以大範圍的視角達成多元包容的目標,但是也有品牌選擇鎖定特定邊緣化族群的需求。

同於 2022 年，NFTY Collective 推出新專案「不假隱藏」
（Unhidden），代表身心問題顯見或隱蔽難見的各類身心障礙朋
友發聲。此專案的發起人 Giselle Mota 希望讓身心障礙朋友「擁
有選擇權，如果這些朋友們希望虛擬身份可以反應自己真實的身
體狀況，那他們應該要能得到相關選項。」他告訴偉門智威智庫：
「真正具備多元包容價值的元宇宙，裡面的人物形象會和他們想
要吸引的客群一樣多元。」

照顧伊斯蘭信仰價值的 MetaKawn 是新興元宇宙平台，他們
推出以包容價值、多元族裔、性別平權等為主題的 Huffaz NFT
系列作品。本身是穆斯林的虛擬造型設計師 Idiat Shiole，為
Decentraland 這類遊戲平台打造了一系列符合奈及利亞獨特美
學的時尚設計，包含伊斯蘭頭巾、部落紋身、辮子頭飾等等。

近期 Meta 和萬事達卡為了照顧 LGBTQ+ 社群，與兩位在虛擬實
境平台 Horizon Worlds 打造出社交體驗「真我世界」（True Self
World）的設計師展開合作——RhondaX 和 Skitter。「真我世界」
是讓成員和社團好友可以在其中碰面、互動的社群體驗。

數位創作者兼元宇宙設計師 Yiran Shu 總結了上述專案的共同
目標，向偉門智威智庫解釋道：「元宇宙更需要呈現出多元代表性，
我們想讓人們覺得受到歡迎，感受到自己並未受人忽視，你不只
是隨便的另一個虛擬化身而已。我們看到你在這個世界中能發揮
的超能力，我想這是我們有所不同的地方，我們選擇的途徑，要
能代表形形色色的人物。」

值得關注的原因：
品牌有責任打造包容、多元的元宇宙，而做法就是確保其中的虛
擬化身、空間、論述都能涵蓋各色光譜，兼容並蓄。

多重宇宙品牌

各大品牌開始推出主打未來科技的限量神秘商品。

偉門智威智庫在《改變未來的 100 件事：2020 年全球百大趨勢》一書中，於〈走進多重宇宙〉篇章裡首次提及消費者的心態轉變，消費者因為對現代生活平凡無奇而感到厭倦，所以開始尋找出口與冒險行程，希望覓得更令人癡迷的趣味經驗。品牌從這個先見趨勢出發，催生出耐人尋味、不同凡響的產品。傳統產品注重原料、產地、香氣和口味等特色，新一代實驗商品則擁抱未來科技，並以元宇宙語言為依據。

可口可樂的創意平台「樂創無界」（Coca-Cola's Creations）於 2022 年上線，「旨在透過魔幻且意想不到的飲料口味、特色時刻與合作計畫，來驚艷、逗樂並吸引全球觀眾」。平台推出的首款飲品是以外太空為主題的「星河漫步」（Starlight），據說味道「讓人聯想到在營火旁觀賞星星的時刻，同時又有彷彿在外太空旅遊的冰冷感受。」後續推出的商品還有「位元組」（Byte）和「夢幻世界」（Dreamworld），口感描述和普通的可樂不同，據說喝起來像像素和夢境。可口可樂商標全球類別總裁 Selman Careaga 對《The Drum》表示，這些特色飲品創造出的互動量比平台 2022 年的其他企劃多了一倍之多。

聯合利華旗下的體香膏品牌 Lynx 也顛覆了同類商品的傳統銷售模式，與瑞士香精公司芬美意（Firmenich）共同發表「Lynx 人工智慧身體噴霧」。發表會中未提及任何描述香氛或氣味的用詞，而是主打未來科技，宣稱此限量商品「透過人工智慧驅動」，使用了 46TB 的儲存量、涵蓋 6 千多種原料，且可創造出 350 萬種不同的排列組合。Lynx 表示這場產品發表會的目的是希望「利用 Z 世代對科技和加密商品的著迷」來為 Lynx 體香膏創造銷量。

值得關注的原因：
品牌開始跨出現實世界，模糊了真實與虛擬世界的邊界。由於現在創意變得更不受限，品牌開始把消費者傳送至特別的宇宙一探究竟（詳見第 61 章〈多宇宙設計〉與第 74 章〈星際奢華〉）。

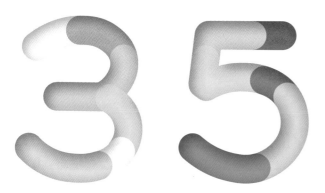

由於現在創意變得更不受限，品牌開始把消費者傳送至特別的宇宙。

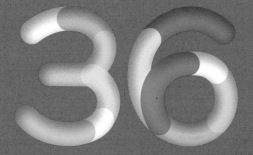

36

貴賓專屬 NFT

NFT 正在改變品牌忠誠度的遊戲規則。

品牌開始利用 NFT 解鎖元宇宙世代的顧客忠誠度目標，為顧客提供限定商品及服務。

紐約的第一間 NFT 餐廳正在動工。會員限定的高級海鮮餐廳 Flyfish Club 以 NFT 為入場門票，預計於 2023 年敞開實體大門歡迎饕客。這張 NFT 會員卡有潛力成為「有價資產」，買家可以按月使用、外租、販賣這種特別的會籍資格。

知名音樂節 Coachella 推出一組 10 件的 NFT 作品 Coachella Keys，每個買家皆可獲得該音樂節的終身門票，在其 NFT 市集購買作品的人還可享有 2022 年音樂節場次的額外福利，包含名廚晚宴及活動前排位置的資格。全球第一個 NFT 限定娛樂節目由 Mila Kunis 和 Ashton Kutcher 推出，買家購買 NFT 後便可觀賞他們的線上影視作品《Stoner Cats》。

購買軒尼詩 NFT 的消費者可獲得軒尼詩第八代珍稀干邑「Hennessy 8」僅此一檔的實體與數位版限量酒款。買家可隨時要求軒尼詩將實體「Hennessy 8」送至他們手中，此一套裝商品包涵紀念雕塑、鑲嵌法國手工吹製的玻璃瓶身、汲酒器、開瓶器、原裝禮盒及原廠認證標牌。

龍舌蘭酒品牌 Patrón 也推出品牌第一套 NFT 藏品：總數達 150 件，以品牌典藏酒款 Chairman's Reserve 為設計理念，每件皆為獨一無二的限量商品，並搭配一款數位瓶身及一瓶實體龍舌蘭酒同時販售。這款加密商品可於 BlockBar 線上購入，附有數位鑑定紀錄及所有權戳記；實體商品則可從線上市集 BlockBar. com 預定配送、交易買賣或贈予他人。

「我們在看一雙虛擬鞋款的時候，看的不是只有那雙鞋本身」，Nike 旗下虛擬工作室 Nike Virtual Studios 的副總裁兼總經理 Ron Faris 如此說道。他所屬的工作室負責利用自家平台 .Swoosh 來為該品牌找出全新的 Web3 品牌忠誠度公式（詳見第 69 章〈元宇宙宅一起〉）。「這雙虛擬球鞋未來有一天也許會成為預定實體鞋款的資格金鑰，或者進入品牌設計師秘密群組的門票，在裡頭和設計師聊天，共同打造出新款商品。我們發現購買虛擬商品不是購物旅程的終點，反而是起跑點。」

值得關注的原因：
NFT 改寫了品牌忠誠度的未來規則，買家能享有 NFT 持有者限定的品牌精選體驗。

37

力挺多元背景創作者

呼籲廣告業追求多元代表性的聲浪日漸上升，
促使品牌與身為邊緣族群的創意人才展開合作。

根據偉門智威智庫完成的一份 2022 年全球報告《下一波包容浪潮襲捲全球》(Inclusion's Next Wave) 顯示，86% 的人認為品牌若要支持弱勢族群，就該與他們合作，而不只是為他們而做。品牌開始擴大他們和邊緣族群的合作範圍，與來自這些社群的創作者、藝術家、網紅攜手合作，希望使品牌溝通更全面、更符合現況。

Herman Miller 集團、Gap、Airbnb 等大品牌於 2021 年在美國共同成立了倡議聯盟 Diversity in Design，致力協助年輕的非裔創意人才進入設計與創意產業。此聯盟著眼於具有潛力的創意人才，幫助他們踏入設計領域，這些人包含高中生、大學生或社會新鮮人都有可能，該聯盟也因此成為美國知名雜誌《Fast Company》2022 年創新設計獎 (Innovation by Design Awards) 的總體傑出獎得主。Snap 同樣注重社會新鮮人的培育，

2022 年 6 月,他們成立創意加速器幫助年輕非裔創意人才,為他們提供導師培訓及財務資源,讓他們能透過 Snapchat 來打造自己的事業。

苦尋不著創意夥伴的品牌,可以轉往數量越來越多的「人才合作社」尋才,這些合作社由過往在創意產業中的邊緣族群所成立,例如英國機構 TripleC。該機構致力為聽障、身障或腦神經迴路與眾不同的人們如自閉症、過動症等,尋找進入藝術媒體產業的機會,他們目前正為一項尋才計畫作準備,希望能為身障藝術家及身障創意人才提供與潛在業主媒合的機會。

於 2022 年 5 月公開的亞洲創意人才索引 The Asian Creators

Index 也採行相同邏輯,該索引由設計實踐團隊 Anak 製作,希望全面展現亞洲形形色色的藝術家與創意人才。該索引主打多元類型的人才,並以視覺化、可供搜尋的形式呈現,為想尋求多元背景合作夥伴的品牌提供簡易的查詢管道。

值得關注的原因:
消費者會支持由品牌提出真正多元包容價值的概念,而且有 66% 的人表示他們更願意支持為平等、多元價值發聲的品牌。把話語權交給邊緣族群,並且與之互動,可讓品牌真正實現多元代表性、為弱勢賦權、提供平等機會等企業使命。

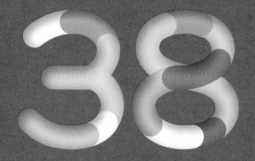

元宇宙中的品牌安全策略

如何在元宇宙中保護品牌聲譽呢？

Gartner 預測在 2026 年前，每四人當中就會有一人每天至少花一小時悠遊在元宇宙當中，所以品牌跨入此一市場實屬合理。了解不斷演進的元宇宙世界，對律師事務所及企業法務部門來說也日益重要，因為有越來越多品牌開始推出新的數位方針。

許多品牌早已為其元宇宙事業申請商標保護，包含 Hermès、美國連鎖藥妝店 CVS、可口可樂、Nike 和萬事達卡等品牌，都已為他們在元宇宙中的公司名稱、logo、虛擬商品及數位資產申請商標。勞力士也已向美國專利商標局（the United States Patent and Trademark Office）提出申請，受保護的應用範疇涵蓋「虛擬物件的線上拍賣服務」與「販售虛擬錶款及其零件等商品的線上買賣空間」。

除了申請專利保護之外，WPP 集團全球資料保護部門的 Gareth Burkhill-Howarth 也與偉門智威智庫分享了其他可行的防護措施。其中包含應用在元宇宙的相關技術，例如虛擬世界中提供交易、所有權註記、進入管道的「智慧合約」；觀察其他品牌的作法，並從他們的成敗經驗中學習；最後也不要忘記現有的品牌安全防護措施。Burkhill-Howarth 說道：「元宇宙雖然看似是個前所未有的全新空間，但還是要套用 Web2.0 和實體世界中的經驗法則。」

Burkhill-Howarth 相信元宇宙不會消失,「但不要認為元宇宙中的互動模式會和現在一樣。」使用者會成為形塑元宇宙風貌的主力,虛擬世界、數位資產、所有權概念會依其需求而演變。關注元宇宙的發展動態對品牌來說相當重要,如此才能確保品牌的未來發展方針不會因為數位世界的變化而失效。

值得關注的原因:
品牌得為元宇宙做好充足準備,且現在就得抓住時機,才不會遠遠落後。Burkhill-Howarth 說道:「我建議品牌要集結旗下法務、資產、財務、法遵、網管以及行銷團隊共同研議,確保他們了解相關機會、風險與挑戰,並準備好合適的元宇宙執行策略。不要到最後才要追趕其他品牌的腳步。」

「不要到最後才要追趕其他品牌的腳步。」

Gareth Burkhill-Howarth
WPP 集團全球資料保護部門

39

大眾共融品牌

企業開始將多元共融商品大眾化。

「在我們將無障礙設計當作設計原則時，甚至可以幫助到更廣大的族群。」《錯配：包容性如何指導設計》的作者 Kat Holmes 如此說道。這也是消費者對品牌的期許。據偉門智威智庫的調查報告《新興多元包容風潮》顯示，72% 的全球受訪者認同此一概念——我們不是要校正身心障礙問題，而是要校正這個世界，讓它能符合身心障礙者的需求。有越來越多品牌開始了解無障礙商品的潛在商機，於是紛紛準備向大眾市場推出相關產品。

2022 年 7 月，美國家具零售商 Pottery Barn 以其最熱賣的 150 種商品為藍圖，重新推出一系列符合適性設計原則的家具。此系列商品的設計獲身心障礙人士成立的倡議機構 Disability Education and Advocacy Network 協助，對於行動不便的消費者來說，更能符合其需求。此系列改版商品可從線上或實體商店購得，且價格與原版的設計品完全相同。

美國成衣零售業者 Kohl's 也擴大其成衣品項，推出適性設計商品。2022 年 9 月，Kohl's 宣布會於旗下品牌 Sonoma Goods for Life 及 Tek Gear 推出適性服飾，也會引進他牌的適性商品於線上商店販售。

包裝產品也開始進行全面調整。Strauss 是以色列最大的食品製造商之一，他們於 2022 年 2 月宣布會調整其零食包裝設計，方便身障人士自行開封。在歐洲，家樂氏針對全系列麥片產品加入 NaviLens 代碼，讓視力受損的人士可以透過手機掃描代碼以獲取營養及其他資訊。

值得關注的原因：
據 Return on Disability 的報告《2020 年全球無障礙經濟》（Global Economics of Disability 2020）評估，身障人士及其家屬的消費力達到 13 兆美元。品牌可以考量更廣泛的使用需求，善用共融設計帶來的機會，進而為所有消費者打造更優質、更無障礙的商品。

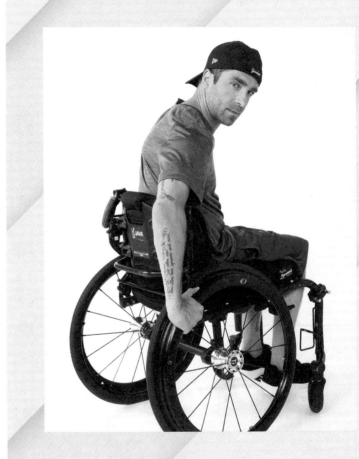

40

玩樂不分年齡

無倫你是哪個年紀，品牌都要鼓勵你盡情玩樂。

麥當勞希望協助大眾重新找回童趣、快樂的兒時感受。2022 年 10 月，這家連鎖速食店為成人推出「快樂成人餐」，套餐附有一件玩具及熱門餐點品項。該公司表示：「大家都記得小時候第一次吃到快樂兒童餐時的經驗，還有那種打開盒子時興奮、坐不住的感覺，這個紅色小盒子能把一個平凡的星期二變成最棒的一天。而現在，我們希望可以用全新的方式讓大家找回這樣的感受，只是這次我們要服務的對象，是成人顧客。」

Moxy 飯店則為旅客提供「趣味旅宿」。該餐旅品牌位在曼哈頓下東區的最新據點於 2022 年 11 月開張，他們將其形容為「童趣的避難所」，其中的設計「以過往紐約包厘街（Bowery）成排的馬戲團和早期動物園為概念」，提供「以荒唐趣味為核心精神的各式娛樂設施」，邀請住客一起「到 Moxy 玩耍」（使用標籤 #atthemoxy）。

加拿大的大麻公司 Houseplant 為旗下商品增添了些許趣味元素。該品牌於 2022 年 4 月公開發表以樂高積木為設計理念的全新包裝，而負責此次設計的是 Pràctica 設計工作室，其共同創辦人 Javier Arizu 對《Dezeen》雜誌表示：「我們想發揮 Houseplant 童趣、創意的品牌精神，設計出可以收藏、再利用的包裝」。

值得關注的原因：
在經歷了未來難以預測的幾個年頭後，大眾開始尋求可以釋放情緒的片刻時光。品牌於是利用消費者對於樂觀主義及孩童般無憂無慮生活的嚮往，重新設計出可以帶給人們喜悅與樂趣的產品與服務。

品牌於是利用消費者對於
樂觀主義及孩童般無憂無慮
生活的嚮往，重新設計出
可以帶給人們喜悅與樂趣的
產品與服務。

41

食品＆飲品

50

勇於嚐鮮

成為一個美食探險家，
體驗不尋常而非凡的美食饗宴。

願意敞開心胸的饕客們，現在正接受不同以往的餐飲體驗，包括創新的菜單、表演般的烹調過程，以及極端的用餐環境。

倫敦的 Bompas & Parr 是一家以多重感官體驗聞名的設計工作室。2022 年 2 月，該工作室在沙烏地阿拉伯歷史悠久的城鎮阿路拉（AIUla），端出以熔岩烹煮而成的晚宴，該地區獨特的砂岩峽谷以及如月球表面般的黑色熔岩高原而聞名。過程中，岩漿調控技術員會負責控制機具以倒入岩漿，熔岩傾瀉而出的畫面十分壯觀；一旁專業的主廚則會將當地農產品，以攝氏 1,350 度的高溫岩漿進行燒烤烹調。

瑞典航空公司 OceanSky Cruises 計畫於 2024 年在航向北極的飛行船上供應高檔精緻的餐點。在這趟 38 小時的旅程中，旅客除了能在空中享用美食，也能體驗在漫天雪地的戶外用餐是什麼氛圍。

「在太空熟成的葡萄酒，超凡出世的滋味。」，拍賣公司佳士得如此描述。去年的拍賣會上，收藏家爭相競標一支 2000 年出產、在國際太空站（ISS）上繞行了 14 個月的的柏翠酒莊（Petrus）紅酒。這批紅酒在零重力的環境下熟成，並熬過長達 3 億公里的漫長太空旅程。

值得關注的原因：
消費者開始挑戰一成不變的生活。他們揮別中規中矩的用餐環境，享受難忘的餐飲體驗。

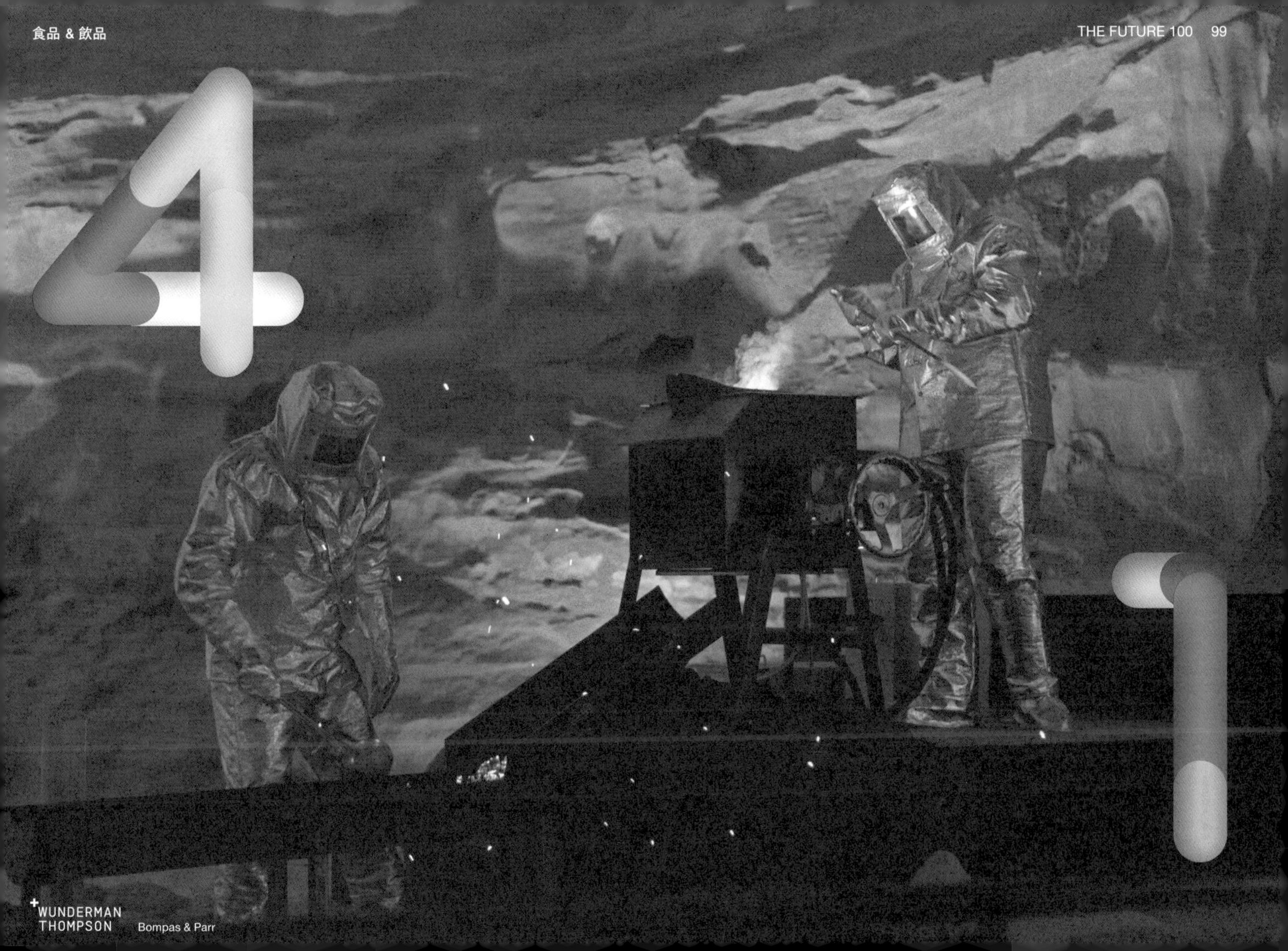

Bompas & Parr

42

虛擬食境

如果元宇宙能品嚐，它會是什麼滋味？

元宇宙影響了餐飲業的發展，它不僅啟發了新風味，也打破了人們對飲食的想像。

2022 年 5 月，可口可樂推出全新口味氣泡飲品，靈感來源超乎想像：元宇宙。該公司首先在線上遊戲《要塞英雄》中推出這款新口味可樂─「字節限定無糖可樂」（Coca-Cola Zero Sugar Byte），風味嚐起來有如像素。可口可樂全球策略資深經理 Oana Vlad 表示：「我們以像素為靈感，深信遊戲能實現各種可能，進而打造出創新風味。此外，如同像素促成數位連結般，『字節限定無糖可樂』也能促進人與人之間的連結。」

其他品牌也相繼以「連結」為主題，重新想像並創造出元宇宙中的餐飲體驗。比如墨西哥建築師 Rojkind Arquitectos 與實驗型設計工作室 Bompas & Parr 合作，為金快活（Jose Cuervo）龍舌蘭酒在 Decentraland 平台上創造了虛擬酒廠。該工作室的共同創辦人 Harry Parr 表示：「希望將人們現實生活中品酒的豐富感官享受，帶入 Decentraland 這個充滿無限可能的世界。」

該設計公司也正重新詮釋飲食在未來數位生活中所扮演的角色，並著重飲食與生活連結，使人共感的特質。Arquitectos 表示：「金快活酒廠的建築結構靈感取自植物龍舌蘭的根。如果仔細觀察它的根部，就會有股防護及鞏固的感覺油然而生。此外，金快活元宇宙酒廠（The Jose Cuervo Metadistillery）致力於成為兼容並蓄的社群中心，協助人們建立更緊密的連結。」

值得關注的原因：

飲食曾經是獨特的生理感官經驗，但各大品牌卻開始思索如何將飲食帶入虛擬世界，以及如何在現實世界重塑虛擬宇宙中的飲食感官體驗。隨著虛擬實境逐漸深入日常，相信未來還會出現更多創新的飲食方式，豐富人們的元宇宙生活。

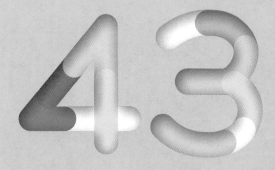

43

無酒精生活

清醒世代逐漸崛起，希望不靠酒精就能嗨起來。

《Vice》於 2022 年 9 月的文章中寫到「酒精已失去吸引力」，且酒吧及餐廳開始提供消費者更多無酒精品項，甚至有些消費者選擇滴酒不沾。這樣的趨勢特別來自於 Z 世代的年輕人選擇無酒精生活。《衛報》報導，英國人不喝酒的年齡層主要介於 16 至 24 歲之間，其中有 26% 的人甚至完全不喝酒。

「隨著健康及養生的意識抬頭，很多人發覺酒精對人體傷害極大，且社會也逐漸接納那些選擇不喝酒的人群。」Z 世代調查機構 Imagen Insights 的共同創辦人 Jay Richards 如此告訴偉門智威。

提倡無酒精飲品的清醒酒吧越來越多。NoLo 是杜拜第一間無酒精酒吧，它於 2022 年 7 月開始試營運，提供消費者無酒精版的健康特調。同年在舊金山開幕的無酒精地下酒吧 Temperance Bar 則採邀請制，提供消費者逾百種無酒精烈酒、調酒及飲品。2021 年 4 月在墨爾本開幕的 Brunswick Aces Bar 則是澳洲第一家無酒精酒吧。

不僅僅是酒吧，洋酒行也開始提供多元的無酒精商品吸引不飲酒的客群。The Zero Co 於 2022 年 12 月在亞特蘭大開幕，成為當地第一間專賣無酒精飲品的酒商，他們要服務的對象是選擇酒精含量低或無酒精飲品的顧客，因為這類需求日漸升高。The Zero Co 店內有逾 300 款無酒精烈酒、葡萄酒及啤酒，甚至設

有品酒空間。2022 年 9 月，快閃店 Sèchey 在紐約西村（West Village）開設了第一間永久店面，並設有品酒櫃檯，其創辦人 Emily Heintz 致力推廣健康的無酒精替代品，讓人們可以免於宿醉的痛苦。2022 年，Free Spirit 在新加坡開幕，成為該國第一間無酒精洋酒行。

值得關注的原因：

過去幾年，我們可以觀察到選擇低酒精或無酒精的消費者穩定上升，而品牌也推出更多精緻的無酒精替代品。現在，多虧了設有品酒櫃檯的無酒精酒類販售商及時髦的無酒精酒吧，無酒精商品將更加走入人們的日常。

零酒精
是新的趨勢。

44

荒野尋味

使用戶外摘採的野生食材－荒野飲食正逐漸萌芽。

人們現在能好好品嚐野人菜單的驚奇了。串流平台 Hulu 的新節目《名廚在野對戰賽》（Chefs vs. Wild），每集都會帶領觀眾跟隨兩位世界名廚的腳步嚐鮮。兩位主廚會被丟在偏遠地區後，想方設法採集、獵捕野生食材入菜，再烹調成高檔佳餚。該影集於 2022 年 9 月開播，節目中每位廚師會與一位野外求生專家搭檔，以確保他們不會誤食有毒的動植物，或在過程中受傷。

想參加節目的廚師必須具備戶外採食與屠宰的相關知識與經驗。確定入選後，他們必須採集食物、捕魚打獵，再將捕獲的食材帶到「野外廚房」製作美味的餐點予兩位主持人試吃——探險家兼專業主廚 Kiran Jethwa 和野味專家 Valerie Segrest。

值得關注的原因：

該影集反映出人們對於以大自然為靈感、採集並料理野生食材的飲食方式越來越感興趣。從摘採野生植物製作特調雞尾酒的趨勢逐漸演化（詳見《改變未來的 100 件事：2022 年全球百大趨勢》第 41 篇），消費者開始將環保理念結合回歸自然的生活態度，在日常生活中實踐。

44

45

俱樂部餐廳

會員專屬的餐飲俱樂部成為頂尖上流社會的飲食新寵。

私人俱樂部與餐廳結合，提供高度客製化的專人服務及頂級美食，並僅限「付費加入」的會員進入其中。

位於邁阿密的餐廳 Haiku 採邀請制，想成為會員，消費者除了須支付年費，每年還須預約至少 4 次奢華的 12 道無菜單料理盛宴。同樣發跡於邁阿密的 ZZ's Club 則早已將俱樂部餐廳的概念帶到紐約，在哈德遜廣場一處佔地 700 坪的三層樓建築中，有廣受歡迎的義大利餐館 Carbone 進駐、還有一間日式餐廳和幾間酒吧，空間只開放給繳交年費的會員進入，且入會年費金額只有在申請加入時才會曉得。預計在 2023 年初於曼哈頓開幕的 Flyfish Club 則將會員概念結合科技潮流，吸引關注加密貨幣的精英階級。以海鮮為靈感的 Flyfish Club 則是隸屬 VCR 餐旅集團旗下，共有兩家分店，會員資格需透過加密貨幣的 Flyfish NFT 來購買。

倫敦頂級餐廳 Casa Cruz 於紐約建造樓高四層的分店，並將俱樂部餐廳的概念發揮到極致。該分店的主要餐廳及休息室對外開放，但四樓的餐廳及屋頂露臺只有繳納 25 萬美金以上的會員才能進入。

值得關注的原因：
高級餐廳正為上流人士提供更高檔的精英飲食體驗，除了僅限會員進入，也迎合幣圈精英的喜好。

高級餐廳正為
上流人士提供更高檔的
精英飲食體驗。

46

WEB3 酒廠

顛覆葡萄酒業既定規則的時機已成熟，
Web3將促進傳統酒廠轉型並升級。

總部位於加州的葡萄酒公司 Evinco 受加密貨幣及元宇宙啟發，以去中心化自治組織（DAO）的形式成立。這種分散式領導的結構是將所有權及決策權交給酒廠的社群，只要擁有該公司的 NFT，每個人都有平等的投票權，能決定公司未來的走向。

「一直以來，葡萄酒廠在製程以外的部分都沒什麼創新，接觸到的消費者也都停留在同一世代。沒有人嘗試要把葡萄酒和烈酒的世界遊戲化，也沒有人讓消費者覺得他們擁有自己支持的品牌所有權。而現在，我們要把品牌忠誠度及社群概念引領至其中。」Evinco 的共同創辦人 Joy Pathak 說道。

沒有人嘗試要把葡萄酒和烈酒的世界遊戲化

Joy Pathak，Evinco共同創辦人

而其他酒廠同樣也在探索 NFT 帶來的獨家福利、流暢度及透明性。Cuvée Collective 是以 NFT 為運作基礎的葡萄酒俱樂部，其 NFT 持有者可在加州葡萄酒之鄉享受 VIP 體驗及專人服務。而奢華 NFT 市集 BlockBar 及自詡為全球第一個以區塊鏈為基礎的葡萄酒投資俱樂部 WiV，則雙雙推出以實體酒瓶及酒箱為設計樣本的 NFT，如此一來，消費者便能透過區塊鏈上的 NFT 來驗證實體商品的真偽與來源，葡萄酒藏家也能順暢地以數位方式進行交易。

值得關注的原因：
去中心化自治組織的用途越來越廣泛，能以去中心化、民主化、透明化及社群共享所有權的方式，重塑傳統產業的結構。

47

全球三大熱門食材

原住民風味料理及道地的傳統菜餚將決定
未來一年的當紅食材。

胭脂樹果實

胭脂樹果實是墨西哥菜裡常見的食材,有著各式各樣的形狀。胭脂樹的英文「Achiote」一詞來自古阿茲提克語系中的納瓦特爾語(Nahuatl),意指「有光澤的種子」。該食材帶有泥土香氣,味道強烈,常用於墨西哥雞肉與魚肉料理,可增添橙紅色的色澤與風味。胭脂樹果實的原產地眾說紛紜,目前主要產於中南美洲、加勒比海、亞洲和非洲國家。

近期胭脂樹果實的流行反映了人們對原住民料理及菜餚的興趣逐漸增加,於是許多新進主廚及餐廳老闆開始將自身文化裡的傳統食材融入菜單。2022 年 8 月,Chipotle 宣布將推出新口味的墨西哥雞肉料理,並以胭脂樹的果實作為明星食材入菜,將香氣提升到新的境界。

日本山椒

山椒是日本料理中的熱門食材，滋味奔放，用途廣泛，適用於多種料理，各種烹調難度皆可使用。2022 年 9 月調味料新品牌 Cabi 以日式料理為靈感，推出一系列調味料，其中的明星商品三入組就包含了一罐結合山椒與味噌口味的醬料。根據品牌官網的食譜，該產品最適合用來烹調鮭魚及絞肉。

當今最為多元的 Z 世代帶動了嘗試多元文化菜餚的風潮，歷史悠久且具文化意義的食材也以嶄新的配方入菜，成為菜單上及廚房中的美味來源。

代茶冬青

代茶冬青來自美國原生的冬青樹，是美洲大陸唯一含天然咖啡因的植物。它以香甜的風味及泥土氣息著稱，美國原住民常將它用於花草茶及淨化儀式中。

製造代茶冬青的茶商有佛羅里達州的 Yaupon Brothers、北卡羅萊納州的 Yaupon Tea Co. 以及德州的 CatSpring Yaupon 等。2022 年 10 月在德州奧斯汀開幕的新餐廳 BBQ Ramen Tatsuya 便在其調酒 Melo-Byrd 中加入冬青茶、索托酒、梅酒、餐前酒以及梅子鹽粉。在 2023 年，代茶冬青勢必會在出現在各大菜單中，敬請拭目以待

細胞培養餐點

細胞培養的食材從實驗室移往商品陳列架上，
而第一個受惠的可能是高級餐廳。

以細胞培養方式生產肉類及乳製品，這種提供動物蛋白質來源的方式充滿前景，不僅能免除動物的痛苦，也能避免環境惡化。然而，細胞培養食材的成本，直到最近仍居高不下。

細胞培養的過程首先要從活體動物身上取得細胞，再將這些細胞置於生物反應器裡的培養基裡，以利生成脂肪與肌肉。2013 年，第一個由實驗室培養出來的漢堡耗資 20 萬歐元，到了 2021 年，其成本已下降到低於 10 歐元。根據 Crunchbase 的調查，在 2021 年，全球在人造肉新創公司的投資額已將近 10 億美元。

由於投資人挹注了大把資金發展人造蛋白質替代品，所以讓高級餐廳優先運用其成果顯得相當合理。2021 年，大阪大學的科學家利用 3D 列印的技術，製造出含有完整條狀脂肪的和牛，而荷蘭科學家則針對人造魚子醬進行試驗。

2022 年 9 月，以細胞培養牛奶的新創公司 TurtleTree 聘請主廚 Dominique Crenn 作為其食物創新顧問，Crenn 曾在 Netflix 影集《主廚的餐桌》（Chef's Table）裡大展廚藝。

Crenn 在舊金山的旗艦餐廳 Atelier Crenn 榮獲米其林三星肯定。該餐廳以海鮮素料理聞名，希望能將對地球的影響降到最低，以詩的形式呈現菜單也是該餐廳的知名特色。

「我誠摯地相信,我們將會再次製造出令人驚豔且愉悅的誘人食物,屆時,食物革命才真正展開。」TurtleTree 的創辦人兼執行長 Fengru Lin 向《The Sacramento Bee》如此說道。TurtleTree 的總部位於新加坡,並在加州薩克拉門托(Sacramento)設有工廠。

2022 年初,以人造雞肉聞名的加州公司 Upside Foods 決定進入高檔市場,收購以人造海鮮,尤其是人造龍蝦聞名的威斯康辛公司 Cultured Decadence。此外,Upside Foods 也和 Crenn 合作,一旦主管機關批准人造雞肉可對外銷售,就會將該食材加入 Crenn 的餐廳菜單中。

值得關注的原因:

細胞培養出來的蛋白質能否商業化還有待商確,到目前為止,仍只有新加坡一個國家允許人造雞肉販售。不過對某些消費者來說,他們嘗試的第一口人造肉可能會來自高級餐廳的餐桌,而非從超商架上自行購入與烹調。

超「現實」餐飲體驗

能源危機掀起餐飲業的創新風潮。

隨著比利時布魯塞爾的能源價格飆漲，餐廳老闆及主廚正在嘗試不用瓦斯、火爐，改採用低電量的方式烹調。Brasserie Surrealiste 餐廳僅提供冷盤及輕度火烤的餐點，並使用炭火來燒烤，餐桌也改以蠟燭為光源。該餐廳供應的餐點包括生白鮪魚、豆烤豬肉、窯烤佛卡夏以及布里歐麵包佐鯷魚等。

Racines 餐館的老闆 Francesco Cury 說到：「我們的靈感是重回山頂洞人時代，提供一系列只需花幾秒鐘燒烤即可食用的料理。」他的員工會在小餐館裡完成料理及上菜工作。

2022 年 10 月，一家位於英國弗羅德舍姆（Frodsham）的餐廳 Next Door 在沒有主電源的情況下營業。該餐廳供應顧客九道料理，而為了抗議能源成本不斷上漲，他們選擇以燭光為燈源，使用炭烤、煙燻、醃製和發酵等技巧料理食材，並以火煮茶、加熱飲品和食物。Next Door 不使用冰箱，而是以地窖保存食材，並僅限現金付款。主廚 Richard Nuttall 使用創新的手法料理及保存每項食材，他向《BBC》表示：「我們用木碳燒烤洋蔥及紅蘿蔔，並將香草置於火爐旁乾燥。」

值得關注的原因：
歐洲餐飲業者著實感受到能源危機帶來的財務壓力，許多主廚正採取極端作法，希望打造新穎的用餐體驗，同時降低能源成本、維持財務穩定。

Next Door restaurant (both images)

50

超循環設計

部份餐廳正著手投入循環設計。

未來的用餐趨勢不再只是減少食物浪費或使用再生原料，而是連整體的用餐環境都會以環保為設計考量。

位於瑞典哥特堡的餐廳 Vrå 採用的家具由廚餘及副產品製成。這些家具由當地設計師 Carolina Härdh 設計，希望能讓顧客親眼見證廚餘經過妥善處理及再利用後可發揮的價值。

Härdh 設計的椅凳及茶几組合是由碎貝殼、米澱粉、魚骨製成，雖然材料是生物原料而非水泥，看起來卻像磨石子一樣。而顧客用餐後留下的食物殘渣，也會用來製成肥料灌溉屋頂的園圃，或做成日式料理所需的筷架。

Härdh 告訴《Dezeen》，她選擇原料的方式是「查看該餐廳的廚餘桶」。她希望透過親眼目睹及親身使用這些家具，「能讓顧客有不一樣的體會，並開始思考食材從盤中美食變成廢棄原料及家具的過程。」

值得關注的原因：
餐飲業的永續實踐正在改變。品牌不再只是減少食物浪費，還會透過餐廳及社交空間的再生循環設計，創造環保飲食的下個篇章。

51

美容

60

51

生理時鐘護膚模式

肌膚保養之道開始將人體的生理節奏融入其中。

美容覺的概念啟發了新的肌膚保養妙方,品牌的最新產品開始跟著肌膚的生理時鐘滴答前進。

科學保養品牌 Nobel Panacea 於 2022 年 2 月創立,其晚安面膜 The Chronobiology Sleep Mask「以肌膚自然的生理節奏為調控基礎,精準地將活性成分導入肌膚當中」。這款面膜會在夜間以三個階段的程序來活化肌膚:在晚間 11 點至凌晨 4 點間的排毒階段,會釋放水基果酸(PHA)及益生元、益生菌、後生元;在修復階段,面膜會釋出視黃醇及胜肽;在最後的滋潤階段,因為肌膚的吸收能力達到最高峰,所以面膜會釋出神經醯胺與玻尿酸。

4AM 的精華液與 La Prairie 的保養油也雙雙主打可以維護生理時鐘運作且與之同步的特性,藉此減緩肌膚老化。

美妝保養品牌 Mutha 將自創成分「生理調節肌膚保養因子」(Circadian Dermablend)加入頂級乳霜當中,該產品的設計是為了調節肌膚每晚的生理節奏。這款產品於 2021 年 6 月推出,其中的草本配方會在夜間修復平日受到外在物質傷害的肌膚,使其恢復滑順與年輕活力。

值得關注的原因:
愛好保養的消費者開始利用生物學來讓肌膚保養再升級。

美容覺的概念啓發了新的肌膚保養妙方，品牌開始跟著肌膚的生理時鐘滴答前進。

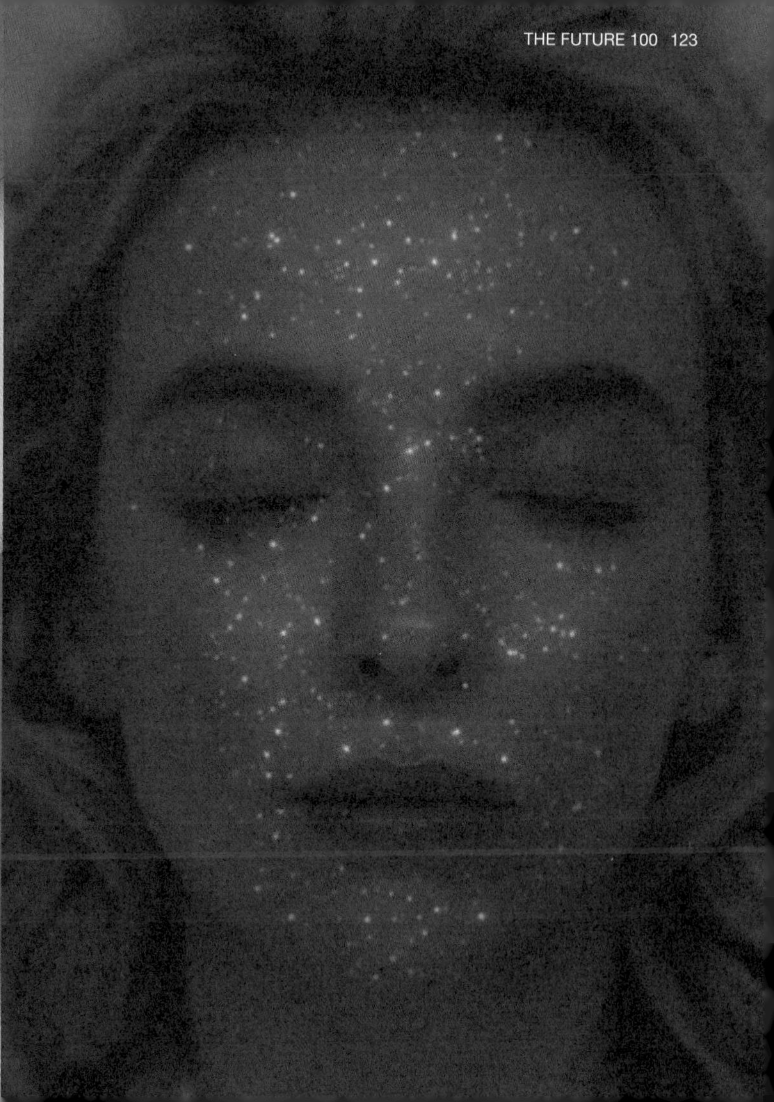

Noble Panacea, courtesy of Facebook

精神皮膚學

美妝品牌開始嘗試更多樣化的肌膚保養成分，
希望同時滋潤消費者的肌膚與心靈。

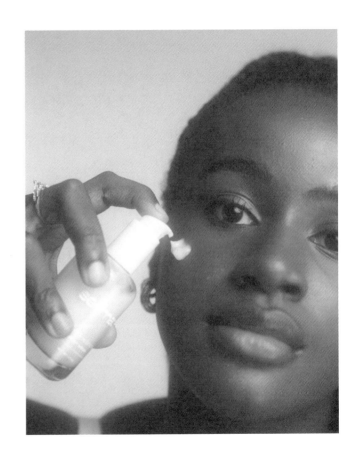

日本護膚品牌 Tatcha 打算運用精神皮膚學——也就是肌膚與心靈間的連結為保養概念，利用特定的保養步驟與成分來強化身心互動，例如甜茴香可提升專注力，檜木油則可以放鬆身心。聯合利華旗下品牌於 2022 年夏季做的一份調查顯示，有 69% 的受訪者在過去十二個月間覺得心力交瘁，70% 的人甚至認為壓力使他們的膚況惡化。這進一步證明了消費者對於能夠同時照顧身心靈的保養成分與儀式感的需求確實存在。

2020 年成立的 Selfmade 是「第一個關注情緒問題的個人護理品牌」，他們將精神皮膚學和情緒健康視為核心價值。該品牌與心理健康專家及年輕的 Z 世代顧問團隊合作。品牌創辦人暨執行長 Stephanie Lee 向偉門智威智庫表示，由於 Z 世代特別注重

「精神皮膚學則是能探討大腦和肌膚間連結的一門學問。」

Stephanie Lee，Selfmade創辦人暨執行長

解決心理健康問題，因此能讓品牌「立基於可信賴的心理健康科學基礎之上。」這也反映在我們對投資人與經營團隊及產品的描述當中。

Lee 解釋道：「我們的壓力太大，但沒有一個有效的機制能讓我們了解並達成身為人類的需求。而精神皮膚學則是能探討大腦和肌膚間連結的一門學問。」Selfmade 的精華液 Self Disclosure Intimacy Serum 與磨砂膏 True Grit Resilience Scrub 等產品，著實展現了這份精神。2022 年 9 月，他們推出的乳霜產品 Corrective Experience Comfort Cream，含有自我修復成分，主要以 Cortinib G 使肌膚透亮的維他命 C 為關鍵原料，藉此降低皮質醇並紓緩壓力。

值得關注的原因：
根據 Tatcha 的調查顯示，74% 的人有意識到心理狀態與肌膚健康之間的連結。美妝品牌開始供應能有效對抗壓力的產品，透過精神皮膚學儀式和有效的成份來同時照顧肌膚與療癒心靈。

53

原料復育

品牌開始尋回早已消失與被遺忘的味覺記憶。

品牌開始搶救已遍尋不著的花香，將其加入品牌最新的香氛產品中，讓原料成為通往過去的任意門，並為後世保留這種感官經驗。

擁有倫敦中央聖馬丁學院未來材料碩士學位（MA Material Futures）的 Tetsuo Lin 近期與 Haeckels 展開合作，為美妝產業搶救已經消失的香氣。他們打算利用花朵樣本的一小部分 DNA 來進行基因工程，重新創造出已消失的香味，這也成為 Haekels 實踐永續的重要里程碑。在實驗室生產的香味不需使用實體花卉或精油來提煉，免除資源密集型的作物種植過程對環境所造成的影響。

在歐洲，研究計畫 Odeuropa 利用人工智慧（AI）來復刻僅存在於過去的氣味。該計畫的研究人員運用 AI 技術來探勘 16 至 20 世紀早期的圖文及文獻歷史檔案，藉此找出「過去利用不同語彙描述氣味的方式，了解其淵源地、應用場合與特殊用途，以及氣味與不同情緒之間的關聯」。他們希望彰顯歐洲豐富的嗅覺記憶史。

值得關注的原因：
復育已滅絕的原料不只是為了吸引消費者的目光，還能同時保留當今的自然環境樣態，為未來的世代留下生態紀錄。

Above: Haeckels
Right: Odeuropa

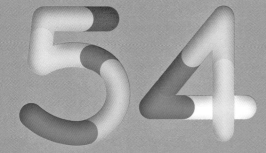

適應原雙重保養

機能保健啓發了美妝產品新配方。

2022 年 8 月成立的美妝新品牌 Herbar 以「美妝保養也能很療癒」為理念，採用近年風靡歐美的適應原（adaptogens）作為配方，他們認為適應原是「無毒、無害、養生的植物，常用來提升人體抵禦能力，對抗各種有害的生物、物理及化學物質。」該系列新品僅使用提煉自「動植物或菌類」的成分，並均具備內在與外在療癒的雙重功效。

品牌首款商品為臉部保養油，主打三種關鍵的適應原成分，包含以排毒、保濕功效聞名的成分銀耳，可降低發炎、浮腫、抗老化並對抗自由基危害的靈芝，以及富含鐵與維他命 C，可對抗痘痘、消除黑斑及疤痕等的大棗。

Allies of Skin 於 2022 年推出進階亮白精華（Advanced Brightening Serum），使用含有靈芝與香菇的適應原配方，來加強肌膚健康與保濕。Hydrafacial x JLo Beauty 於 2022 年 10 月推出一款強效精華，主打使用發酵適應原的配方。

值得關注的原因：
美妝保養日漸納入健康照護的類別中，其產品也從美妝商品櫃位移往健康養生專區。

虛擬香氛

美妝與香氛品牌開始為元宇宙改寫香氣代表的意義。

2022 年 8 月，Gucci 在《機器磚塊》（Roblox）這款遊戲上推出虛擬香水 Gucci Flora，此款產品不具任何氣味，而是由一系列的體驗組成，包含挑戰關卡、遊戲與互動學習模組，還有以香水瓶為設計靈感的虛擬後背包，讓 Roblox 的玩家可以「穿戴」此款香水。

香氛品牌 Byredo 和虛擬潮流品牌工作室 RTFKT 則以不同的形式來呈現他們的虛擬香氛。2022 年 6 月，他們共同發表虛擬香水 Alphameta，以可配戴的氣息來演繹其香氣，推出 26 款帶有不同情緒氛圍，例如「敏銳」（acuity）、「天真」（naivety）等，並鼓勵使用者自行組合不同的情緒來「提煉」個人化的氣息。這些香氣以限量收藏的「元素」形式呈現，可於 RTFKT 所謂的「虛擬化身生態系」中獲得。

自詡為「未來香氛」（profuture）的品牌 Altra 同樣也在虛擬環境中將情緒與氣味連結在一起，並於 2022 年 2 月推出虛擬的「香氣地景」（scentscape）。品牌共同創辦人 Beckielou Brown 對《哈潑時尚》表示：「我對香氣這類感官體驗跨入虛擬世界的方式深感著迷。」他形容這類的香氣地景是「一種沈浸式的數位氛圍，在日益數位化的環境中，提供觀眾另一種對氣味的新想像，並能喚起相關的情緒。」

值得關注的原因：
目前為止，虛擬環境大多以視覺元素組成，而這些在元宇宙發展初期出現的創意，讓我們看到未來的數位互動如何更具沈浸式氛圍：重新想像虛擬世界中的感官體驗。

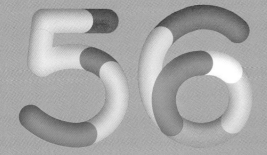

肌膚循環

居家保養的新風潮包含極簡保養品項，
與每隔幾日使用的特定保養品。

美妝消費者開始
將維護心理健康的習慣
應用在肌膚保養上。

抖音網紅往往會帶起新的美妝風潮，而席捲該平台的最新潮流是「肌膚循環」概念（skin cycling）。截至 2022 年 11 月，該標籤在抖音上的觀看人次高達 35 億，這些短片中宣導的是交替使用保養品與留幾天當肌膚修復期的好處何在。雖然抖音網紅的保養步驟各異，但大概念是以四天為一循環，先使用活性成分，例如酸類產品或視黃醇，一次最多用兩天，後兩天則留給肌膚休息。

雖然皮膚保養專家過往一直鼓勵民眾交替使用不同的活性成份，但是創造「肌膚循環」一詞的人是獲得紐約資格認證的皮膚科專家 Whiteney Bowe 博士。2022 年 Bowe 在一個播客節目《好好生活的藝術》（The Art of Being Well）中擔任客座來賓，並在裡面談到：「要讓膚況達到最佳狀態，就要在夜間循環使用不同的保養品」，接著強調給予肌膚充足的時間休養能「修復其天然屏障並讓微生物群系的生長狀況恢復正常」。

品牌也開始著手運用此趨勢來行銷產品，推出循環保養套組，讓消費者可以輕鬆「重置」肌膚保養程序。By Beauty Bay 推出的「肌膚循環保養套裝」（The Skin Cycling Kit）含有四款精華及夜間循環保養教學。Nip & Fab's 的套裝則含有保濕乳液、甘醇酸與視黃醇等活性產品，組合中也有四天為一循環的使用教學，讓消費者可以按部就班地輕鬆完成循環保養步驟。

值得關注的原因：
美妝消費者開始將維護心理健康的習慣應用在肌膚保養上，他們支持休息日帶來的好處是能更徹底地了解身體需求，不再一昧追求成效與結果。

57

實驗室美妝新品

最新保養成分以生物科技技術製成，
讓美妝產品的生產過程能更符合永續價值、
提高產品功效並縮短生產時間。

雅詩蘭黛旗下的英國美妝保養品牌 Haeckels 於 2022 年 9 月推出升級版品牌 Haeckels 2.0。由實驗室生產的新產品線使用永續且可分解的包裝，降低生產過程中的碳排放，並讓生產時間減半。此次產品發表是該品牌革命性永續美妝實踐的最新成果。

聯合利華已承諾要投入 1.2 億美元與總部位在聖地牙哥的生技集團 Geno 合作，希望打造一系列僅使用植本配方的美妝保養、居家與個人護理產品。聯合利華的研發長 Richard Slater 表示，打造可取代棕櫚油或化石燃料的替代產品成份，讓品牌可以在「科學與永續的交鋒位置坐穩寶座」，也讓品牌可以成為「適應未來趨勢的企業，同時符合消費者、股東與地球的利益」。

實驗室生產的配方也為產品提升了功效。英國肌膚保養品牌 Cellular Goods 於 2022 年 2 月推出以實驗室生產的大麻二酚為成分的新款保養品。生技美妝品牌 Ourself 於同年成立，預計仿效門診手術流程生產一系列生技美妝成分的保養品。

保養品化學專家 Jen Novakovich 告訴《Allure》雜誌，生技成分可以依需求客製出「你想要的任何功效，可以只提高特定成分的用量來達成特殊需求。」使用生物技術來生產成分更可符合永續目標，Novakovich 說道：「許多的產品生命週期分析（追蹤成分生產過程的土地與水資源使用情況，藉此評估對環境造成的影響）都顯示，生技產品對達成永續目標更有助益。」

值得關注的原因：
美妝品牌開始啟用實驗室生產的生技成分，來達成產品永續目標與精準保養的雙重功效。

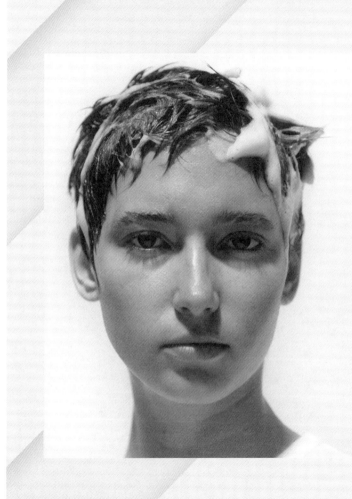

58

全球三大熱門成分

心理健康與天然配方引領今年的美妝保養趨勢。

檜木

2022 年 9 月，日本美妝品牌 Tatcha 推出能同時療癒身心的新系列身體保養品，其中的主成分檜木是原產於日本的扁柏屬植物，帶有能放鬆身心的森林香氣。檜木有「樹王」的美稱，也反應出日本人「泡森林浴」的習慣—走入森林與自然中讓自己能好好放鬆。Credo Beauty 的共同創辦人暨營運長 Annie Jackson 告訴《Well+Good》：「品牌開始利用森林中找到的藥用成分來提升肌膚的免疫力，並達到舒壓的效果。」

紅毛丹

這項來自東南亞的熱帶水果開始帶起肌膚保養潮流，可以取代視黃醇，並對抗黑斑、皺紋。紅毛丹已經過證實能有效對抗魚尾紋，它能促進皮膚中膠原蛋白與彈力蛋白的增生，提供抗氧化物，且致敏性遠低於市面上眾多的視黃醇及其衍生物製成的產品。通過資格認證的皮膚專家 Hadley King 認為，整顆紅毛丹都對肌膚有益，她告訴《Well+Good》：「紅毛丹的果皮、果肉、種子都富含糖分、單寧、類黃酮等等具抗氧化功效的物質。」Dr Loretta、Alpyn Beauty、Indie Lee 和 Holifrog 等品牌都相繼推出含有紅毛丹的新款精華與乳液，並將其列為 2022 年的明星保養成分。

植物奶

米奶、椰奶和堅果奶開始成為肌膚與美髮護理產品中日益受歡迎的成分，因為他們具有保濕、去角質的功效。從咖啡杯到梳妝台，植物奶已成為許多頂級保養品牌的愛用配方：Dermalogica 的去角質產品 Daily Milkfoliant 使用脫水椰奶與研磨燕麥製作而成。Fresh 的牛奶身體保養乳系列是 2022 年推出的全新植物奶系列商品，改版自該品牌從 1996 年即推出的牛奶保養品系列。Sol de Janeiro 將巴西堅果、大花可可樹（cupuaçu）、巴巴蘇棕櫚（babaçu）加進免沖洗護髮產品 Brazilian Joia Milky Leave-In Conditioner 當中以滋潤秀髮。

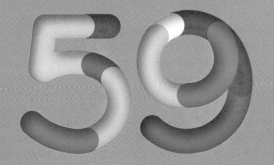

超級秀髮充電站

預防勝於治療的道理現在開始適用於頭髮護理。

市面上的頭髮護理產品琳瑯滿目,因為疫情帶來的壓力、基因、甚至單純穿戴伊斯蘭頭巾等眾多因素都可能導致頭髮脫落、受損。

女性掉髮問題開始四處浮現,從光鮮亮麗的雜誌到 NBC 的節目《今日秀》(Today Show)都曾談及此議題,該節目曾於 2022 年 5 月播出讓人寒毛直豎的影片,紀錄紐約一名醫師在病患頭皮注射「高濃度血小板血漿」的經過。不過對頭髮日漸稀疏的女性來說,較常見的做法是綜合使用含有玻尿酸這類成分的口服營養保健品、外用藥膏、精華乳液與洗髮產品。開架保養品牌如 L'Oréal 和 Rejoice 也已推出「預防掉髮」的系列產品。

據 Coherent Market Insights 的調查顯示,2028 年以前頭髮護理產品的全球市場規模就會達到 1,500 億美元以上;而 The Insight Partners 的預測報告也顯示,單看預防脫髮的產品,在 2028 年前其規模就會超過 3,100 萬美元了。

2022 年 5 月,大勢妝髮品牌 Ouai 針對掉髮問題推出頭皮精華 The Scalp Serum 與純素保健膠囊 Thick & Full Supplements。這兩項產品都加入了知名的護髮成分,包含胜肽、生物素、玻尿酸、豌豆苗萃取物等來強韌秀髮並促進頭髮生長。「我們每件產品的誕生都是源自於自家消費者給我們的回饋,我們一直有收到下列需求,例如想要解決頭皮乾癢、頭髮分岔斷裂等問題。」Ouai 的執行長 Colin Walsh 如此說道。

英國品牌 Nue Co 於 2022 年 1 月推出兩項能促進頭髮生長、讓頭髮更茂密的產品。其一為口服保健食品「生長階段」(Growth Phase),可促進頭髮生長並減少脫落;另一項產品「超級濃密」

（Supa Thick），則是洗髮前使用的外用產品，可為頭皮去除角質同時幫助頭髮生長、預防脫落。Nue Co 的創辦人 Jules Miller 告訴《Glossy》雜誌，這兩項產品是為「掉髮情形比平常更嚴重的女性所設計，而且據統計，我們每三個人當中就有一個人會遇到這種狀況。」

頂級沙龍護髮品牌 Oribe 於 2022 年 2 月推出 Hair Alchemy 系列產品，主打能對付頭髮分岔問題。產品研發經理 Gabriella Raccuia 告訴《哈潑時尚》：「預防性商品一直是肌膚保養品項中的重要類別，而現在也開始進入頭髮護理領域，因為消費者越來越知道自己想要什麼了。」

值得關注的原因：
預防保養的趨勢已從肌膚保養與身體護理延伸至秀髮健康領域。

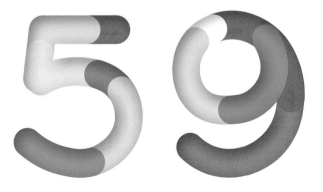

「預防性商品一直是肌膚保養品項中的重要類別，而現在也開始進入頭髮護理領域，因為消費者越來越知道自己想要什麼了。」

Gabriella Raccuia，Oribe產品研發經理

美妝認同

「美妝」成為身份探索與玩味生活的要角，
更是一種展現自我認同的方式。

Isamaya Ffrench 正在重塑美妝的定義，她認為妝容是探索自我身份與多重自我形象的工具，她在 2022 年 6 月推出的同名化妝品品牌 Isamaya，儼然已成為自我形象建構的先鋒。該品牌目前已推出的兩個產品系列都代表了獨特的身份認同。首發系列「工業風」（Industrial）彰顯「硬派」風格，靈感來自「皮衣與乳膠衣著、穿環與橡膠，還有肉身、力量、鎮定」等概念。

最新發表的「狂野新星」（Wild Star）系列則是「要向我們心中的牛仔女孩致敬」，並為「頑強堅韌、據理力爭、勇敢堅持」的精神賦予實體形象，Ffrench 如此說道。「她知道自己是誰且從不妥協，她能順應心中的意念來感受自己的美麗與力量。她內心有個狂野的靈魂。」

Donni Davy 是在電視節目《高校十八禁》（Euphoria）中打造出亮眼妝容的化妝師，她在 2022 年 5 月推出個人品牌 Half Magic，搭上該節目帶起的狂歡妝容風潮（詳見《改變未來的 100 件事：2020 年全球百大趨勢》第 51 章〈高校十八禁仿妝〉）。Half Magic 的產品獲一家娛樂公司支持，讓相關妝容與劇中人物的形象更加緊貼在一起。Half Magic 的總經理 Michelle Liu 告訴《Allure》雜誌：「Half Magic 之所以會成立，是受到《高校十八禁》全球各地的粉絲所帶起的美妝文化現象鼓舞。節目幕後的創作者重聚一堂，繼續延伸相關對話，探索自我身份與自我表達的方式。」

The Fabricant 則把同樣的概念帶入虛擬國度中。這家虛擬時尚品牌於 2022 年 10 月推出能妝點臉部的虛擬產品 Xxories，品牌創意總監 Amber Slooten 表示：「數位美妝有潛力把我們的自我

形象推展至從未出現過的境地」，也讓美妝愛好者可以「在實體世界以外嘗試更多不同的身份並探索其他面向的自我。」

值得關注的原因：

The Fabricant 的內容總監 Michaela Larosse 對新加坡《Vogue》雜誌表示：「過去美妝只是為了打造令人賞心悅目的視覺容貌，但現在它還能傳達我們個人的信念、感受與觀點。」在數位世界中，妝容將能展現使用者不斷變化的情緒狀態，為數位身份能帶來的無限可能敞開了大門。Larosse 接著說道：「我們未來可以套用多種不同的虛擬形象，彰顯當下的心情寫照，只要輕輕一按就能改變個人形象。」

61

零售&商業

70

多宇宙設計

如夢似幻的異世界設計在創意新紀元
改變現實世界的空間風貌。

現實生活中夢幻奇異的新設計，將人們帶往奇幻世界與另類實境。隨著數位環境和虛擬世界的日新月異，促成新一代的創意風格，以無邊際的奇特狂想，來掙脫現實世界的束縛。

2022 年 4 月，巴黎世家（Balenciaga）以粉紅色的絨毛鋪滿整間倫敦門市，從牆壁、地板到商品架上，每處都以粉紅色絨毛包圍，給顧客一種趣味又超現實的夢幻世界。

2022 年 5 月，時裝設計師 Simon Jacquemus 為英國百貨公司 Selfridges 推出一系列的快閃裝置藝術。根據 Selfridges 的說法，該系列以浴室的「超現實想像」為靈感；設計師 Jacquemus 則表示他目的在「創造與水、浴室意象相關，既瘋狂又超現實的裝置藝術」。

2022 年 6 月，路易威登（Louis Vuitton）在巴黎羅浮宮打造一座仿真大小的玩具賽車場，作為 2023 年春夏時裝發表會的背景。該品牌表示「這座亮黃色的巨型兒童賽車場，讓人聯想起綠野仙蹤裡的黃磚路，不僅激發人們的想像力，更為他們開啟一條進化之路，將童年幻想化為現實。」

上海連鎖餐廳小大董以「傳遞富有情感的夢幻用餐體驗」為構想，在餐廳內光線採用神秘的藍紫色調，照亮具雕塑美感的隔間與深色牆面，搭配「迷幻」的音樂，以及讓餐廳顧客與服務生看起來扭曲顛倒的鏡面天花板，來營造「該空間的夢幻氛圍」。

值得關注的原因：
隨著元宇宙的展開，我們正準備迎接創意的下個黃金世代。日漸複雜的數位設計，解放現實世界中的創意束縛，不論線上或線下，通往多宇宙設計的大門都已開啟。

共同創作的雙贏模式

在下一個零售世代中，我們將能看見使用者與
品牌共同創造出虛擬產品及店面陳設。

Nike 全新的 Web3 平台 .Swoosh 讓消費者能自行設計並銷售
他們的虛擬運動鞋。該平台於 2022 年 11 月推出測試版，希望結
合虛擬交易市集、VIP 社群及創作者經濟於一體。在平台上，民眾
可以購買及交易 Nike 的虛擬商品、參與社群挑戰以解鎖活動及
產品的獨家消息，甚至共同創作 Nike 的運動產品。

Nike 預告明年將擴大 .Swoosh 的社群挑戰規模，贏得比賽的會
員有機會和該品牌的設計師共同設計 Nike 的虛擬產品，甚至能
在上市後收取權利金。「我們希望重新定義何謂創作者」，Nike
旗下虛擬工作室 Nike Virtual Studios 的副總裁兼總經理 Ron
Faris 如此說道。

Forever 21 邀請顧客在 Roblox 平台上策畫並經營他們的虛擬店面。該品牌在 2021 年 12 月推出 Forever 21 Shop City 企劃，引導由使用者負責決策的零售模式。用戶能開店、進貨並經營自己的 Forever 21 虛擬加盟店，包括管理倉儲、協助顧客、操作收銀機、雇用員工及裝飾店面窗櫥等；也能自行設計店面，挑選喜歡的家具、藝術品、燈光及音樂；甚至規劃想在當季銷售的品牌產品，從 Roblox 上每期與實體店面同步更新的產品型錄中，親自挑選想進貨的品項。

元宇宙商機正在擴張，同時也為零售業帶來新靈感。根據彭博（Bloomberg）的統計，元宇宙市場規模將從 2020 年的 4,790 億美元上升至 2024 年的 7,830 億美元。目前 Nike 成長最快

速的部門是其數位部門 Nike Digital，占了總營收逾四分之一（26%）。該品牌在 Roblox 平台上搭建的虛擬世界 Nikeland，可讓用戶自行客製 Nike 球鞋，截至 2022 年 11 月已吸引了 2,600 萬人造訪，旗下 Web3 產品更在 2022 年 8 月前就已累積了 1.85 億美元的營收。

值得關注的原因：
共同創作將是虛擬零售業未來的發展方向。隨著 Web3 時代的到來，創意成為新的地位象徵（請見第 2 章〈創作者社群〉），而品牌也開始調整虛擬世界中的行銷策略，將傳統商品融入創意及共同創作的成分以利銷售。在未來，我們將看到更多品牌開始將虛擬商業活動的策劃權下放，提供消費者更多揮灑創意的空間。

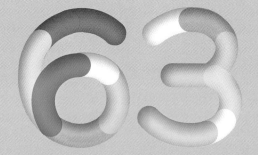

暮光商店歡迎你

以混合模式操作為「影子商店」（dark store）
增添社群歸屬感。

疫情加速了人們對極速快遞的需求，提供隨選服務的物流公司於是利用散落大城市中各個地點的「影子商店」來縮短送貨時間，讓消費者最快在 10 分鐘內就收到商品。然而，近期這些影子商店或廚房卻受到城市居民反彈，認為他們浪費了社區的寶貴空間，導致某些國家必須採取措施加以禁止。在法國，影子商店被重新歸類為倉儲而非店面，使地方當局有權將其移出市中心。同時，該行業的大型業者如 Gorillas、Getir 及 Zapp 也因供過於求，開始縮減部分國家的影子商店數量。

由於影子商店的長期發展性開始受到質疑，業者於是將社群元素重新融合至其商業模式中，讓影子商店搖身一變成為混合型的「暮光商店」（twilight stores）。有別於過往不對外開放的商業模式，暮光商店加入與消費者面對面接觸的元素，不僅能與當地居民互動，也能從未預約、直接走入店面的顧客身上獲益。

有別於過往不對外開放的商業模式，暮光商店加入與消費者面對面接觸的元素。

德國快遞服務 DPD 在柏林開設了兩用的暮光商店，不僅可作為微型倉庫以電動自行車在當地送貨，更是能協助店鋪解決不便收發包裹的問題。同樣地，按需服務快遞公司「戶戶送」（Deliveroo）旗下的戶戶超市（Deliveroo's Hop）不僅是倫敦鄰近地區的民生用品快遞據點，更是顧客能取貨、路人能順道下單的窗口。

自稱非影子廚房的「外送至上餐廳」Taster 在其倫敦的兩間快閃店推出英國名廚傑米·奧利佛（Jamie Oliver）的外送品牌 Pasta Dreams。Taster 的執行長 Anton Soulier 表示，混合外送與餐廳的優勢在於不僅將效率最大化，又能讓品牌「與顧客建立直接關係」。

值得關注的原因：
影子商店固然方便，卻不能在人口密度高的地區將空間善加利用。這樣的困境促成了暮光商店的誕生，一種利用空間、便利性及社區感來獲利的混合零售模式。

聰明錢進元宇宙

金融機構及金融科技（Fintech）品牌努力
揭開元宇宙經濟的神秘面紗。

2022 年 3 月，美國財政部開始推動計畫，希望教育大眾加密貨幣的潛在風險。該部的金融素養委員會（Financial Literacy Education Commission）負責發行教育刊物並籌辦相關推廣活動，希望讓大眾了解加密資產如何運作，以及它們與其他付款方式的差別。

根據《路透社》報導，美國財政部負責國內金融事務的副部長梁內利（Nellie Liang）表示，隨著加密貨幣從金融市場的小眾躍升成為主流，財政部希望採取行動，提升公眾對投資數位資產的風險認知。「我們耳聞越來越多投資人與家庭進場購買加密資產，也意識到有些數位資產的運作十分複雜，所以我們認為在這個領域多加教育大眾並喚醒公共意識，應該會有所助益」，梁內利說道。

除了政府，金融品牌也投身加密貨幣教育的行列。2022 年 4 月，富達投資（Fidelity Investments）在元宇宙設立了金融教育中心。該中心設立於 Decentraland 平台之中，是棟八層樓的虛擬學習中心，教導訪客投資的基本原理、何謂元宇宙，並介紹富達的元宇宙 ETF。該品牌表示，建立此中心的目的是希望「教育新一代的投資人」。

2022 年 2 月，萬事達卡擴大其諮詢服務的範圍，將加密貨幣、NFT 及開放銀行（open banking）納入其中。而這一系列的新服務能協助銀行及企業啟用加密貨幣及 NFT 等數位資產，也能對數位貨幣及 NFT 進行風險評估，並針對數位錢包、加密貨幣信用卡及加密貨幣酬賓方案的開發設計提供建議。

Visa 於 2021 年 12 月為金融機構與商家推出加密貨幣諮詢服務。該公司表示，其服務對象包括想透過加密貨幣產品吸引或留住顧客的金融機構、希望深入了解 NFT 的零售業者，甚至是想研究數位貨幣可行性的各國中央銀行。

值得關注的原因：
元宇宙及 Web3 將開創新型態的零售途徑與數位產品經濟，進而改變人們的消費模式，創造全新的加密經濟生態系統。然而，這一切的先決要件是教育。Web3 商業市場的未來不僅仰賴品牌及消費者的採用，更需要兩者都具備足夠的相關知識才行。

無障礙購物站

品牌藉由先進的語音辨識科技，將現實世界及虛擬世界
轉化為所有人皆能自在徜徉的無障礙空間。

科技巨擘如亞馬遜、蘋果、谷歌、Meta、微軟皆相繼投入美國伊利諾大學的「無障礙語音辨識計畫」(Speech Accessibility Project)，希望透過強化語音辨識功能，來幫助因疾病而導致說話方式與眾不同的人。該計畫將蒐集患有肌肉萎縮性脊髓側索硬化症（路格裡克氏病）、帕金森氏症、腦性麻痺、唐氏症患者中具代表性的語音樣本，以建立語音資料庫來訓練機器學習模型，希望進一步發展語音辨識技術以回應這些特定人士的需求。

透過這類語音辨識技術的發展，實體零售商及電商將更有能力打造具包容性的無障礙銷售管道。阿里巴巴旗下的網購平台「淘寶」便擴大其語音搜尋功能，帶頭讓中國的電商平台變得更加友善，幫助居住在一級城市外的年長消費者輕鬆購物。過去僅能識別華語的搜尋功能，現在也能聽懂天津、山東、河南及河北地區的方言。

星巴克致力於「設計、檢驗並擴大更具包容性的設計及相關體驗，將它們帶給全球消費者」，並宣布將在實體門市中試用語音轉換文字的科技，如此一來，消費者及員工便能即時看到點餐過程的對話，使其服務對聽障及重聽族群更加友善。

值得關注的原因：
若品牌無法設置全方位的無障礙空間及服務，便會失去一大客群。因此，語音辨識及語音轉換文字的科技進步，不論對線上或線下的零售通路來說，都在品牌邁向無障礙服務的路上扮演著關鍵的角色。

零售危機成轉機

在財務危機的困境下，
品牌正站出來幫助最弱勢的消費者。

許多品牌在疫情高峰時主動採取行動，確保消費者可取得必要的民生物資。而在全球消費者因面臨基本生活費危機而導致購買力下降時，各大企業又再度挺身而出。

零售商正盡力降低商品價格或提供較為划算的替代品，以協助經濟極度拮据的消費者。土耳其快遞平台 Getir 將民生必需品的價格調降至 1990 年代的水準，讓民眾能以最低降至目前售價 20% 的價格來購入麵包、義大利麵、巧克力、牙膏及洗碗精。隨著加拿大的通膨率在 2022 年 9 月來到 41 年來的新高 11.4%，超市 Loblaws 也凍漲了平價民生品牌 No Name 共計 1,500 項產品的售價。在日本，無印良品也投入居家用品平價化的行列，推出以百元商店為靈感的「無印良品 500」商店，讓民眾以低於 500 日圓（約台幣 115 元）的價格購買居家用品。

消費者正在尋找省錢的
生活小撇步，希望以最低
的價格買到最多的物品。

英國超市 Sainsbury 則採取不同作法，希望教育消費者採取更
加節儉的生活方式。該超市的《Recipe Scrapbook》網站教導
大眾如何以不到 5 英鎊（約台幣 180 元）的價格烹調家庭料理，
而其倫敦快閃店 Sainsfreeze 也提供課程，教導大眾如何在將用
剩的新鮮食材冷凍後還能於他日另做使用，協助消費者將每次
的採買物盡其用。英國平價超市 Iceland 也肩負起教導的角色，
與能源供應商 Utilita 合作開辦「聰明購物、精明烹煮」（Shop
Smart Cook Savvy）計畫，在店內及產品包裝上標示如何以最
划算、最低耗能的方式烹煮食物。

值得關注的原因：

由於維持基本生活越來越困難，消費者正在尋找省錢的生活小撇
步，希望以最低的價格買到最多的物品。而品牌在此扮演關鍵角
色，透過不同方式協助消費者度過難關不僅可以凝聚品牌社群，
更能培養消費者的長期忠誠度。

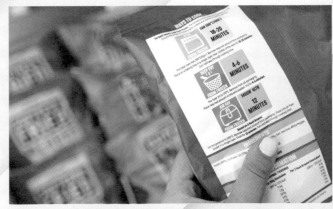

WEB3 未來市集

全新「鑄造」的商品市集正改變電子商務的未來。

隨著消費者購物習慣改變，新興電子商務及零售平台開始提供消費者更具沉浸式氛圍的互動購物體驗。

Draup 是一個即將推出的數位時尚平台，志在建立一個可以買賣、交易及展現數位時尚的市集。Draup 將成為「策畫及展示數位時尚，甚至讓成果得以轉移至其他虛擬環境的平台。」Draup 創辦人兼執行長 Daniella Loftus 在 2022 年 1 月的報導中如此寫到。Draup 目前已獲得 150 萬美元的種子輪資金，希望能「為數位原生世代的創作者及消費者打造一個社群，提供他們所需的資源及教育，將他們在數位時尚產業的獲益最大化」。

在紐約的蘇活區（SoHo），Zero10 和充滿創意點子的 Crosby Studios 合作，將數位時尚帶到這個受歡迎的購物區。Zero10 是一間擴增實境零售快閃店，讓顧客能在類似店面的實體環境中試穿虛擬衣物。

Zero10 共同創辦人兼執行長 George Yashin 向偉門智威智庫表示：「隨著擴增實境在時尚界的應用越來越廣，時尚產業將會朝向更永續、更具互動性的方向發展。而回到實體商店時，包含 Z 世代在內的消費族群也在期待擴增實境所帶來的全新沉浸式體驗。」Yashin 預測，若零售商能結合類似 Zero10 所開發的這類擴增實境穿衣鏡或擴增實境試穿應用程式，「就能推銷那些店內沒有庫存、但可提供預購的商品，而人們也能先透過擴增實境試穿衣服，避免店家生產衣物後又造成浪費。」

值得關注的原因：
這些作法都讓我們得以一窺 Web3 購物的未來。

理財的信仰

金融科技應用程式正在改變伊斯蘭世界的銀行業。

符合伊斯蘭教義的金融科技應用程式正在市場上興起。這些程式的開發者脫離傳統銀行，將自身於金融與科技領域的專業才能與宗教信仰結合。

伊斯蘭金融和傳統金融業最大的不同處在於伊斯蘭律法（sharia）禁止（haram）任何不勞而獲的利潤（riba），所以伊斯蘭金融機構多以分享利潤的方式運作。除此之外，伊斯蘭律法也禁止投機行為及賭博。

根據紐約研究諮詢機構 DinarStandard 的統計，2021 年全球伊斯蘭金融資產為 3.6 兆美元，較前一年上升了 7.8%。

東南亞最大的幾間電商正在探索伊斯蘭金融產品的潛力。隸屬叫車服務暨電商巨擘 GoTo 的印尼公司 GoPay 近期和印尼清真寺委員會（Indonesian Mosque Council）合作，讓民眾能在數千間清真寺以數位管道繳納「天課」（zakat），有能力的教徒都需奉獻的部分所得。另一家電商巨擘 Bukalapak 則推出符合伊斯蘭律法的投資應用程式 BMoney，該程式與資產管理公司 PT Ashmore Asset Management 合作開發，最低只需 1,000 印尼盾（約台幣 2 元）就可進行投資。

此外還有 Alami。自 2018 年起，Alami 即為中小企業提供點對點（P2P）的商業融資媒合服務。其共同創辦人兼執行長 Dima Djani 先前曾在雅加達的花旗銀行及法國興業銀行（Société Générale）工作。

截至 2022 年 8 月，Alami 平台在應用程式、網站及直播聊天室一共累積了 9.5 萬名使用者，發放逾 3 兆印尼盾（約台幣 59 億）的信貸，且無任何不良債權或呆帳，公司甚至在疫情之下仍逆勢成長。2021 年，Alami

收購了當地銀行 BPRS Cempaka Al-Amin，並在隔年重新掛牌且改名為 Hijra Bank，成為該公司旗下符合伊斯蘭律法的數位金融應用程式。

Alami 執行長 Dima 向偉門智威智庫表示：「不論你的職業為何，只要你的意圖是以敬拜（ibadah）為依歸，信奉阿拉的旨意（insya Allah），那麼你在來世（akhira）以前一定會找到一條奉獻的途徑。而對全體穆斯林來說，所有的行為舉止都必須以伊斯蘭律法為依歸。」

值得關注的原因：
以伊斯蘭教為大宗信仰的國家，其政府正積極鼓勵伊斯蘭金融業的發展，希望藉此振興經濟、刺激出口。伊斯蘭金融科技儼然成為此一趨勢的最新成果。

2021年全球伊斯蘭金融資產為3.6兆美元，較前一年上升7.8%。

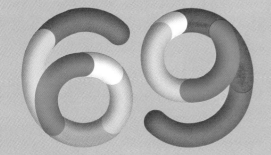

元宇宙宅一起

零售業者正在為遊戲中的虛擬化身設計虛擬家居環境。

零售家居設計業者開始透過虛擬遊戲開發 Web3 商機。

手遊新創公司 Robin Games 最近為其「居家遊戲系列」增加了 Playhouse 這款室內設計遊戲，並將遊戲與購物體驗結合在一起。Playhouse 讓消費者能夠在虛擬房屋內新增並擺放家具及家飾，打造屬於自己的空間及房間，可以加入沙發、壁畫、植栽、桌子，也能依照喜好改變家具的大小並將它們堆疊擺放。

人們開始棲居於數位空間之中，所以也開始著重其中的居家設計，希望在元宇宙中有個溫馨舒適的家。

雖然由 CrowdStar 發行的 Design Home 以及 Playtika 發行的 Redecor 玩法也類似於此，但 Playhouse 還與設計公司與家具品牌合作，讓玩家能直接從應用程式中購買家具，把虛擬居家遊戲的成果帶進現實生活的家中。Playhouse 的合作品牌包括 Article、Lulu & Georgia、Lulu & Georgia、Jenni Kayne 和 Society6。透過該款遊戲，玩家只要動動手指就能改造他們現實生活的居家風貌，將虛擬世界的創意點子化為現實。

2022 年 10 月，西榆家飾（West Elm）在 Roblox 平台上推出了該品牌的第一個元宇宙體驗 West Elm Home Design。西榆家飾將逾 150 件的自家家具數位化，使用者可選擇需要的物件客製自己的家，或者造訪西榆俱樂部（West Elm Hub）的虛擬店面及咖啡廳，甚至替他們的虛擬化身蒐集西榆的衣飾品。

值得關注的原因：
人們開始棲居於數位空間之中，所以也開始著重其中的居家設計，希望在元宇宙中有個溫馨舒適的家。

當修補成為潮流

近期，高階時尚品牌也開始提供
店內縫補衣物的新選擇。

通膨壓力加上環保考量，讓越來越多人重新考慮以修補代替購買。過去被視為名牌特權的修補服務，如今也有越來越多高階時尚品牌提供該服務。

Uniqlo 近期在倫敦攝政街的門市擴大了縫補服務的範圍，以應付廣大消費者對補丁、滾邊、刺繡及其他基本縫補服務的需求。除了現已提供縫補服務的柏林及紐約，該日系品牌也打算將此服務擴展到歐洲各地。

H&M 也開始提倡修補。作為快時尚巨擘，H&M 在其阿姆斯特丹的卡弗街（Kalverstraat）門市舉辦「重補與重製」（Repair & Remake）工作坊，幫助顧客翻新 H&M 及其他品牌的衣物。

Nike 則採用高科技的做法協助顧客修補球鞋。2022 年底，該品牌在倫敦的店面開始試用「機器人延年益壽實驗室」（Bot Initiated Longevity Lab），英文簡稱 BILL，是一個能協助縫補及清理球鞋的「機器人增強系統」。這款機器人會透過 3D 掃描偵測球鞋磨損的區域，並讓消費者自行選擇補丁的材料。

過去幾年，消費者已盡力減少消費（請見我們在〈The Future 100:2020〉這份報告中關於反對過度消費主義的報導），而現在的物價危機又進一步削弱了民眾的購買慾。根據 Primark 旗下的愛爾蘭服飾品牌 Penneys 於 2022 年 7 月所做的調查，有 62% 的民眾會為了省錢而選擇修補物品，該比例在 Z 世代中更佔了 95%。

英國零售商 Toast 自 2018 年以來便為民眾提供縫補服務，其社
會責任傳播專員 Madeline Michell 向偉門智威智庫表示：「雖然
就我們的立場，向消費者提倡減少購買、多加縫補，似乎有些矛盾，
但我們仍希望改變民眾的消費習慣、提倡注重品質及使用壽命的
概念，讓消費者不再將新鮮感置於耐用度之前。」

值得關注的原因：
縫補服務不再是奢侈品牌的專利，而是一般消費者在經濟壓力以
及愛護地球的考量下所做出的明智之舉。

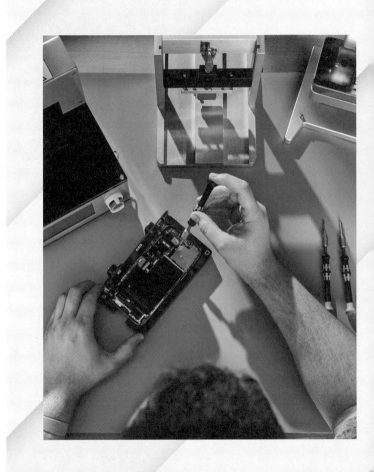

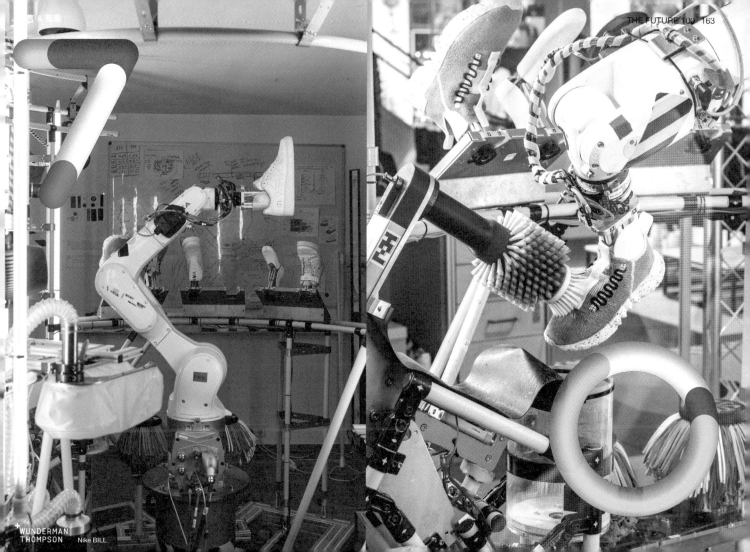

WUNDERMAN THOMPSON Nike BILL

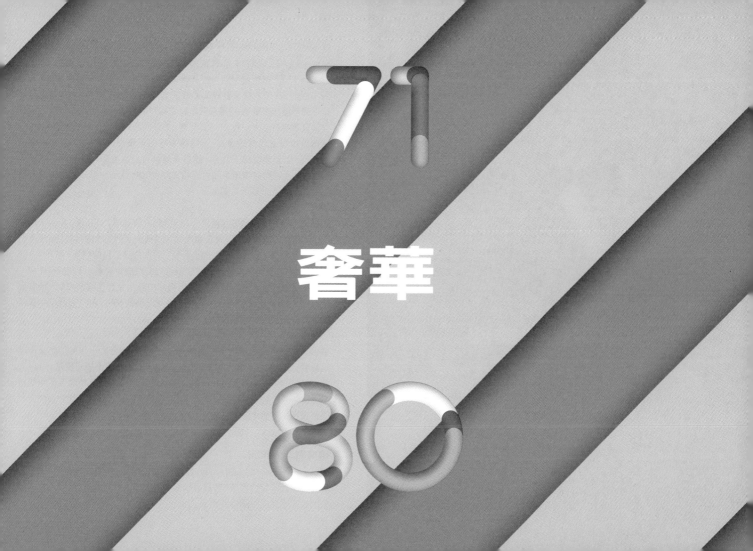

71

奢華

80

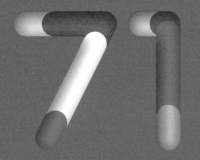

加密會員俱樂部

去中心化時代的會員限定俱樂部，會是什麼模樣呢？

Friends With Benefits 被稱為「去中心界的蘇活俱樂部（Soho House）」與「加密幣圈創意階級的 VIP 室」，它是由一個非正式的 Discord 聊天室所發展而來的高檔數位會員俱樂部，其市值在 2022 年達到 1 億美元。加入會員要購買最低規定量的 $FWB 幣，$FWB 幣是該俱樂部的專屬加密貨幣，可用來解鎖特定福利與服務。根據《紐約時報》報導，會員只要持有至少一枚 $FWB 代幣，就能閱讀會員電子報及部落格文章；持有五枚以上代幣的會員，可獲得有限的權限進入 FWB 特定 Discord 聊天室，以及參與線下活動。購買全球通行的會員費用是 75 $FWB（在 2022 年 11 月時該幣值金額大約相當於 4,000 美元），該會員擁有進入旗下所有 Discord 聊天室的權限。

熱愛旅行的幣圈投資客可選擇「幸運猿旅行俱樂部」（Lucky Ape Travel Club）推出的旅行 NFT，每位買家都可獲得一系列的專屬福利：高級度假村的房間鑰匙、邀請制活動的通行證、前往異國景點的門票。基本上，該俱樂部將 NFT 轉換成多項實體旅遊福利的虛擬兌換券，只要持有任何一件 NFT 作品，即可從參與計劃的俱樂部中獲得免費住宿的權利。擁有這款 NFT 也可說是獲得進入奢華旅遊會員社群的資格，可結識社群中其他熱愛旅遊與文化探索的會員。

奢侈品品牌也透過導入加密貨幣付款方式，來迎合新一代的加密奢侈品消費者，Gucci 在 2022 年 5 月宣布將在北美店面接受加密貨幣付款。同年，高級健身俱樂部 Equinox 開放會員在紐約市的所有旗艦店面中使用加密貨幣支付會費。有報導顯示，該健身品牌已有計畫要將加密貨幣支付服務擴展至其他地區的分店。

值得關注的原因：
摩根士丹利（Morgan Stanley）認為對高端消費市場來說，元宇宙擁有著 500 億美元的獲利商機。會員俱樂部的概念開始進入虛擬世界，服務的對象則是新崛起的幣圈精英們。

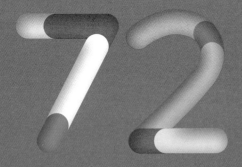

超稀有的味覺饗宴

稀有即是另類的奢華象徵。

從亞馬遜雨林捕捉到的螞蟻到手工收割的野生稻米，再到熟成 15 年的香檳。許多企業因為能尋獲稀有的食材或是風味而脫穎而出。

位於美國明尼亞波利斯的著名餐廳 Owamni by The Sioux Chef，以其「去殖民化」菜單聞名，他們避免使用歐洲殖民者帶到美洲的食材，從麵粉到乳製品，以及現代的家禽／家畜，例如雞和豬。該餐廳在 2022 年被詹姆斯‧比爾德基金會（James Beard Foundation）評選為「美國最佳新餐廳」。Owamni 提供的是美國在地食物，像是藍玉米、麋鹿、野牛，還有手工收成的珍稀野生菰米（manoomin）。根據《紐約客》雜誌對這家餐廳的報導，菰米只生長在五大湖周圍，且和北美原住民歐吉布威族（Ojibwe）的淵源有關，他們在幾世紀前從東岸搬遷至內陸，為的就是尋找這種「水中生長的食物」。菰米的採集方式仍沿用著古老的方法，也就是划獨木舟到有菰米生長的湖泊邊緣，並從稻稈的頂部敲下麥穗來收成。

在巴爾的摩，有一間由委內瑞拉當地人所管理的 Alma Cocina Latina 餐廳，其以亞馬遜森林採集的罕見食材為其酒吧亮點。這些食材包含調酒增添柑橘風味的檸檬蟻，還有蘭姆酒中能增添暖意的巴西小米椒（murupí pepper）。根據《富比士》報導，Alma Cocina Latina 的食材供應商是一間致力保留傳統作物與料理的機構，該機構為這些作物的生產者建立一套有利可圖的商業模式，讓他們得以藉此維生，不必非法挖礦。

Owammi 與 Alma Cocina Latina 這兩間餐廳部分動機是為了實現社會正義與身份認同才選用稀有食材，但也有許多餐廳單純是為了利用稀有性來創造尊絕不凡的感受。總部位在杜拜的阿聯酋航空（Emirates），在 2022 年秋季的某段期間中，為頭等艙的旅客供應極為稀有的香檳王 P2（Dom Pérignon Plénitude 2），這瓶佳釀必須經過 15 年窖藏，有萊姆和烘烤過的礦物香氣，尾韻則帶有乾燥杏桃、蘋果、糖漬覆盆莓及無花果的風味。「它的口感豐富卻又溫和，飽滿並帶有恰到好處的活力，尾韻在口中縈繞留香，辛辣中還帶點鹹味。」該航空業者如此形容道。

值得關注的原因：
餐飲企業在餐點品項中加入稀有食材，不僅能藉此穩固自身品牌在市場的定位，在某些情況下，甚至還能支持當地的小型生產者。

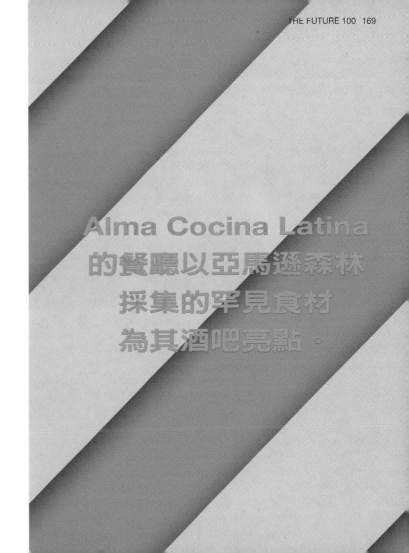

Alma Cocina Latina 的餐廳以亞馬遜森林採集的罕見食材為其酒吧亮點。

73

精英級睡眠

各個品類的高檔品牌開始將
「一夜好眠」化為最新的奢侈品品項。

諸多奢侈品牌開始意識到睡眠可以帶來潛在商機，於是推出豐富的新商品及服務。

2022 年 5 月，Gucci 與芬蘭健康科技公司 Oura 共同推出可追蹤睡眠狀況的戒指。這款售價為 950 美元的追蹤器，戒身以合成黑剛玉製成，上面鑲有 18K 的黃金。Gucci 以此產品踏入睡眠領域是相當有趣的第一步。

零售業與睡眠在 2022 年夏季產生交集，因為高檔百貨 Selfriges 開設了「性愛與睡眠」（Sex & Sleep）快閃店。對有意想改善睡眠狀況的消費者來說，這裡可以找到許多助眠的花草茶、精油及保健食品。除了快閃店面，Selfridges 更在商場內的電影院中舉辦睡眠課程，邀請消費者入內補眠，充飽電後再繼續逛街。

豪華旅遊品牌也加入此行列，協助旅客養成良好睡眠習慣，儘管旅行結束後也能夠維持下去。渡假飯店 Rosewood Hotels & Resorts 於 2022 年 1 月推出「睡眠鍊金術」（Alchemy of Sleep）企劃，開發崛起中的睡眠觀光商機。旅客可以選擇為時一晚的「夢境之地」（Dreamscape）或是持續五晚的沈浸式「睡眠改造體驗」（Sleep Transformation）。這些休閒活動為旅客提供一個機會，讓他們能全心投入冥想和充分的休息時光，並在離開飯店回到家後也能持續維持這樣的習慣。

值得關注的原因：
Oura 告訴偉門智威智庫：「疫情促進社會大眾對健康的優先關注度。」如同我們在新冠肺炎（COVID-19）疫情初期所做的預測，現在每個企業都成了健康企業。奢侈品牌也開始建立與健康養生有關的資歷，並且瞄準那些將「睡眠」視為最新穎的投資奢侈品品項的上流消費者。

星際奢華

奢侈品品牌以冒險與驚奇的精神，
在實用主義當前的時代中，推出
神秘且有趣的企劃而自豪。

Burberry 於 2022 年 10 月推出了「暗夜物種」（Night Creatures）的宣傳活動，並以此讚揚「好奇心與探索未知領域的力量」。故事線跟著三位主角的腳步前進，他們會遇到一隻來自異世界的科幻生物。該影片與創意團隊 Megaforce 共同創作，內容橫跨於現實與想像世界之間，也讓人不禁聯想起童話故事的氛圍。Megaforce 說道：「我們想要展現出深入未知領域時的勇氣與大膽態度，也就是在探險旅程中無懼又調皮的精神。」

Gucci 也開始探索未知世界。該品牌於 2022 年 5 月首次舉辦品牌系列時裝秀「宇宙起源」（Cosmogonie show）—「銀河系」（galactical）的系列新裝作品。並表示其靈感來自「神秘的偶遇與神話的國度」，其品牌總監 Alessandro Michele 將舉辦這場時裝秀的地點描述為「地球與天空之間的星際通道」。

這場秀以「星宿的隱喻」為靈感，「那是過去未知的現實，現在卻已能打破傳統框架的限制。」Michele 如此描述道。舉辦這場秀的目的更是因為「宇宙世界的碎片散落各處，我們讓它們有了連結。而我在尋找的是魔幻又有神話色彩的地方，讓我可以踏入其中並迷失自我。」

值得關注的原因：
奢侈品品牌開始突破現實的界限，從神秘和魔幻的領域找尋靈感。經過兩年優先考量實用主義以及採納嚴肅穩重的調性，奢侈品品牌開始反映出市場對探索與驚奇的渴望。Michele 對《女裝日報》（WWD）說道：「時尚會說話，它不是精英階級專屬的象形文字，而是談論一種生活態度。時尚是一面鏡子。」

精品業新局面

奢侈品零售模式正在經歷重大變革。

奢侈品網購平台 Farfetch 於 2022 年 8 月談下一筆破天荒的交易，準備透過買下競爭對手 Yoox Net-a-Porter 的大量股權，成為奢侈品電商巨擘。這筆交易預計於 2023 年底完成，意味著奢侈品電商將會整合的未來趨勢。Yoox Net-a-Porter 母公司 Richemont 的董事長 Johann Rupert 表示，這是「為精品產業打造一個獨立且中立的線上平台」的一步。

早在幾個月前，Farfetch 已於 2022 年 4 月與美國最大全通路奢侈品零售商 Neiman Marcus Group（簡稱 NMG，旗下主力精品品牌包含 Neiman Marcus 與 Bergdorf Goodman）共同發布策略性聯盟的消息，要「顛覆整合性精品零售的未來」。Farfetch 的創辦人、董事長暨執行長 José Neves 為此解釋：「這次的策略性聯盟，是為了顛覆奢侈品零售產業在線上與線下的全球佈局，整合 NMG 在美國的影響力，以及 Farfetch 對奢侈品零售業的視野與技術。」這次結盟也讓 NMG 獲得 Farfetch 電商工具與科技技術的使用權，他們將來用來改造 Bergdorf Goodman 的網站與行動應用程式。

疫情帶動了虛擬消費的風潮，根據美國人口調查局 2022 年的報告顯示，電商銷售額於 2020 年大幅成長了 43%。線上購物的盛行，加上亞馬遜等第三方電商平台開始販售奢侈品所帶來的壓力（過去許多精品業者拒絕在亞馬遜上經營官方店面，但自從亞馬遜在 2022 年 10 月開始與二手物零售商 What Goes Around Comes Around 合作後，消費者便可在亞馬遜上購入這些品牌的二手精品），上述因素讓精品品牌開始重新思考市場策略。

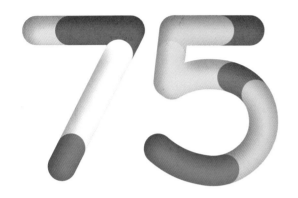

Neves 說道:「我相信美國奢侈品市場正處在一個重要的轉振點。雖然美國一直以來都是精品產業重要的成長動力來源,由於對精品具高度興趣的年輕世代逐漸增加,因此企業必須大幅提升數位能力,同時強化線上與線下的顧客購物體驗,才能夠滿足這群新興客群的期望,在未來幾年競爭相當激烈的領域中,仍保有領先地位。」

值得關注的原因:
繼〈精品百貨之死〉(《改變未來的 100 件事:2020 年全球百大趨勢》第 68 章)與〈百貨公司生活圈〉(《2022 年全球百大趨勢》第 66 章)之後,大型奢侈品零售業者開始將資源導入新興領域,探索新的銷售途徑。隨著品牌開始邁入零售業的下個時代,未來預計可以看到更多精品產業在商業佈局上的變動,以及更多品牌聯名合作的推廣計畫。

「美國奢侈品市場
正處在一個
重要的轉捩點。」

José Neves,
Farfetch 的創辦人、董事長暨執行長

76

健康養生聚

新型聚會場所結合
高級健身房與社交俱樂部兩項功能。

消費者對以健康為中心的社群及全人照護的需求日益增加，於是專為社交與身心健康設計的空間紛紛成立。

Remedy Place 自詡為「社交健康俱樂部」於 2022 年 9 月在紐約市開幕，成為一家全新健康導向的清醒社交空間。其創辦人 Jonathan Leary 博士告訴《Vogue》雜誌，Remedy Place 是「一間沒有誘惑及毒素的俱樂部，可以同時提升健康與社交生活品質。它提供的不只是自我照顧而已，更具有社交元素的自我照顧。」該俱樂部供應冰浴（ice bath）、呼吸練習、引導課程、桑拿、針灸、維他命 IV 注射套裝等設備與服務。

在洛杉磯，Heimat 為放鬆的社交氛圍設計了全新的空間。這間私人的健身與生活俱樂部讓會員可以在健身房與健身課程之外，還能享受頂樓露天泳池、體能訓練戰鬥營、米其林星級餐廳、SPA 會館。Heimat 提供頂級、私密的環境，讓重視養生的社群成員可以互動、放鬆並重新找回活力。

教父級社交俱樂部 Soho House 於 2022 年 9 月深化旗下健康事業的營運範疇，推出純素食、零殘忍的 Soho Skin 肌膚保養品系列。此系列產品的原料皆有科研背書，都是頂級醫美使用的保養原料。顧客可在 Soho House 旗下的某些分館中免費使用，也可以在紐約市的 Bloomingdale's 百貨進行購買。

值得關注的原因：
消費者正在將自我照顧社交化。Leary 博士告訴《Vogue》：「自我照顧最重要的一環是人與人之間的連結，人們需要一段真誠的關係。」

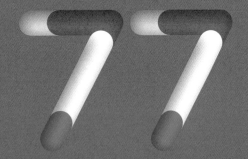

77

療癒系頭等艙

頭等艙開始供應各種能帶來滿足和愉悅感的飛機餐。

在疫情期間,許多人開始投向療癒飲食的懷抱,希望可以從家常料理、美食節目和美食部落格中,重新找回安定的時光。在客機重返天際時,有些航空公司開始利用這樣的思維來調整頭等艙的飛機餐品項,供應能讓人想起家的療癒美食。

2022 年 8 月,達美航空 (Delta) 與榮獲 2022 年詹姆斯・比爾德「傑出美國主廚獎」的 Mashama Bailey 合作,為頭等艙的旅客供應南方療癒系飲食。頭等艙的新菜單出自美國東南方喬治亞州的薩凡納 (Savannah) 由 Bailey 經營的餐廳 The Grey,菜色的品項包含佐以白芙美白酒 (Blanc Fumé)、青蘋果、馬鈴薯、小白菜、大頭菜的比目魚和生蠔料理，或是搭配辣洋蔥醬（kanni sauce）與煙燻芥蘭菜的牛小排，還有拌入烤蕃薯與北非香草辣醬（chermoula sauce）的純素蔬食塔吉鍋（tagine），甜點則是優酪乳和玉米粉做成的特蕾斯蛋糕，再搭配金桔和橘子蜜餞。

「我們的食物能讓遠離家鄉的人產生共鳴，是專為尋求療癒美食者設計的菜單。」Bailey 如此告訴《Food and Wine》雜誌。

達美航空國際線的高級座艙也讓乘客可以 DIY 自己的聖代冰淇淋，上面可以加入糖漬莫雷洛櫻桃、巧克力醬和餅乾碎。

新加坡航空（Singapore Airlines）邀請加州的 Golden Door 健康養生會館一起合作，為飛機餐增添更多色彩風味。這間高級水療會館的行政主廚 Grey Frey Jr 研發了一款波特菇「肉丸子」，搭配蔬菜高湯燉飯一起上菜，療癒卻又不負擔。Frey 對「美國全國廣播公司商業頻道」（CNBC）表示：「這吃起來很有飽足感，也可以品嘗到各種甘甜風味。而且最棒的是，在吃完的一個小時後，你並不會覺得後悔說：『啊，好希望剛剛沒有貪嘴吃了那些肉丸子』。」

值得關注的原因：
在旅客重返天際時，航空公司開始利用各種療癒舒心的特色來吸引旅客，其中一項即為療癒飲食菜單，藉此希望消費者能購買獲利率最高的頭等艙座位。

「是專為尋求療癒美食者設計的菜單。」

Mashama Bailey，主廚

78

超限量奢華體驗

奢侈品品牌將高檔服務再升級，
只為金字塔頂層客戶而開的貴賓室大門。

2023 年，Chanel 計畫在亞洲開設只服務頂層貴賓的私人精品店。這間總部位於巴黎的精品品牌，在 2021 年有將近一半的營收來自亞太地區，獲利近 160 億美元，比 2020 年成長了近乎50%。

此舉在社群平台上引發一場論戰：Chanel 是否變得過於勢利？

加上該品牌在近期，不僅全面調漲了手提包款的售價，一些夢幻設計款更限制每位消費者所能訂購的數量。

同為法國時尚品牌的 Dior 也依循相同策略，於 2022 年 6、7 月的時裝秀期間，邀請頂層貴賓到巴黎塞納河畔，展開一趟奢華遊輪之旅。在兩個小時的航程裡，首先享受一小時的頂級護膚水療服務，再盡情飽覽河畔景緻。每趟只接待五位賓客，需提前預訂。此次企劃的靈感，源自 19 世紀誕生於巴黎新橋（Pont-Neuf）一艘豪華遊輪上的浴場—莎瑪麗丹浴場（Bains de la Samaritaine），該浴場也是現代 SPA 中心的始祖。此外，Dior

也在巴黎開設兩間常駐的頂級水療會館，分別位於雅典娜飯店（Hôtel Plaza Athénée），與白馬莊園飯店（Cheval Blanc）。

除了精品品牌，頂級飯店集團 Nobu Hotels 也規劃一套專攻頂層客戶的行程。

Nobu Hotels，由日本主廚松久信幸（Nobu Matsuhisa）、好萊塢影星 Robert De Niro 與電影監製 Meir Teper 共同創立，靈感來自傳統日式旅館（ryokan）。他們在 2022 年與私人飛機公司 Schubach Aviation 合作，推出「日式旅館度假旅程」（Ryokan Retreat），包含以私人飛機接送旅客往返該飯店集團位於加州兩處的分館：馬里布（Malibu）與帕羅奧圖（Palo Alto），旅客能在兩個分館各宿兩晚，以及一頓兩人份的無菜單晚餐料理。

值得關注的原因：
奢侈品品牌，一直以來都以頂級服務來維持品牌高度。其中一些品牌開始運用限制人數的頂級體驗，進一步地提升在人們心中的高度。

天涯海角的高級餐廳

地處偏遠的當代高級餐廳，
讓饕客們即使跋山涉水也要前往用餐。

美好的用餐體驗，其實從出發的那一刻便開始。

位於北大西洋海上的法羅群島（Faroe Islands）的米其林二星餐廳 Koks，原址已非常偏遠，但在 2022 年夏季至 2023 年間，他們又暫時搬遷至同樣難以抵達的地點一位於北極圈內的格陵蘭島上，名為 Ilimanaq 的小村莊。想要嚐到這間米其林二星餐廳的料理，需要從最近的城鎮 Ilulissat 搭船航行一小時才能抵達。《BBC》記者 Adrienne Murray Nielsen 在 2022 年 9 月的一篇文章中，將這趟旅程比喻為「一場漫長而驚奇的歷險」，過程中需要乘船穿梭於冰山尖塔之間，讓這場體驗更像是「一趟史詩級的美食之旅」。Koks 將在 2024 年搬回法羅群島，而他們目前正在搭建新址。

在挪威西北部的海岸邊，有一間座落於峽灣間的高級餐廳—Kvitnes Gård，於 2021 年底開幕。想抵達這間餐廳，必須從鄰近城鎮搭船前往，且要求所有賓客都得在那裡住上一晚。因為 Kvitnes Gård 想為顧客帶來的是「一場體驗，而非僅是一客餐點」。

值得關注的原因：
如今高級餐廳不僅提升菜品的質量，更將前往餐廳的路程，設計為美食體驗的一環。由於高端的消費客群，更願追尋小眾、限量的獨特體驗，預期未來將能看到更多需走進天涯海角才能嚐鮮的餐廳。

WUNDERMAN
THOMPSON   Koks, Ilimanaq, Greenland

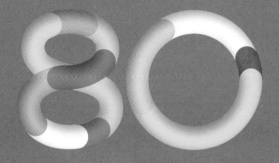

80
頂級海上住宅

世界各國工作的數位遊牧（Digital Nomad），
以海為家將成為未來的趨勢。

郵輪新創公司 Storylines，日前已公開發表首艘奢華住宿郵輪船的概念。這艘有著 18 層甲板的 MV Narrative 郵輪預計於 2025 年啟航，船上有 547 間房間，提供 11 種半客製化的房型，共可容納 1,000 名來自世界各地的旅客，能提供長達一輩子的無限航程。據《Insider》雜誌報導，有些房型已經完售。感興趣的買家有多種選擇，包含：售價 100 萬美元，約 6.6 坪的工作室；售價 800 萬美元，約 55.3 坪且有樓中樓設計的四房公寓。

每間房都設有收納空間、衣櫥、壁掛電視、廚房及一間衛浴。遠距工作的居民還可以租用私人辦公室。這艘海上住宅提供全包式的服務，其費用中涵蓋食物、醫療服務、進入泳池與港口的權限、健身設備，甚至設有保齡球館。當然也可以在每次靠港時，自由進出包含土耳其、希臘、義大利、蒙特內哥羅等國家。

2022 年 10 月，麗思卡爾頓飯店（Ritz-Carlton）推出每週要價 6,000 美元起跳的奢華郵輪之旅，由旗下連鎖五星級飯店 Evrima 操刀辦理。這趟從西班牙巴賽隆納到法國尼斯的航程中，提供米其林星級主廚的料理，更設有四座游泳池、香檳酒吧、雪茄室、夜店與水療設施。

值得關注的原因：
購入海上住宅的消費者，想買下的是最頂級的遊牧生活。

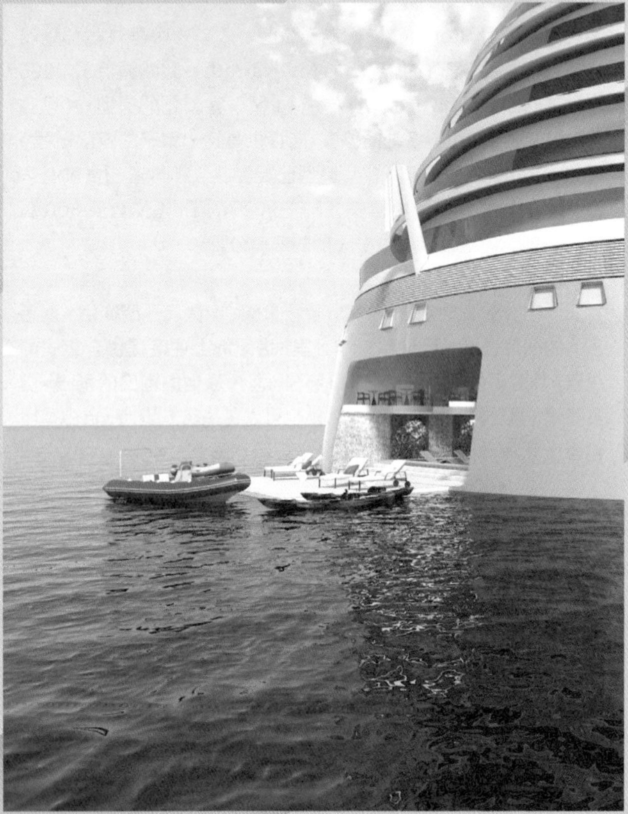

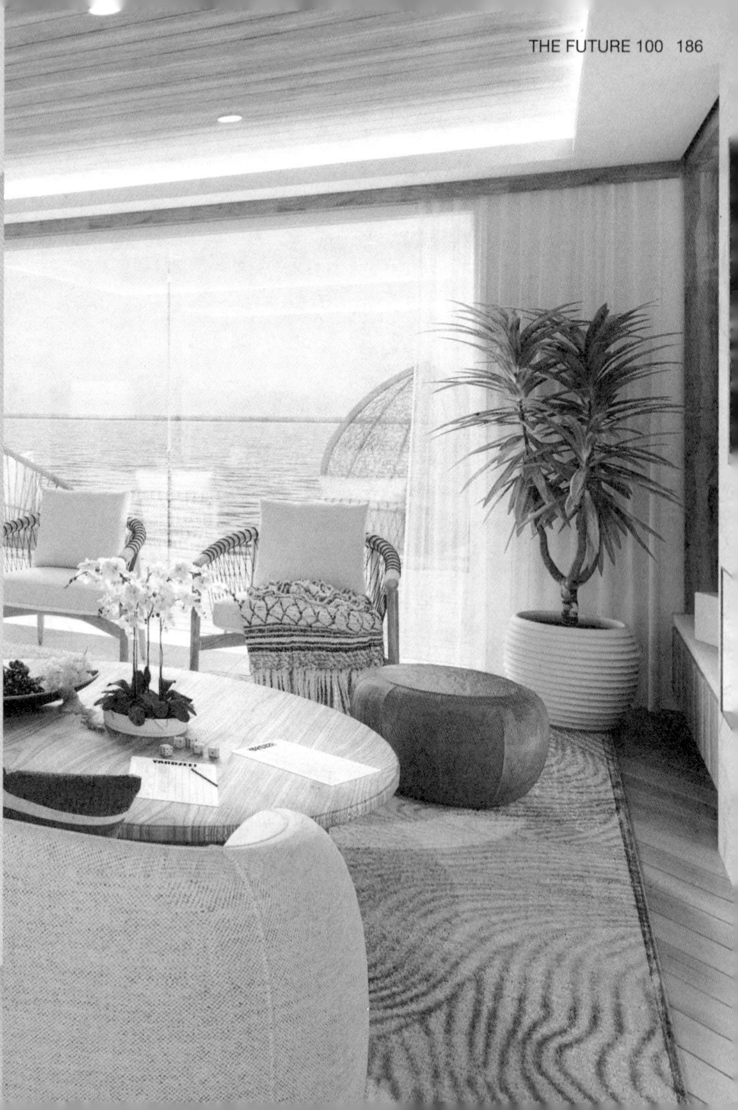

Storylines (both images)

81

健康

90

81

至尚真我

愛自己的模式全面啓動。

人們對身心健康的看法正逐漸改變。

「走出疫情陰霾後,人們意識到追求生活平衡和身心健康,不該是偶爾想到才做的小事。」半島酒店的品牌及集團營運總監—羅瑞思(Gareth Roberts)向《華爾街日報》如此說道。根據該集團的觀察,近年養生旅遊逐漸興起(請參考第84章〈「療癒」旅宿〉),足見身心健康已成為民眾的首要考量。

英國百貨公司 Selfridges,鼓勵消費者以更宏觀的角度看待自我照護與身心健康。該品牌將自己重新定位成「快樂泉源」的提供者,希望促進消費者思考何謂「活出自己最好的樣子」。2022 年更提出「Superfutures 至臻未來」的品牌計畫,涵蓋產品、服務與內容—從風格選品,到閱讀文章、收聽 Podcasts 放鬆身心的「感官體驗」。該計畫也包含 Selfridges 所提出的「新型零售療法」,將自信教練(confidence coach)、呼吸療法專家、性治療師推薦給消費者。

「我們將健身、永續、美妝、食品及創意等多元的自我照顧方式推廣給消費者,協助你成為更好的自己——『Superfutures 至臻未來』。」該品牌的代理創意總監 Emma Kidd 這麼說道。

值得關注的原因:
我們過去在《改變未來的 100 件事:2022 年全球百大趨勢》一書中,已經點出人們對心理健康愈發重視,而今針對「健康」的概念更全方位擴展。「愛自己」的定義,如今涵蓋了自我身心健康及外在環境健康,唯有內外兼具,才能成就更好的自己。

HOW TO DISCOVER YOUR SUPERSELF:

SUPERCHARGE
FROM WITHIN

BIOHACKING TREATMENTS
BY DR VALI, COMING SOON

82

精神益生菌

腸道健康，會成為讓心靈健康的新途徑嗎？

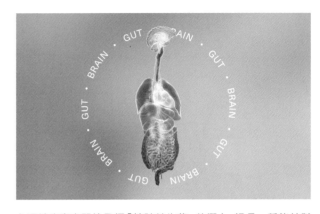

心理健康專家開始發揮「精神益生菌」的潛力，這是一種能針對神經系統帶來好處的益生菌。

屢獲殊榮的益生菌和益生元保健品牌—Seed Health，在 2022 年 7 月與生技公司 Axial Therapeutics 合作腸腦開發計畫。該品牌使用加州理工學院的研究，進一步找出腸道微生物(microbiome)對於舒緩焦慮、壓力與憂鬱的潛在功效。加州理工學院是第一個指出腸道微生物與神經精神疾病有所關聯的實驗機構，讓人們能更了解微生物菌種療法對身心健康的潛在好處。

追求心靈健康的消費者，對腸腦健康連結帶來的益處趨之若。根據 Research and Markets 的調查，全球益生菌市場從 2016 年的 390 億美元，成長至 2021 年的 580 億美元。市面上的益生菌也逐漸以強化認知功能、改善心情及提振精神為行銷賣點。

2022 年 8 月，美國生醫公司 Bened Life 研發出專利益生菌—PS128，並推出第一款有益腦部的益生菌保健品「Neuralli」。該公司聲稱這款產品能「幫助平衡血清素、多巴胺、皮質醇以及其他影響情緒、心智及行為的分子，同時有助於調節消化道健康。」

Bened Life 的科學傳播總監 Cassandra Arendt 博士，向偉門智威智庫表示：「經過長期觀察，近年有關『腸腦軸線』（gut-brain axis）的科研文獻數量呈指數成長，代表這股熱潮正持續擴張，現在連大眾對該項發展也開始感興趣。現在有越來越多人受心理疾病所苦，我們需要更安全、更低副作用的治療方法，因此對某些人來說，精神益生菌或許可以滿足這項需求。」

同月，泰國及加拿大也批准了益生菌 PS128 的相關註冊。這款益生菌聲稱「會對神經系統及心理健康有潛在益處，如改善睡眠品質及緩解焦慮症、憂鬱症、自閉症及帕金森氏症會出現的症狀」。

值得關注的原因：
隨著消費者對於全方位身心健康的重視度逐漸提升，各個保健品牌開始探索，試圖找出腸道健康能為心理健康帶來哪些益處。

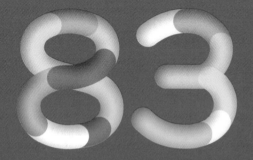

快樂健身法

專為提振精神而設計的運動，能為人們帶來快樂。

根據世界衛生組織的統計，新冠肺炎疫情導致全球焦慮症及憂鬱症人口增加了 25%。人們為了改善心理健康，決定從身體健康著手，擁抱運動的美好。而健身品牌看準此商機，開始思考：如何透過品牌服務內容，滿足消費者維持心理健康的需求。

心理學家 Kelly McGonigal 在《紐約時報》的專欄中向大眾介紹了「快樂健身法」(joy workout)。該健身法包含：彈跳、伸展、搖擺、愉快地跳躍，以及一種被 McGonigal 稱為「慶祝」，類似灑五彩碎紙的動作。根據運動相關研究指出，這些動作能激發人們的正向情緒。McGonigal 寫道：「快樂健身法只是以律動提振精神的一種方式。」除此之外，還有許多「經科學實證，能透過運動有效舒緩情緒的做法」。

Fitbit 的電子手環能幫助配戴者追蹤並管控心理壓力數值，將生理與心理健康連結在一起。該品牌於 2022 年 8 月推出的 Sense 2 手環，搭載全新生理反應追蹤功能，能偵測心跳、體表溫度及流汗程度等。當配戴者體溫產生急劇變化，該手環會立刻跳出通知，提醒配戴者留意自身身心狀態。

該健身法包含：
彈跳、伸展、
搖擺、愉快地跳躍，
以及「慶祝」，類似
灑五彩碎紙的動作–
根據運動相關研究指
出，這些動作能激發
人們的正向情緒。

達特茅斯學院（Dartmouth College）學者於 2022 年 8 月發表的研究顯示：「追蹤人們健身數據時，我們發現記憶力、心理健康、特定肢體動作之間，有一定的對應關係。」該研究證實，雖然運動對記憶力及心理健康的影響，會隨著體力消耗而有所差異，但肢體活動確實能以非侵入式的方式，影響認知能力及心理健康。如同重量訓練可僅針對特定肌群，進行強化或改善特定生理表現一樣，這個原則也能適用在改善部分認知功能及心理健康上。

值得關注的原因：
健身品牌能幫助消費者同時改善「生理」及「心理」健康。有別於過去只講求雕塑體態。如今大眾對心理健康的重視程度，也可能改變未來對「健身」的定義。

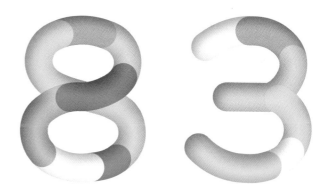

「療癒」旅宿

最新的養生飯店，將餐飲住宿結合醫療保健，
從靜脈注射到幹細胞治療，無所不包。

根據 Grand View Research 於 2022 年 6 月發布的報告顯示，全球保健旅遊市場在未來 8 年，預估會以每年 10% 的幅度成長，並在 2030 年突破 1 兆美元。「疫情使人們開始關注日常健康狀態。」曼哈頓養生品牌 The Well 的共同創辦人兼創意總監 Kane Sarhan 向《華爾街日報》如此說道。

最近精品酒店也開始提供高科技的醫療服務，以搭上養生旅遊的商機。比如位於夏威夷的酒店—The Four Seasons Resort Maui at Wailea，便與洛杉磯的預防與診斷醫學中心—Next Health 合作，提供飯店賓客一整套的醫療服務，包括靜脈注射、能提高血氧濃度來增進免疫力與活力的臭氧療法、每小時療程要價 12,000 美元的幹細胞治療。在全新的計畫內，甚至提供基因生物標記測試，賓客啟程前可先於紐約或洛杉磯進行檢測，抵達夏威夷後便能與 Next Health 的人員會談，依照個別檢測結果，擬定高度客製化的飲食、活動及療程。

2022 年 7 月，醫美水療中心 Lanserhof 在德國設立新據點，主打高級的醫學療程，包括在房內設置生物節律燈、駐館專業心理學家、模擬缺氧環境以增強粒線體功能的 CellGym 課程，甚至備有磁振造影及電腦斷層掃描等儀器。

養生水療酒店 Ranch Malibu 也在義大利的新據點，派駐了 8 位醫師，為賓客提供血液檢測等醫療診斷。

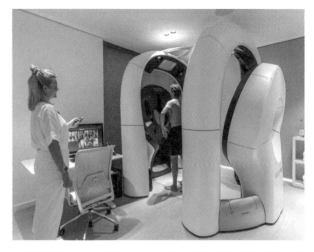

「健康不該是你在踏入水療中心時才想到的事，那種催眠自己『現在踏進健康世界了』的想法既過時又無法真正解決問題。」半島酒店的品牌及集團營運總監羅瑞思（Gareth Roberts）如此告訴《華爾街日報》。

值得關注的原因：
健康養生逐漸成為旅遊新趨勢，由此誕生結合旅館與醫院的新興旅宿，引進科學實證療法，以吸引注重健康的消費者。

淋巴健康

淋巴系統成為健康新焦點。

刮痧,是一種透過在皮膚上刮動來疏通淋巴的傳統中醫療法。不僅在西方名人圈成為風潮,更席捲了全球的高級水療中心。

在刮痧過程中,需先在皮膚上抹上精油潤滑,再以刮痧板刮拭,此時皮膚表層會出現一粒粒如沙般的紫紅色瘀點。過程中會讓血管神經受到刺激,使血管擴張,讓血流與淋巴運行速度加快,提升免疫系統中的淋巴細胞與血液中的吞噬細胞的作用速度與搬運能力,加速體內毒素廢物的排除,以協助人體對抗疾病感染。

美國影星暨養生達人葛妮絲·派特洛(Gwyneth Paltrow)的公司 Goop,正在出售心型玫瑰石英刮痧板。該刮痧板由超模米蘭達·寇兒(Miranda Kerr)的品牌 Kora Organics 所生產,並附上臉部圖示教學,引導購買者如何使用刮痧板刮拭皮膚。

位於紐約哈德遜廣場的飯店 Equinox Hotel,自稱是讓賓客「如獲重生的聖殿」。2022 年 8 月,該飯店的水療中心 The Spa by Equinox 與健康儀器公司 Skin Science Solutions 合作,導入淋巴引流治療法,提供賓客手持的淋巴按摩設施,不僅可替身體排毒消腫,更能雕塑身形及臉部輪廓。

淋巴健康療程,日漸受到亞洲高級水療中心的重視,成為館內必備的療程之一。草本磨砂及熱石按摩也一樣受歡迎。

目的是讓血流與淋巴
運行速度加快，提升
免疫系統中的淋巴細胞
與血液中的吞噬細胞的
作用速度與搬運能力，
加速體內毒素廢物的
排除，以協助人體對抗
疾病感染。

坐落於泰國北方大城清萊的度假飯店—The Anantara Golden Triangle Elephant Camp and Resort，提供 60 分鐘的臉部刮痧療程，使用植物萃取物及泰國傳統配方一起進行。此外，該飯店亦於叢林環繞的露天涼亭中，提供 90 分鐘的背部排毒按摩。

位於峇里島小鎮 Ubud 近郊的新加坡豪華度假村—The Como Shambhala Estate，為顧客提供 60 或 75 分鐘的淋巴排毒療程，其主打輕柔的按摩手法，帶走身體內的毒素及廢物。

值得關注的原因：
繼針灸和腳底按摩等養生風潮之後，現在在養生會館中最受歡迎的療法是傳統中醫的刮痧。

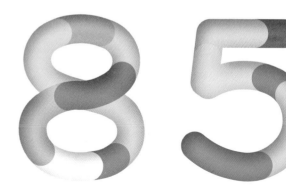

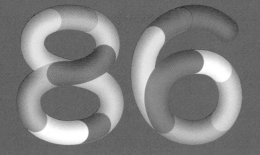

休息大革命

許多社群網紅開始提倡慢步調的生活方式。

最近越來越多人開始提倡休息和復原的重要性，並倡導自我修復與自我療癒的概念，因為對弱勢族群而言，這兩者是對抗創傷、壓力、歧視的有效工具。

致力「發掘午睡力量」的組織 The Nap Ministry 在全美各地舉辦集體午睡及做白日夢的活動。創辦人暨午睡教主 Tricia Hersey 在 2022 年 10 月出版了《休養即反抗》（Rest Is Resistance: A Manifesto）一書，內容和該組織的宗旨相呼應，皆在提倡將休息視為一種自我療癒的方式，並抨擊那些強調刻苦耐勞、不可懶怠的工作文化。該書認為休息對弱勢族群尤其重要，能賦予他們力量，讓他們可以與體制問題長期抗戰。

健康應用程式 Exhale 取自相同靈感，於 2020 年夏季推出，以回應當時的社會動盪，希望提供非裔族群、原住民以及有色人種女性（合稱為 BIWOC）一個避難所。該應用程式預計於 2023 年重新上架，希望創造安全舒適的環境，引導使用者進行冥想、練習正向樂觀的思維、把理想具象化，及具有療癒力的呼吸練習。

WUNDERMAN
THOMPSON　Exhale

『你已經做太多了，可以休息了，放輕鬆，休息。』這樣就是革命了。

Tricia Hersey，
The Nap Ministry 創辦人

The Mae House 也針對最需要休假卻較難負擔度假行程的家庭提供健康養生的住宿，其中包含非裔、原住民及有色族群（合稱 BIPOC）。該旅宿以「休養生息」（Rest as Residency）為主題，將距離紐約市 2.5 小時路程的農舍翻新成豪華民宿，自 2022 年 6 月起開放入住，並制定不同價格等級的方案來維持此計畫的運作。

雖然提倡休養生息的多是弱勢族群，但在講究高產能的時代，一般大眾也能對休息的重要性感同身受。如同 Hersey 在書中提到的：「光是聽到一段簡單卻大膽的宣言：『你已經做太多了，可以休息了，放輕鬆，休息。』這樣就是革命了。如果能相信這句話，並持續找到休養生息、自我修復及療癒的方式，那便是解放」。

值得關注的原因：
將休養詮釋為一種反抗工具，替養生概念增添了不同色彩。品牌可以透過提倡休息的權益，幫助轉型健康的概念，讓社會脫離庸庸碌碌的工作循環。

更年期靜修

從介紹更年期荷爾蒙療法到提供營養攝取建議，專為
更年期消費者打造的靜修空間越來越受歡迎。

2022 年夏季，Amilla Maldives 首度推出「更年期靜修」（Menopause Retreat），活動為期五天，內容包含荷爾蒙平衡講座、呼吸療法及抱樹療法等。Amilla 的這項女性專屬靜修計畫是希望正視這個人生階段可能會遇到的挑戰，目標是「傳遞知識並賦予女性力量，啟發她們展開新的生活方式」。

義大利南提洛省（South Tyrol）的養生度假村 Preidlhof 提供旅客為期六天的更年期休養行程，結合了醫療保健課程及傳統療法；而位在澳洲大洋路的養生度假村 Great Ocean Road Resort 也預計在 2023 年開設 5 期的更年期靜修課程。

許多參加更年期靜修的女性都從套裝行程中獲益。「你們讓我再度容光煥發」、「謝謝你們幫助我改善睡眠」、「我覺得自己又活過來了」……　這些都是參加英國 Menoheaven 三日更年期靜修活動的旅客所給的好評。2017 年開幕的 Menoheaven 坐落在英國薩塞克斯郡海邊，致力於改善人們對更年期缺乏關注的情形，許多人在更年期之前與中間的階段都在盲目摸索。其共同創辦人 Tania Smith 向偉門智威智庫表示：「過去在英國並不存在這樣的行程。而現在，我們的靜修活動讓參與的女性有機會把自己放在第一順位，也能真正地停下腳步來，開始關注自己、向專家學習、分享並傾聽他人的經歷，並反思自己的生活是否需要做出改變。」

Menoheaven 也提供一對一的課程，內容涵蓋更年期荷爾蒙替代療法及心靈療癒等。Smith 表示：「在艱難的時刻同時滋養自己的身、心、靈，效果十分卓越，我們也發現這對接近更年期和正處於更年期的女性來說很有效」。自從 Menoheaven 開幕以來，越來越多接近更年期的女性前往靜修，提前為人生的下一階段做準備。

值得關注的原因：
根據 Grand View Research 在 2022 年 11 月的調查顯示，全球更年期市場的規模預計在 2030 年前達到約莫 244 億美元。因應這樣的市場需求，飯店及度假村正擴大他們的服務範疇，為這個過去鮮少受人關注的人生階段提供服務。

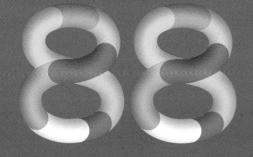

元宇宙正念

元宇宙開始傳達正能量，幫助真人使用者和
虛擬角色放鬆身心。

偉門智威智庫的調查顯示，美、英、中三國有 56% 的人認為科技
對於提升他們的心理健康有所幫助，更有 81% 的人會透過數位
科技來達到休息放鬆的效果。

2022 年 2 月，瑜珈品牌 Alo Yoga 在 Roblox 平台上推出沉
浸式瑜珈及冥想體驗，希望藉此推廣身心健康。這個名為 Alo
Sanctuary 的虛擬空間以「療癒身心的靜修處」為設計理念，讓
人們能進行引導式冥想，也可隨時開啟每日瑜珈課程，沈浸於頌
缽聲浴中。

Roblox 全球品牌合夥副總裁 Christina Wootton 表示：「我們
已經聽聞許多用戶將 Roblox 當作療癒平台及救生浮木的感人故
事。而現在，我們的社群又多了一個空間向頂尖健康養生專家直
接學習正念及冥想的重要性。」

Tripp 也致力創造正向的元宇宙。該公司利用虛擬實境技術，讓民眾「練習正念，並學習利用其他情緒掌控自己的感受」，Tripp 執行長兼共同創辦人 Nanea Reeves 向偉門智威智庫如此說道。2022 年 6 月，該公司募得逾 1,100 萬美元來強化虛擬冥想體驗，其中包括來自亞馬遜、高通及 Pokémon Go 開發商 Niantic 的投資。

值得關注的原因：

元宇宙和正念兩者並不互斥。人們將提升身心健康的習慣帶進元宇宙，並期望商業品牌能帶給他們一場元宇宙正念之旅。

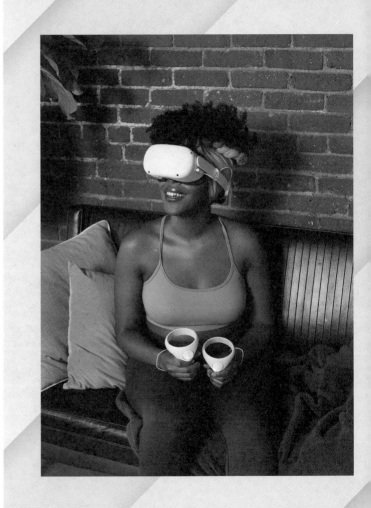

越來越多研究強調，文化對於精神疾病或慢性疼痛的患者具有治療效果。

位於布魯塞爾的布魯格曼大學附設醫院（Brugmann University Hospital）近期推出一項為期 6 個月的試驗計畫，讓醫生針對憂鬱症、焦慮症及其他心理疾病患者開出免費參訪文化機構的處方。在五間參與計畫的文化機構中，患者能前往其中一處進行參訪，如布魯塞爾早期的下水道系統，或是專門展示尿尿小童服裝的 GardeRobe 博物館。

布魯格曼大學附設醫院的精神科醫師 Dr Johan Newell 向偉門智威智庫表示，文化處方的目的在於讓患者重新與世界產生連結。「參觀藝術能讓我們與自己的內心世界產生連結、放慢步調，並專注於當下。同時也能讓長期受到精神疾病所苦的人們找到出門的意義，讓他們在瞬息萬變的社會中找回一席之地。」

在美國，由麻州文化協會（Mass Cultural Council）所資助的當地計畫 -CultureRx，也提倡讓患者多加參與藝術、科學及文化活動。2022 年 6 月，該計畫於試行三年後獲得良好成效，更預計在 2023 年擴大合作對象。另一方面，希臘文化部也推動一項計畫，支持藝文機構如國立當代藝術博物館（National Museum of Contemporary Art）、雅典管弦樂團（Athens State Orchestra）等提供民眾創新的文化展演作為處方。

值得關注的原因：
隨著人們了解到文化活動對健康有益，「健康」一詞的定義也持續擴大、邊界更加模糊。文化活動不再只是單純的休閒娛樂，而是讓人能療癒身心、以有意義的方式與外界互動的醫師處方。

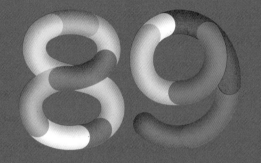

89

文化處方

醫生正為患者的心理健康開出文化處方，
鼓勵他們參訪博物館、畫廊及其他藝文場所，
以協助他們改善自身的心理健康。

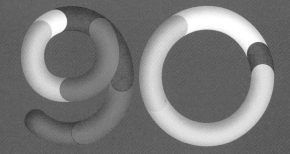

滋養全身肌膚

皮膚做為人體最大的器官，正在得到更全面的營養升級。

「就像我們日常飲食會攝取不同營養成分一樣，我們的皮膚也需要均衡攝取不同營養」

「皮膚健康也是健康的一環，而皮膚微生物菌相就像腸道微生物菌相一樣，能夠影響整個身體。」iota 共同創辦人 Monique Meneses 向偉門智威智庫如此說道。iota 於 2022 年 9 月底在紐約創立，作為「第一個全身肌膚的營養品牌」，iota 著重在脖子以下的肌膚護理。該品牌旗下產品包括「超維他命沐浴乳」（Supervitamin Body Wash+）及超植萃身體精華（Superplant Body Serum+）。該精華蘊含 24 種皮膚必需的營養成分，能平衡微生物菌相，增進肌膚健康。Meneses 將 iota 產品比擬為皮膚的營養餐，「就像我們日常飲食會攝取不同營養成分一樣，我們的皮膚也需要均衡攝取不同營養」。

根據美國皮膚科學會（American Academy of Dermatology）調查，美國最常見的皮膚問題是青春痘（痤瘡），每年影響近 5,000 萬人。此外，美國平均每 10 人就有 1 人曾得過異位性皮膚炎，還有 1,600 萬人有玫瑰斑／酒糟性皮膚炎（rosacea）的困擾。因此，iota 致力於提升大眾對皮膚健康的認知，希望透過旗下產品，協助民眾解決皮膚問題。Meneses 解釋道：「近年研究顯示，較差的皮膚健康，容易發炎、產生自體免疫疾病、心臟病及過敏的風險也較高。而 iota 是將顧客全面性的健康放在心上的品牌。」

皮膚保養品牌 Advanced Nutrition Programme 也專注於提升皮膚健康，針對特定皮膚問題打造營養保健品，如該品牌的「肌膚活力綜合維他命」（Skin Vitality）就富含 28 種能滋養肌膚的營養成分。

值得關注的原因：
身體護理的時代已然到來。過去為臉部肌膚打造的產品已相當多元，而今品牌將焦點轉向脖子以下的身體肌膚，為消費者的整體健康打下良好基礎。

91

工作

100

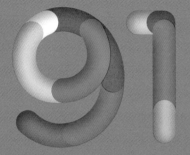

共融創業家

來自關注度較低的族群以自身的需求為本，帶頭設計出
創新的產品與服務，掀起共融企業潮。

身障運動迷在前往體育場館觀賽的途中可能會遇到重重阻礙。在出生時即患有腦性麻痺，所以在說話與行動時會稍微受限的 Victor Ocando 也對此深感挫折，於是他決定創立 Adapt The Game 來為所有人提供一個正常、良好的觀賽體驗。從自己位在美國的新創公司出發，Victor Ocando 設計出一套可以檢視體育場館座位的行動應用程式，讓身障觀眾選擇符合自己需求的無障礙座位。不管是美式橄欖球賽、足球賽或籃球賽，他的終極目標是要讓身障運動迷獲得更佳的觀賽體驗。

倫敦企業家「ay Reid 深感更年期教育的不足，於是決定展開「上班族的更年期」（9 to 5 Menopause）計畫，為所有族裔的受薪階級女性提供更年期教育與適應秘訣等相關資源。Reid 對偉門智威智庫表示：「我從 46 歲開始出現更年期症狀，但當時在談更年期的都是富裕、不用工作的白人女性。她們推薦的做法是拜訪私人診所、尋找個人營養師或做瑜伽，但我不適用這些，我還有工作要做。所以我決定展開「上班族的更年期」計畫，因為在過去，職場女性從來沒討論過這個議題。」Reid 以在社群媒體上分享自己的經驗談開始這項計畫，目前也密切地和英國企業合作，讓他們了解如何制定合適的公司政策來保障員工在這塊領域的福祉。」

英國創業家 Charlotte Fountaine 對心理健康應用程式中，一成不變的內容感到厭倦，於是開發了專為 LGBTQ+ 族群設計的心理諮詢應用程式 Kalda。LGBTQ+ 族群承受的壓力常常會比其他

人更大，若還得從異性戀價值觀的環境尋找心理健康相關資源，那對他們來說，無非也是一種壓迫。2022 年上架的 Kalda 是自助式的心理健康工具，內容由同屬 LGBTQ+ 族群的諮商師開發設計，每週會固定提供團體諮商時段，也都有許多社群成員每日上線給予彼此支持和鼓勵。

值得關注的原因：
共融企業家們以自身族群的需求缺口為原點，開創了新世代的產品與服務。企業或品牌有機會可以與他們合作、將他們列為旗下供應商或者投資這些企業，以展現對這些族群的支持。

虛擬執行長

未來出現在會議室中的企業高層，
有沒有可能都是虛擬人物呢？

現今企業想提升效率，將機器取代人力，使更好、更快且以更低成本完成的工作自動化。所以人工智慧對他們來說已成為一項不可取代的重要工具。過往，這些人工智慧都躲在幕後，但擁有先驅思維的企業如今開始探索人工智慧的潛力，讓這些虛擬員工擔任起團隊中受人景仰的領導職位。

中國遊戲公司「網龍」旗下的產品包含多人線上遊戲與應用程式，而近期，他們為福建分公司指派人工智慧的虛擬角色唐鈺女士擔任執行長，此舉也被視為藉由人工智慧的潛能探索如何改變企業的治理結構，是該公司元宇宙部門的重要里程碑。唐鈺的首要任務是簡化公司流程、提升產品品質、改善執行效率，她同時也是該公司的即時資料核心與分析師，協助企業進行每日決策與風險管理。

關注 Web3 發展的高檔蘭姆酒品牌 Dictador 同樣也聘用人工智慧機器人來擔任執行長，並取名為 Mika。該機器人由 Hanson Robotics 製造，會參與並主導該烈酒公司旗下去中心化自治組織 Arthouse Spirits DAO 的經營會議，也會代表品牌與組織成員溝通。先前 Dictador 已推出蘭姆酒相關 NFT 並建立去中心化社群，所以此刻將機器人拱上大位，是擁抱科技潛能的他們自然會下的一步棋。該品牌的歐洲區總裁 Marek Szoldrowski 表示，創新「會不斷改變我們對現有世界的認知。」

虛擬領導「會不斷改變我
們對現有世界的認知。」

Marek Szoldrowski，歐洲區總裁

值得關注的原因：

我們在 2018 年時就已首次提出數位人力資源的概念，當時企業讓虛擬人物擔任發言人或接待人員來平衡人力與科技的應用比例，改善職場環境也提升顧客體驗。隨著元宇宙中人力資源逐漸發展成型，公司高層會受到什麼樣的影響，值得拭目以待。

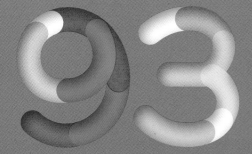

退而不休

退休，落伍。
退而不休（rewirement），正夯。

2022 年 8 月，網壇名將小威廉絲（Serena Williams）宣布退役，並將重心轉移到她的家庭和其他事業上。

在《Vogue》雜誌的封面故事中，小威廉絲談到她這麼做的動機：「我一直不喜歡『退休』這個詞，聽起來很不符合現代生活。比較適合形容我現階段狀態的說法可能是轉換跑道，我離開網壇，轉而著重其他對我來說相同重要的人事物。」

小威廉絲不是唯一一個揚棄退休觀念的人。理財顧問們從幾年前就已開始使用「退而不休」這個新詞彙來與打算退休的客戶溝通，而現在這個用詞也拓及到財務管理以外，涵蓋了生活中更多不同的面向。

退役記者 Jackie Crosby 過去十分勤於工作，她於 2021 年自《明尼亞波里斯明星論壇報》(The Minneapolis Star Tribune)退休，她向偉門智威智庫表示：「『退而不休』這個詞我是從朋友口中聽來的，之後我當然也愛上這個說法，因為『退休』畢竟聽起來太老套、無趣了。」這位曾兩度榮獲普立茲新聞獎的記者現在把時間花在音樂上，目前身兼三個樂團的貝斯手，其中一團名為「化學實驗組」(Chemistry Set)。這是她幾十年以來第一次真正以自己的步調生活，她非常享受這份自由自在的感受，也可以花時間陪伴身邊關心的人，不用再不停地為了報刊截稿日忙碌奔走。

法國的 Chris Welsch 是名半退休的攝影師與編輯，他決定離開過往的生活重心巴黎，搬到偏遠的勃艮第定居，而促使他做出決

定的因素之一是新冠疫情。他告訴偉門智威智庫：「我不想終其一生都窩在巴黎狹小的公寓裡，不想在窗外沒有樹木的地方老去。現在我想一步步融入勃艮第當地的社區，也就是我現在的家。」

退而不休也不代表要減低工作量。Welsch 近期成為歐洲微軟傳播部門的全職記者，跑遍全歐洲報導科技對人類與地球造成的影響。

值得關注的原因：
疫後、生活、工作，現在開始有了全新定義，接下來的幾十年也更將如此。退而不休族現在開始重新審視生活中的優先順位，重新了解自己，並把時間花在自己有興趣的事物和家人身上。

94

平權福利

**共融型企業現在開始將員工福利範圍擴大，
藉此改善員工的生活，並照顧以往受到邊緣化的族群。**

想在多元、平等、包容等面向取得領先地位的雇主，現在開始調整缺乏彈性的員工福利政策，希望了解來自邊緣社群的員工，並改善他們的生活條件。雇主們開始正視並處理當前的弱勢問題，努力讓職場成為對所有人而言更平等、更具多元包容力的環境。

正視多元族群對健康照護的特殊需求，是企業往平權邁進的方式之一。在中國，阿里巴巴為員工提供的健檢福利除了適用於員工本身及其子女外，也包含員工的父母，因為該公司意識到照顧高齡長輩所費不貲。

在阿根廷，電商公司 Mercado Libre 協助跨性別員工負擔變性手術的開銷；在英國，PayPal 將更年期照護計劃獨立於員工健保之外，讓更多僱員毋須負擔保險費用亦能受惠；而在美國，亞馬遜、美國銀行（Bank of America）、BuzzFeed 等公司為提升員工的生育健康，推出補助計劃為他們支付跨州墮胎的旅費。

沃爾瑪超市（Walmart）為了促進員工健康並解決不同種族間的生育照護平等議題，他們宣布會自 2022 年 6 月起，在幾個州為工作夥伴提供產婦陪護。在喬治亞州推出此一方案後，該公司也表示會緊接著在路易斯安那州、印第安納與伊利諾州導入此一福利措施，因為此政策似乎能立竿見影地改善這些地區員工的生活。沃爾瑪超市說道，在路易斯安那州，黑人產婦的死亡率比白人高出五倍；在印第安納州，有多達 33 個郡沒有在地的婦產科。沃爾瑪超市合作的產婦陪護都來自當地的社區，對於產婦及其子女的健康都帶來正面的影響，因為他們能理解產婦的文化背景，這是與傳統醫療照護不同之處。

值得關注的原因：
企業開始將弱勢族群的獨特需求列入考量，進一步反思更多元的健康照護議題，同時讓工作環境更人性化。

沃爾瑪超市（Walmart）宣布自2022年6月起，在幾個州為工作夥伴提供產婦陪護。

五星級辦公環境

企業為了持續吸引員工重回辦公室，於是開始從
旅宿業者的服務項目中尋找靈感。

25 米的泳池、200 公尺的頂樓露天跑道、一間舒壓按摩室,這些聽起來像高級飯店的配備,其實是 Google 位在倫敦國王十字區的新辦公大樓的福利設施,且還只是其中幾項而已。這件極具野心的新總部大樓規劃案,因其佔地極廣而有「the landscraper」的暱稱,能讓 Google 員工及附近居民雙雙受益——因為部分設施亦會開放予居民使用。該大樓預計於 2024 年完工。

科技巨擘亞馬遜目前正在美國維吉尼亞州建造第二總部大樓,這座螺旋形建物名為「The Helix」,建築物最外圍會有戶外跑道沿著大樓

盤旋而上,周圍種有來自當地山脈 Blue Ridge Mountains 的植物。對亞馬遜的員工而言,不只是建築物外圍有著可以親近自然的設計,建案中還有一片森林廣場,並搭配瀑布般的水幕,簡直是將親生物設計(biophilic design)應用到極限的絕佳案例。

倫敦機構 Ask Us For Ideas 的地下國度僅以幽微光線照明,與大眾習慣的明亮辦公環境截然不同。此一空間設計於 2022 年完成,由 Cake Architecture 工作室設計,其總監 Hugh Scott Moncrieff 向偉門智威智庫表示,這種環境「比較幽靜、有氣氛,也比較內斂」。硬木地板、粗毛地毯加上中世紀風格的扶手椅,整體空間的設計理念是要跳脫辦公室的既定框架,希望鼓勵員工在辦公之外,也能在此舉辦活動。Moncrieff 說道:「他們會在這裡舉辦一對一心理諮商、呼吸及瑜伽課程。也會辦夜間講座和調酒派對。」

世界級的服務也融進辦公環境。L'Oréal's 位在美國洛杉磯的第二總部大樓於 2022 年 8 月啟用,他們為員工提供的是禮賓服務,可以為員工跑腿打雜,例如加油、收取送洗衣物等,每小時的收費為 5 美元。這項服務讓員工不必擔心日常雜務,能將時間騰出來,也成為進辦公室的額外福利。

值得關注的原因:
新一代的辦公環境再升級,融入五星級服務,希望吸引已習慣居家辦公的員工重回辦公室。企業此時已開始爭相讓辦公環境變得更誘人。

The Soho office of Ask Us For Ideas

WUNDERMAN
THOMPSON   The Soho office of Ask Us For Ideas

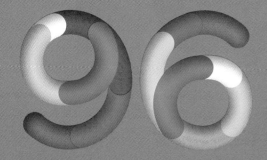

非同步工作

非同步工作讓員工可自行安排工時，
而這種模式會繼續存在。

疫情期間，遠距工作模式讓下班時間變得模糊，這讓許多人心力交瘁，因為他們在此工作模式下很難真正關機休息。但也有許多人認為，這種非同步模式的工作成效不輸過往，甚至能得到比朝九晚五工作模式更好的成果。

家裡有幼兒的家長可以溜出去看場籃球賽，或者在工作間的休息時段下廚做飯，又或者在晚餐後才回覆 email。其他遠距工作者則可以把通勤的時間省下來，拿來慢跑或上瑜伽課。

「非同步工作讓員工可以省下通勤時間，可以在效率低的時段處理行政瑣事，也多出時間可以運動，甚至自己下廚以節省餐費。」倫敦政經學院的行為科學系助理教授 Laura Giurge 向《BBC》如此說道。

受薪階級現已習慣這種彈性工作模式，於是開始要求公司讓他們在疫後也能維持。針對員工所做的調查顯示，很多人希望可以採行混合工作模式，一週內只有幾天進公司，其他天則在家工作即可。

這種非同步模式的工作成效不輸過往，甚至能得到比朝九晚五工作模式更好的成果。

非同步工作的工具與平台現在如雨後春筍般湧現。新創公司 Loom 讓使用 email 傳送影片這件事變得更加便利，而 Slack 和微軟都複製了他們的做法，將短影片訊息整合至旗下產品當中。微軟旗下的平台 Teams 已能讓遠距工作團隊互相協力，現在更推出測試版的應用程式 Places，可以追蹤遠距團隊成員的工作情形。

另一款應用程式 Flown 則可「以數位方式複製身體」，可以模擬另一個人出現在身邊的畫面，或者模擬出「一群」遠距工作者，讓自己身處其中，因而能保持專注並認真工作。

值得關注的原因：
非線性工作模式會持續存在，勞資雙方也都開始漸漸習慣此一作法，並利用新的科技平台與應用程式來改善其缺點，進一步將優點放大。

在岌岌可危的財務危機與股市動盪之下，許多退休民眾正在選擇重返職場。英國樂齡中心 Centre for Ageing Better 的調查數據顯示，65 歲以上的人口中，重回職場的人數在 2022 年第一季中增加了 17.3 萬人。美國退休人員協會（American Association of Retired Persons，簡稱 AARP）在 2022 年 5 月的報告中，引用的求職網站 Indeed 資料指出，在美國提早一年退休的人士中，已有 170 萬人重新進入勞動力市場。

Kim Chaplain 是英國樂齡中心的求職顧問，她向《衛報》表示，該機構「猜測日常開銷上升可能是導致此一現象的原因。」《衛報》也側寫報導了住在英國薩福克郡（Suffolk）的 Bernadette Hempstead，她是一名已退休的人資，領有小額的私人保險及政府發放的退休金，然而這兩筆收入卻不足以應付她的日常開銷。Hempstead 說道：「現在物價越來越貴，生活變得很艱困。」

也有人是為了尋求社交機會才重返職場。美國金融科技公司 Ubiquity Retirement + Savings 的高階副總 Andrew Meadows 向 AARP 說道：「我們國家的高齡人口中，孤獨和憂鬱的狀況非常嚴重，且這波疫情又讓情況更為嚴峻。很多年長者被迫待在家中，時至今日，他們也開始思考要重新進入職場，希望獲得社交互動機會。」

值得關注的原因：
老一輩的人正在重新改寫晚年人生的傳統選項，拋開退休人生並擁抱職場生活。有的人是因為經濟考量，也有人是為了尋求社交互動。

97

不退不休

有一群退休人士現正打算重返職場，
他們尋求的是人際互動的機會，
或者確保財源穩定無虞。

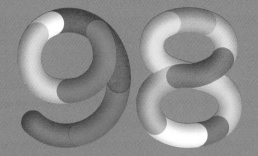

超級通勤族

新一類的通勤者開始出現，他們平日待在城市工作，
週末才回到位於郊區的家中。

因應實體進公司辦公的職場規定，住在城外的通勤上班族紛紛回到都市工作，於視旅宿業者開始為這些居民推出特別的住宿優惠。

《紐約時報》創造了「超級通勤族」（supercommuter）一詞，這群上班族平日選擇有提供住宿優惠的飯店，既讓通勤變得輕鬆，也不會失去週末的郊區生活。

在英國，旗下擁有 The Savoy 與 Pullman London St Pancras 的雅高飯店集團（Accor Group），推出了「通勤住宿」（Commute

and Stay）的優惠方案，提供賓客週間兩晚的住宿優惠、彈性取消以及在工作與客戶會議方面的排程協助。

萬豪酒店（Marriott）於 2022 年初推出的「一日通行證」（Day Pass）計畫，可於旗下飯店享受晚間退房服務並使用共同工作空間。該計畫當時提供住客從鄰近機場搭機往返歐洲及英國各地的機票（現已調整優惠內容），因為有些上班族早已搬離工作城市，現在卻得經常回去工作，這類的通勤族便可受益於此計畫。

美國芝加哥的 The Hoxton 飯店則提供支付固定月費的會員一項優惠方案「工作、住宿、玩樂一把罩」（Work Stay Play）。方案會員可以使用飯店內的共同工作空間，享有工作與娛樂方面的優惠福利，每月還可以在任一分館中住宿一晚。飯店總經理鼓勵訪客「要好好利用『工作假期』（workcation）的優點」。

在 2022 年，有幾間大公司規定員工一定要回到辦公室工作。馬斯克（Elon Musk）在 11 月時明言，Twitter 的員工一週至少得在辦公室待上 40 小時。Apple 和 Google 也相繼祭出政策，要求員工自 4 月起，每週進辦公室至少一到三天。Meta 規定員工在 3 月時得重返辦公室工作。微軟則計畫延續混合工作模式，要員工實際進公司幾天。

值得關注的原因：
隨著工作條件不斷演進，超級通勤族開始選擇長時間通勤並購買飯店的常客方案，以求在必須回到城市工作的同時，還能與城市生活保持優雅的距離。

工作

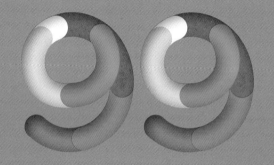

職場健康照護

企業開始為員工提供更多樣的健康照護福利，
希望吸引並留住人才。

雇主開始發揮創意，提供員工更多元的健康照護計畫，因為照顧員工的心理健康已成為越來越迫切的需求。世界衛生組織（WHO）的調查發現，全球僱員每年因為憂鬱或焦慮而無法工作的天數加總為 120 億天，損失的產值相當於 1 兆美元。經濟動盪與工作技能短缺的情況加劇，代表的是全球企業需要更積極地照顧員工的身心健康。

現在有許多企業會提供現成的心理健康計畫，但也有些企業選擇直接讓員工放假休息。資誠會計師事務所（PwC）、人資平台領英（LinkedIn）和 WPP 廣告集團等企業為避免員工心力交瘁，為全公司員工關上辦公室大門，提供所有人一到兩天的心理健康假。印度電商平台 Meesho 則提供了更棒的福利，於 2022 年 9 月宣布要讓員工放上 11 天的長假，這也是該公司連續第二年提供此一假期。

另外，生活開銷增加造成的壓力也對員工心理健康帶來更大的負擔。MetLife UK 於 2022 年的研究顯示，有 64% 的工作人士因為財務狀況而面臨壓力、焦慮及憂鬱問題，同時可能導致他們的生產力下降。英國私人勞工保險公司 Cushon 的價值主張總監 Steve Watson 向《金融時報》（Financial Times）表示：「過往我們都將財務健康與身體健康分開看待，但現在我們得用更整體的角度來思考這件事。」

英國連鎖速食餐廳 Honest Burgers 為員工提供財務管理應用程式 Wagestream 的使用權限，可進行財務健檢並有理財顧問在線服務。該計畫也打進 2022 年英國「最佳雇主獎」（Employee Benefits Awards）的決賽，類別是「小型雇主最佳財務健康策略獎」。近期美國智庫蘭德公司（RAND）位於歐洲的分部有項調查發現，使用雇主提供的財務管理計畫的人，其心理健康表現確實有所提升。

值得關注的原因：
員工福利顧問公司 Mercer Marsh Benefits 的研究顯示，在企業能為員工提供的眾多福利中，最有價值的主要是與增進心理健康有關的照護方案。現在基本的心理健康照護已成為員工福利的標配，可見企業正在改寫能吸引與留住員工的經營守則。

「這在我們都將財務健康與身體健康分開看待，但現在我們得用更整體的角度來思考這件事。」

Steve Watson,
Cushon 價值主張總監

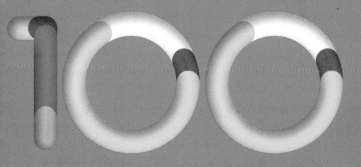

起身世代

員工的期待日漸上升。
儘管當前正處於經濟衰退的局勢，
但權力的天秤會不會仍往勞方的方向傾斜呢？

「人才的戰爭已經結束了，獲勝的是人才！」美國全國廣播公司商業頻道（CNBC）於 2022 年 10 月舉辦了「工作高峰會」（Work Summit），而全球顧問公司資誠（PwC）的美國主席暨資深夥人 Tim Ryan 在該活動中如此說道。Ryan 也表示，僱員現在開始堅持自己有權選擇以更彈性的方式完成工作。

求職網站 Indeed 的執行長 Chris Hyams 也提到，要求提升勞動條件的員工數量越來越多。Hyams 在 2022 年 8 月由《Fortune》雜誌進行的一項訪問中指出，「追求工作和生活平衡的聲量越來越大」，這代表職場契約開始出現變化。勞方此刻正準備大展身手，因而凸顯了此一趨勢的聲量。

具體的例子是重回辦公室的規定，正面臨持續的拉鋸戰。《金融時報》（Financial Times）分析了 Google 追蹤手機位置的資料發現，從 2022 年 10 月中的職場往返通勤紀錄看來，全球前七大經濟體的通勤狀況都遠低於疫情前的規模。

在美國，雖然一直有離職率下降的相關報導，但麥肯錫（McKinsey）引用了證據指出，年長女性轉換工作的速度創下新高，比同齡男性更快。麥肯錫與 Leanin.Org 共同撰述的報告〈2022 年職場女力〉（Women in the Workplace 2022）顯示，女性會為了更好的待遇而離職。

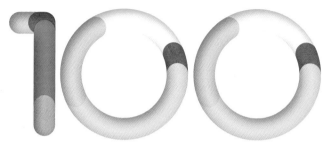

「人才的戰爭
已經結束了，
獲勝的是人才！」

在許多國家勞方的怒火燃燒之下，我們終於看到工會組織再次崛起，在蘋果、亞馬遜、奇波雷墨西哥燒烤餐廳（Chipotle）與星巴克等美國企業當中尤為顯見。雖然有些企業仍堅決抵抗，但也有企業看到傾聽員工聲音的價值。微軟於 2022 年 6 月宣布，他們會正式認可員工加入及組織工會的權利。

雖然有些經濟學家預測，一旦經濟開始衰退，權力的鐘擺又會往資方的方向擺動，但資誠的 Ryan 持有不同的看法：「如果有人覺得權力平衡會回到過往的狀態，那我必須誠實而謙卑地說，我認為他們的判斷有誤。」

值得關注的原因：
隨著經濟緊縮日趨嚴重，企業不該猖狂無視人才的要求。進步的企業會傾聽勞方的顧慮，讓他們感受到自己握有掌控權及彈性。

關於偉門智威智庫（Wunderman Thompson Intelligence）

偉門智威智庫是智威湯遜面向未來思考的研究和創新單位，負責觀察剛興起的現象以及未來的全球趨勢、消費型態變化、創新發展模式，並在進一步解讀這些趨勢後，將其見解提供給品牌參考。本單位提供一系列諮詢服務，包含客製化研究、簡報、聯名品牌報告、工作坊，也勇於創新，與品牌合作，在品牌框架下引領未來趨勢，並執行新產品與概念。本單位由偉門智威智庫的全球總監 Emma Chiu 與 Marie Stafford 所帶領。

如欲瞭解更多資訊，請造訪：

wundermanthompson.com/expertise/intelligence

關於《改變未來的100件事》

這是由偉門智威智庫出版的年度預測報告，除了描繪未來一年的樣貌，也呈現了最受歡迎的趨勢，讓您能掌握潮流。這份報告紀錄了十大領域的 100 個趨勢，橫跨文化、科技與創新、旅遊與觀光、品牌與行銷、食品和飲品、美容、零售與商業、奢華、健康、工作領域。

聯絡人

Emma Chiu
emma.chiu@wundermanthompson.com

Marie Stafford
marie.stafford@wundermanthompson.com

台灣偉門智威
wt.taipei@wundermanthompson.com

封面圖片

Planet City. Courtesy of Liam Young

字型選用

Termina; Helvetica Neue (TT)

+ WUNDERMAN THOMPSON

A REPORT BY WUNDERMAN THOMPSON INTELLIGENCE

+WUNDERMAN
THOMPSON

Trends and change to watch in 2023

100

THE FUTURE

2023 The Future 100
Writer / Wunderman Thompson Intelligence

Editor-in-chief / Emma Chiu
Editor / Emily Safian-Demers
Writers / Marie Stafford, Chen May Yee, John O'Sullivan, Sarah Tilley, Carla Calandra, Jamie Hannah Shackleton, Francesca Lewis
Sub editors / Hester Lacey, Katie Myers

Creative director / Shazia Chaudhry

Cover / Planet City. Courtesy of Liam Young

Assistant editor / Jill Chang, Rita Cheng, Julie Hsueh, Joyce Lu, Raquel Hung, Cassie Chiang, Jessica Chien, Ann Chen, Joyce Lo, Alison Hung, Cloud Kao, Robin Yang, Easy Tsai, Leo Jian, Meg Huang, Ai Hsiao, Kevin Huang, Timothy Yeh, Hailey Lin, Ben Hu

Translator / Rye Lin, Tina Hsieh
Publisher / Wunderman Thompson Taipei
Address / 13F - 5, No.8, Sec. 7, Civic Boulevard, Nangang District, Taipei City, 115, Taiwan
Tel / (02) 3766-1000
Fax / (02) 2788-0260

Agent / China Times Publishing Company
Tel / (02) 2306-6842
Address / No.351, Sec.2, Wanshou Rd., Guisha District., Taoyuan City, 333, Taiwan

Retail price / NTD 500
ISBN / 9789869899239

First published in Taiwan by Wunderman Thompson in April 2023

✛ WUNDERMAN
THOMPSON
A REPORT BY WUNDERMAN THOMPSON INTELLIGENCE

FOREWORD

Community, creativity, and color vibrantly paint 2023, as last year's unbounded optimism shifts to an exuberant need for uplift and play.

All signs should point towards a bleak and chaotic year as a rocky economy, political instability, and environmental deterioration persist. However, people are determined to show resilience, innovation, and joy in the face of continued hardship. Pantone's bright choice for its Color of the Year 2023, Viva Magenta, captures the spritely sentiment: it's "an unconventional shade for an unconventional time," the brand says (page 21). A joyconomy is in motion this year, with brands offering uninhibited play for all ages (Ageless play, page 95) and exercise classes that mimic the feeling of tossing confetti (Joy workout, page 192)—sign us up, please (with arms waving profusely).

The stress of the past years has put an emphasis on optimizing both the mind and body to empower an elevated self (The Superself, page 188). Businesses are increasingly leading with emotional intelligence and making mental health a priority in their brand mission (see Psycho-dermatology, page 124, and Psychobiotics, page 190). A holistic approach to health is evident across all categories as people expect to positively enhance their wellbeing at every touchpoint, suggesting that every brand needs to be a health brand.The lightning pace of technology sees the evolution from building to living the metaverse. Every aspect of life is being explored in the metaverse—from our digital identities (page 36) to the prospect of virtual families (Virtual nurturers, page 26) to constructing virtual homes (Digital nesting, page 159). More importantly, the metaverse is opening the door to a 3.0 future as a decentralized era slowly takes shape in the form of Web3. Communities,

creators, and brands are invited to form a democratic internet that truly belongs to everyone, introducing new formulas for everything from ownership (Next-gen ownership, page 17) to community engagement (Crypto clubs, page 166) to retail (Cocreative commerce, page 146).

In addition, people are demanding that brands use their influence to better society by putting accessibility and inclusion at the fore. Eighty-six percent of global respondents believe that to support a disadvantaged group, brands need to work with them, not just for them. Various brands are already encouraging diverse voices (Amplifying diverse creators, page 88) and more businesses are introducing inclusive products to the mainstream (Mass inclusive brands, page 93).

Get ready for 100 bitesize trends that offer a splash of color, inspiration, and an insightful glimpse into the unfolding year.

Emma Chiu
Global director, Wunderman Thompson Intelligence
wundermanthompson.com/expertise/intelligence

FOREWORD

"New technologies" and "long lasting events"can both set trends, and Future 100 2023 represents exactly the reflection on events as well as the technological advancement.

The Covid-19 pandemic has been around for over three years. As many countries reopened their borders, Taiwan followed suit in October 2022 and gradually lifting the "face mask mandate". When face masks have become a must-have, our daily greetings went from "Are you vaccinated?" to "Have you had Covid?" People seem to be getting ready to live with Covid rather than still panicking about it. Life graudally returns to normal.

Although people are less panicked about Covid-19, the pandemic did change people's beliefs and ways of living. It has put a spotlight on health, and prompted people to relax and seek work/life balance, especially among Gen Z. A sober generation now rises with no intention to get drunk in their gatherings as younger people value health and sustainability more than ever. We also see the boom of "exclusive services" that are offered to the upper echelons. In contrast to that, the trends of "rewirement" or even "unretirement" are taking shape, too. Why don't people retire? One reason is that they are in search of social connection, and the other one is out of economic necessity.

Climate change and environmental challenges are still two big global issues that no one can walk away from. More and more people are getting anxious about climate change, but younger generations are turning their climate anxiety into "climate optimism", believing that it is the best way to combat climate crisis and get motivated to take actions.

There's even a startup claiming Earth is its "only shareholder", funnelling all its profits to protect the Earth.

The Russia-Ukraine War has lasted for a year, and its impact on global supply chains and geopolitics cannot be more pronounced. But travel agencies take a different approach to this issue. They launched guided tours to the dark zone, giving participants a chance to witness the fear Ukrainians experienced so that people get to cherish what they have in their lives.

Maybe it's too cheesy to talk about the metaverse, but now it indeed has a wider application. We see innovative concepts and services such as "Sustainability in the Metaverse", "ATM(etaverse)" and "Metamobility". Immersive technologies also help to bring metaverse to the next level, blurring the lines between the virtual and the real world.

I believe"new technologies" and "major, long-lasting events" are two big drivers of new trends because these factors are profoundly changing people's lives and values. The issuance of Future 100 2023 represents exactly the reflection on these events and the technological advancement. However challenging the future will be, I know we can face it and embrace it more optimistically.

Evan Teng
CEO, Wunderman Thompson Taipei

60 70 80 90 100

01

CULTURE

10

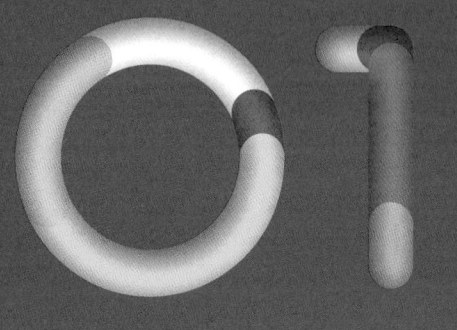

NEW REALITIES

The metaverse evolves.

As metaverse activations continue to advance, the way we think about emerging technologies is becoming much more nuanced and engrained in the everyday—shaping a new reality where physical and virtual living are indistinguishable.

DoorLabs is using technology to advance accessibility in virtual worlds. The company is exploring how to use "new immersion technology in the metaverse to better help and better equip people with different needs in the future," DoorLabs cofounder Kunho Kim tells Wunderman Thompson Intelligence.

Speculative architect and director Liam Young is leveraging virtual reality (VR) to inspire activism. "It changes us from being a passive audience into an active citizen. To be a citizen of an immersive world is a different kind of relationship than being an audience member in front of a screen," Young tells Wunderman Thompson Intelligence.

Apple CEO Tim Cook predicts that augmented reality (AR) will become an integral part of daily life. "Zoom out to the future and look back, you'll wonder how you led your life without augmented reality. Just like today, we wonder: 'How did people like me grow up without the internet?'," Cook told Dutch publication *Bright*. "AR is a profound technology that will affect everything."

Leading tech brands are investing heavily in AR and VR, preparing for the coming reign of immersive technologies. Between 2019 and September 30, 2022, Meta shoveled $36 billion into Reality Labs, its metaverse and VR division, according to *Business Insider*.

Analyst Gene Munster of Loup Funds estimates Google's R&D spending on AR at around $39 billion. Snap is going all in on AR—the company listed investing in AR as one of its top three strategic priorities in its 2022 third quarter financial results report.

WHY IT'S INTERESTING
The next era of digital engagement will see a diversification of immersive technologies and further blurring of the digital and the physical—ushering in a new reality.

O2

CREATOR COMMUNITIES

The next generation of digital communities centers around creativity.

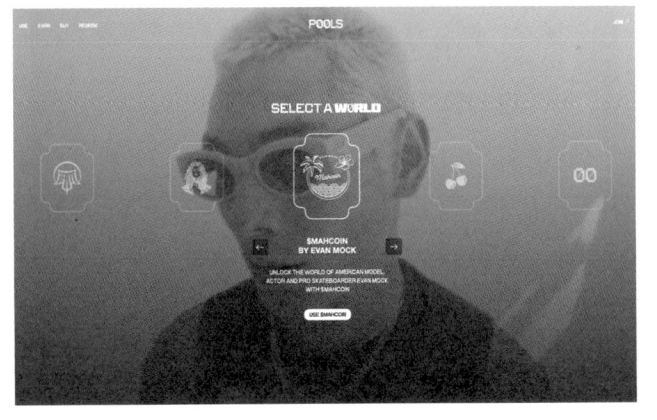

Pools is a creator community that equips creatives and brands with tools to build their own cryptocurrency-enabled communities. "Pools has the power to revolutionize how we view and value creators," supermodel Coco Rocha, who invested in Pools, told *Paper* magazine. In October 2022, the company launched Creator Worlds, a landing pad for each creator's digital ecosystem.

Pools partnered with YSL Beauté in June 2022 to launch creator tokens from musicians Agathe Mougin and Kittens. The tokens grant holders access to the respective artists' Pools communities, where users can unlock bespoke content and experiences, VIP tickets to events, and access to podcasts. Token holders also have privileged access to YSL Beauté's Web3 hub.

"Traditional spheres of influence—from Hollywood to Wall Street and Silicon Valley—are converging more now than ever before, forming a new marketplace with creators and their audiences at the center," Pools states, pointing to social tokens as "a new way for creators to engage directly with their fans through access to real life and metaverse experiences, products, and activities."

Mona is another platform facilitating creator communities. In June 2022, Mona raised nearly $15 million to build a metaverse platform for creators. "Mona is a Web3 metaverse, world-building platform and network built for creators by creators," Justin Melillo, CEO of Mona, told *GamesBeat*. Melillo started Mona in order to "place the emphasis on the creator" with a mission "to make the metaverse a social network where creators can thrive." In July 2022, the company hosted the launch of The Row, a members-only virtual community featuring architectural designs by acclaimed creatives.

Adobe is facilitating creativity in the metaverse. At its Adobe Max conference in October 2022, the company announced new collaboration and artificial intelligence-powered features for its Creative Cloud applications. "We're doubling down on collaboration," said David Wadhwani, president of Adobe's digital media business. "Creativity is increasingly a team sport, whether you're collaborating with other creators or asking for feedback from stakeholders."

WHY IT'S INTERESTING

"We see creators and developers as the backbone for the metaverse," Melillo says. As digital engagement moves from passive consumption to active creation (for more on this shift, see our "New Realities: Into the Metaverse and Beyond" report), the role of brands is evolving. Creativity is becoming the new status symbol for the next digital era—and brands are transforming their offerings to connect consumers and creatives.

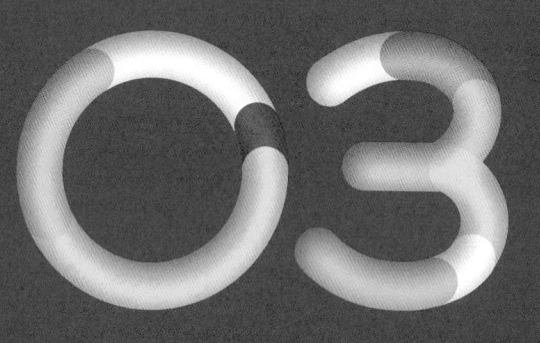

03

REWILDED MINDS

Is it possible to "rewild" ourselves?

Is it possible to rewild the way we think and act? The BBC posed the question in a May 2022 article; Lindsay Baker writes that "we can all find this sense of wonder and meaning in nature. Not only in our connection with it, but in the sense of hope and renewal it seems to offer us."

Gamers are embracing environmentally minded video games that encourage regenerative practices. *Terra Nil*, for example, set to launch in early 2023, will instruct players to reconstruct an ecosystem in the aftermath of a devastating climate crisis event. The concept of the game, which is reminiscent of SimCity's urban-development model, flips the concept to prioritize the environment above skyscrapers and urban infrastructure. *Terra Nil* players will need to restore nature rather than exploit resources to build their city.

According to Wunderman Thompson Intelligence's "New Realities: Into the Metaverse and Beyond" report, 81% of global consumers say they "switch on" to unwind. As gamers turn to their screens and consoles to mentally decompress, they're turning to nature-focused campaigns, rewilding their time-off entertainment of choice.

LL Bean encouraged its audience to replace shopping with ecotherapy in May 2022. The brand replaced its Instagram grid with a "gone fishing" layout and redirected its social media links to the website's landing page, which hosted a message to encourage its shoppers and social media followers to lean into nature for a wellness refresh.

WHY IT'S INTERESTING

Conscious consumers are following nature-minded brands into an age of rewilding and sustainability, reconsidering their habits and habitats as they continue to prioritize their mental health and sustainable lifestyles.

Timberborn game featuring "lumberpunk beavers," by Discord member Cynical Entity, courtesy of Twitter

Is it possible to rewild the way we think and act?

NEXT-GEN OWNERSHIP

An emerging digital framework is introducing a new formula for ownership.

In the coming digital era of Web3, users will not only coauthor but co-own their digital experience.

In the past, if a user created something and posted it on Instagram, Instagram would own that asset. But platforms like Niche are putting control into people's hands. On Niche, the "members are owners," Niche cofounder and CEO Chris Gulczynski tells Wunderman Thompson Intelligence.

"If you think about traditional social media, there is one company that controls everything and has all of the data locked away in their own servers," Zaven Nahapetyan, cofounder and CTO of Niche, tells Wunderman Thompson Intelligence. "What a decentralized social media platform does is distribute that data to other people. It democratizes it, meaning people have ownership and portability over their own data and content."

This adds another layer of value to the Niche user's experience, making people "owners in the same way that someone who has stock in a company is an owner," Nahapetyan says. "As their group becomes more desirable, more exclusive, or gets more media coverage, the value of their ownership stake could go up."

Flyfish Club is experimenting with NFT-based ownership. The members-only restaurant, set to open in 2023, will let members lease their NFTs—which function as membership cards—for temporary membership.

"They own the membership rather than essentially renting a social experience. They own their access."

David Rodolitz, founder and CEO, Flyfish Club

NFTs have "changed the value proposition to our members," David Rodolitz, founder and CEO of Flyfish Club, tells Wunderman Thompson Intelligence. "They own the membership rather than essentially renting a social experience. They own their access."

NFTs—digital certificates of ownership—are also changing how users interact with digital media. As Gary Liu, founder and CEO of Artifact Labs, tells Wunderman Thompson Intelligence, "the internet—Web1, Web2—has fundamentally broken the business model for news because information, once published on the internet, has zero intrinsic value." But, he says, "NFT technologies change that calculus: NFTs allow digital media to have intrinsic value," leading to "new business models, new direct relationships."

WHY IT'S INTERESTING

A paradigm shift is under way. Decentralization is democratizing digital platforms—opening the door to new ownership models that will revolutionize the way brands and consumers interact with digital goods, services, and content.

04

05

CLIMATE OPTIMISM

Gen Z are turning their climate anxiety into climate optimism.

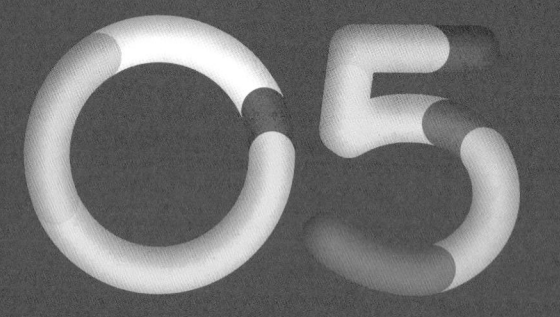

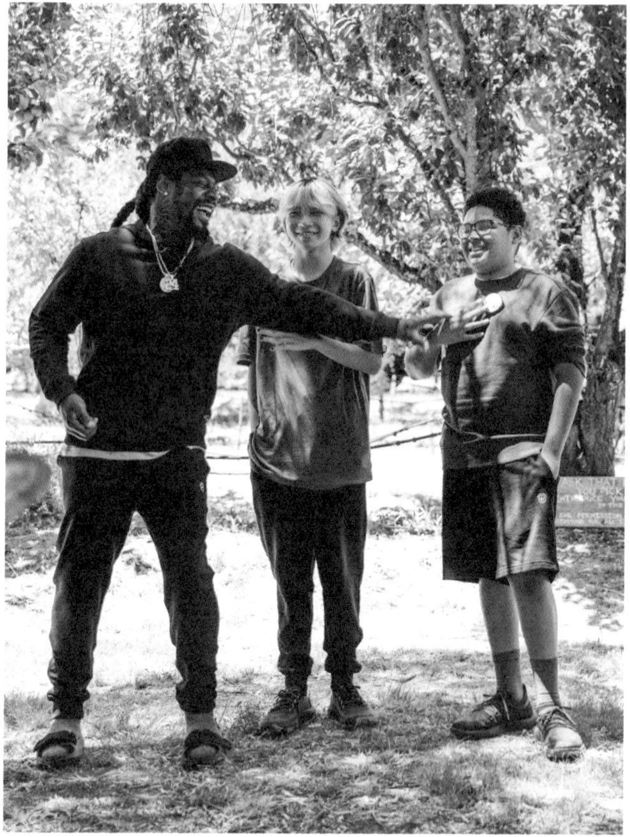

Allbirds Schooled series created with Marshawn Lynch

A 2021 survey for Wunderman Thompson Intelligence's "Regeneration Rising" report finds that 66% of respondents express anxiety about how climate change will affect them personally, rising to 72% of generation Z. To combat their anxiety and climate change's effects, gen Z are taking action.

85% of those surveyed believe that people must be prepared to rethink the way they live and spend to tackle climate change, and 70% are prepared to make dramatic changes to their lifestyle if it will help tackle climate change.

In a *Guardian* series, several gen Zers were highlighted for their ecowork and positive attitudes towards making small steps to improve their communities.

In July 2022, environmentalist Zahra Biabani started In the Loop, the first sustainable fashion rental marketplace, as part of her mission to make sustainable and ethical brands accessible to her generation. Biabani, 23 years old at the time of the interview, told the *Guardian* that "climate optimism is just a framework for unlocking the full potentiality of climate solutions that we desperately need." Thomas Lawrence, also 23 when he spoke to the *Guardian*, is the founder of Good People Inc, an ethical, value-driven sales platform that hopes to provide an alternative to the big players in online retail.

In Louisiana, Franziska Trautmann has founded Glass Half Full, the state's sole glass recycling facility, which uses glass turned to sand to restore Louisiana's eroding coastline. In Florida, Caulin Donaldson posts his daily beach-garbage pick-up to his TikTok

followers, who numbered 1.7 million as of January 2023.

His positivity and love for the environment is contagious, and part of a major trend on the social media platform. As of mid-January 2023, #climatechange had 4.1 billion views, #eco had 2.3 billion, and #ecotok, a community of climate advocates on TikTok, had nearly 835 million views.

WHY IT'S INTERESTING

Gen Z are turning their climate anxiety into climate optimism by taking meaningful action. Brands will need to meet consumer optimism with an uplifting and empowering tone when addressing the climate crisis.

06

ELEVATED EXPRESSIONISM

Vibrancy, strength, and uplift brighten 2023, energizing self-expression and empowerment.

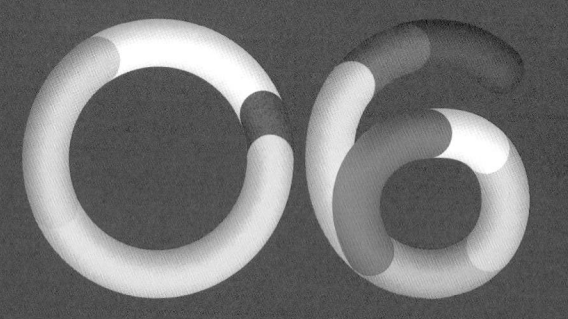

WUNDERMAN
THOMPSON   Artechouse, New York

Viva Magenta, Pantone Color of the Year 2023, is a bold, energetic hue that the company describes as "an unconventional shade for an unconventional time." Against the current global climate of looming recessions, environmental uncertainty, and surging inflation rates, Pantone is offering brightness and hope by channeling inner strength. "It's brave, it's fearless, it depicts optimism and joy," says Leatrice Eiseman, executive director of the Pantone Color Institute. "It is a color that is audacious, full of wit and inclusive for all."

American paint manufacturer Benjamin Moore echoes a similar sentiment with its Raspberry Blush Color of the Year 2023. "As much as we love the muted softer colors, we felt ready to do something a little bolder," Andrea Magno, director of color marketing and development at Benjamin Moore, told *Architectural Digest*. "We're just raring to go and turn up the dial on the saturation of color." The vivacious impact of Raspberry Blush is an unapologetic statement shade that radiates positivity. "It has a very happy quality to it," Magno says. "I think we need some happy."

Luxury fashion brands are painting the runway in punchy hues. At Paris Fashion Week, "bright and bold colors boasted optimism," *WWD* reported. Jean Paul Gaultier's fall/winter 2022/2023 runway was awash in monochromatic bold pinks, reds, and blues, capturing a "sense of fun and irreverence," wrote *WWD*'s Miles Socha in his collection review.

Valentino's fall/winter 2022/2023 haute couture collection also embraced a lively palette, with "a rainbow of hues" including royal blue, neon green, and vivid orange, paired with bold shapes. "Beauty is resilience, not escapism," said Valentino creative director Pierpaolo Piccioli.

WHY IT'S INTERESTING
An unrestrained, impactful, and powerful burst of energy is being injected into the year ahead, arming people with hope, joy, and happiness amid continuing uncertain times.

07

THE ARTISAN WAVE

Disaffection with the daily grind is driving an artisan renaissance.

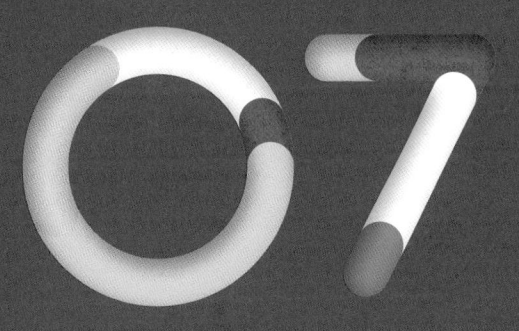

As industrialized economies creak, experts predict the rise of a new artisan economy. In *Return of the Artisan*, published in July 2022, anthropologist Grant McCracken charts the emergence of an American artisanal movement that is shifting from the margins to the mainstream. Prompted by post-pandemic malaise, disillusioned workers are ditching the 9 to 5 to become cheesemongers, bakers, jewelers, and more.

The artisanal life, it seems, offers a sense of control and liberation, while sites such as Etsy make the transition from side-hustle to business easier. In an interview with the *Guardian*, McCracken estimates that two out of every three new jobs in America are now driven by the artisanal movement. In a September 2022 piece, *Vogue* also points to a wave of

Two out of every three
new jobs in America are now
driven by the
artisanal movement.

fledgling fashion brands launched by novice creators during or post pandemic. These include Memorial Day, which has blossomed from crochet hobby to full-time business for former marketing professional Delsy Gouw. "I love the freedom that comes with it," Gouw tells Wunderman Thompson Intelligence. "I like that I'm able to take a walk or go to a park and feel inspired, and I wouldn't be able to do this at a regular office job."

The trend is not restricted to the United States. In July 2022 the *Sydney Morning Herald* reported on surging interest in Australia in crafts-based classes teaching skills from knife-making to ceramics. In the United Kingdom, a November 2021 report by Metro Dynamics for Amazon Handmade reported that artisanal businesses already contributed £4.8 billion ($5.8 billion) to the British economy as of 2020. No doubt noting the rising interest, Amazon Handmade has begun showcasing the creative processes of its artisanal sellers in a new video content series.

WHY IT'S INTERESTING

What started with the rise of micropreneurs two years ago is now evolving into a new artisan economy that could redefine the way we work and shop.

WUNDERMAN
THOMPSON   Memorial Day crochet products

VIRTUAL NURTURERS

Virtual avenues are emerging for digital carers seeking virtual companions.

Catriona Campbell, an artificial intelligence (AI) expert from the United Kingdom, predicts that virtual children will exist in the metaverse within the next 50 years. Campbell believes that the technology that evolves to create these virtual newborns will be embraced by the same consumers who grew up caring for a popular 1990s pet toy: the Tamagotchi generation. She predicts that these virtual children will look like their "parents" and be able to play and interact from within their digital habitat. In an age when many younger generations are reconsidering having families of their own, this outlet might attract a new generation of digital caretakers.

The Petaverse Network, created by Tiny Rebel Games, will launch its first generation of cats directly on Ethereum in early 2023. The Petaverse Network offers a gamified NFT experience that fosters emotional connection and delivers true digital pet ownership.

The Digital Pets Company, developer of digital 3D dogs, launched AI-driven canines authenticated as NFTs; an evolution of Nintendogs for modern digital pet-lovers. Owners will be able to interact with, play with, and care for their digi-dogs across virtual reality worlds, mixed and augmented reality platforms, and mobile and web browsers.

WHY IT'S INTERESTING

People are growing digital families, giving "blended families" a whole new meaning in the era of the metaverse and Web3.

Above: The Petaverse Network, courtesy of Twitter
Right: The Petaverse Network (both images)

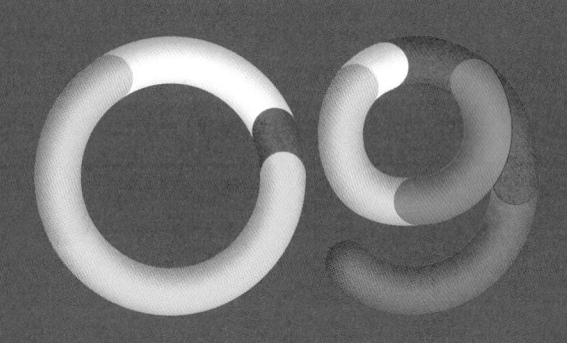

INDIGENOUS INNOVATION

Indigenous techniques are informing regenerative approaches to managing the environment.

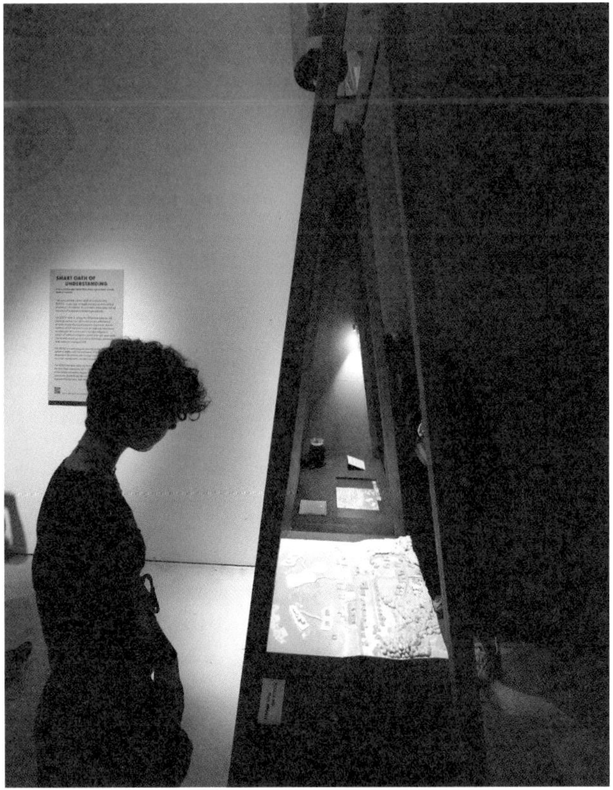

Techniques developed over millennia by indigenous people could augment our collective response to the climate crisis by helping us work with nature, not fight against it. Designers and engineers are reappraising indigenous approaches to urgent issues from flood or drought management to sustainable food production, from forest fires to carbon sequestration.

The Symbiocene, a multimedia piece commissioned for the Our Time on Earth exhibition at London's Barbican Museum in 2022, imagines future urban environments in 2040, and how they might look if we were to harness indigenous knowledge and technologies. The installation was created by representatives from indigenous communities, working alongside Smith Mordak, director of

sustainability and physics at engineering company Buro Happold, and designer Julia Watson.

These communities exemplify the idea of working symbiotically with nature. The Khasi hill tribe from north-eastern India is known for using rubber tree roots to grow living bridges that withstand monsoon rains. The Ma'dan from southern Iraq live in floating thatched villages that are symbiotic with their environment, offering a living example for future water-based development.

Harnessing regenerative approaches that nurture is a growing focus for designers. Super Vernaculars, the September 2022 edition of the design biennial Bio 27, hosted in Ljubljana, examined a return to vernacular traditions and values as a response to climate and biodiversity challenges. The British Pavilion at the 2023 Venice Biennale will showcase the role of diasporic craft cultures in "non-extractive" design. Central Saint Martins art school in London is welcoming students to its first regenerative design MA program.

Watson, author of the 2019 book *Lo-Tek: Design by Radical Indigenism*, says: "Designers should argue for a rebuilding of knowledge through explorations of indigenous philosophies capable of generating new knowledge and dialogues to inform our thinking on sustainability and climate change."

WHY IT'S INTERESTING

In the face of planetary crisis, the expertise of indigenous people—who care for 80% of remaining biodiversity, according to the World Bank—is being rapidly reappraised. Indigenous practices, techniques, and technologies can help shape a regenerative era where we learn to live and work symbiotically with nature.

Lo-Tek: Design by Radical Indigenism by Julia Watson.
Living root bridge, India © Amos Chapple

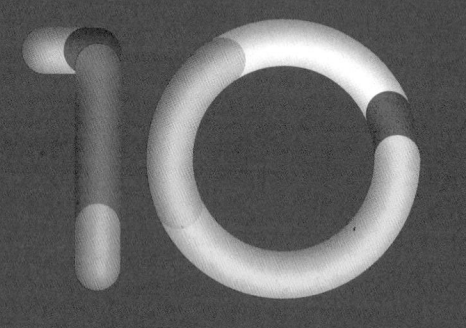

SITUATIONSHIPS

Gen Z are redefining the rules for romantic relationships.

Young generations are intentionally entering temporary partnerships, embracing relationships that ebb and flow between "friends" and "more than friends."

In a September 2022 feature, the BBC highlighted gen Z's tendency to embrace gray-area relationships defined as casual partners and the semi-commitment that goes with them. Elizabeth Armstrong is a sociology professor at the University of Michigan who researches sexuality and, specifically, these new "situationships." Armstrong told the BBC: "Right now, this solves some kind of need for sex, intimacy, companionship—whatever it is—but this does not have necessarily a long-term time horizon."

The topic is a prominent trend on social media. On TikTok, #situationship-tagged videos had over 1.9 billion views as of January 2023. The term was mentioned on the popular reality TV show *Love Island UK* and in Swedish singer Snoh Aalegra's song, "Situationship."

Vice unpacked what makes these relationships work in a feature with relationship coach Ben Goresky and his wife, relationship counselor Sheleana Aiyana. "It's about being really clear about what each of you want, and setting the guidelines and rules of engagement," Goresky said. "Committed or not, it's important to communicate," said Aiyana.

Cami, a 27-year-old from London, defines situationships for Wunderman Thompson Intelligence: "There's a more of a fluid boundary between friendship and relationships. I think

a lot of what you call situationships is just more of a blurred understanding between friendship and sexual relationships, a transition between the two." Cami goes on to unpack why these relationships have gained popularity recently. "There's an element of uncertainty in the state of the world: the environment, the political situation. You're less likely to get into a traditional monogamous relationship if you're not certain that there is going to be stability in the future."

WHY IT'S INTERESTING
For younger daters, situationships are a legitimate relationship status based on open communication and acceptance. Gen Z are embracing the middle ground in a healthy way, approaching some ever-changing boundaries with open minds.

"You're less likely to get into a traditional monogamous relationship if you're not certain that there is going to be stability in the future."

Cami, gen Zer

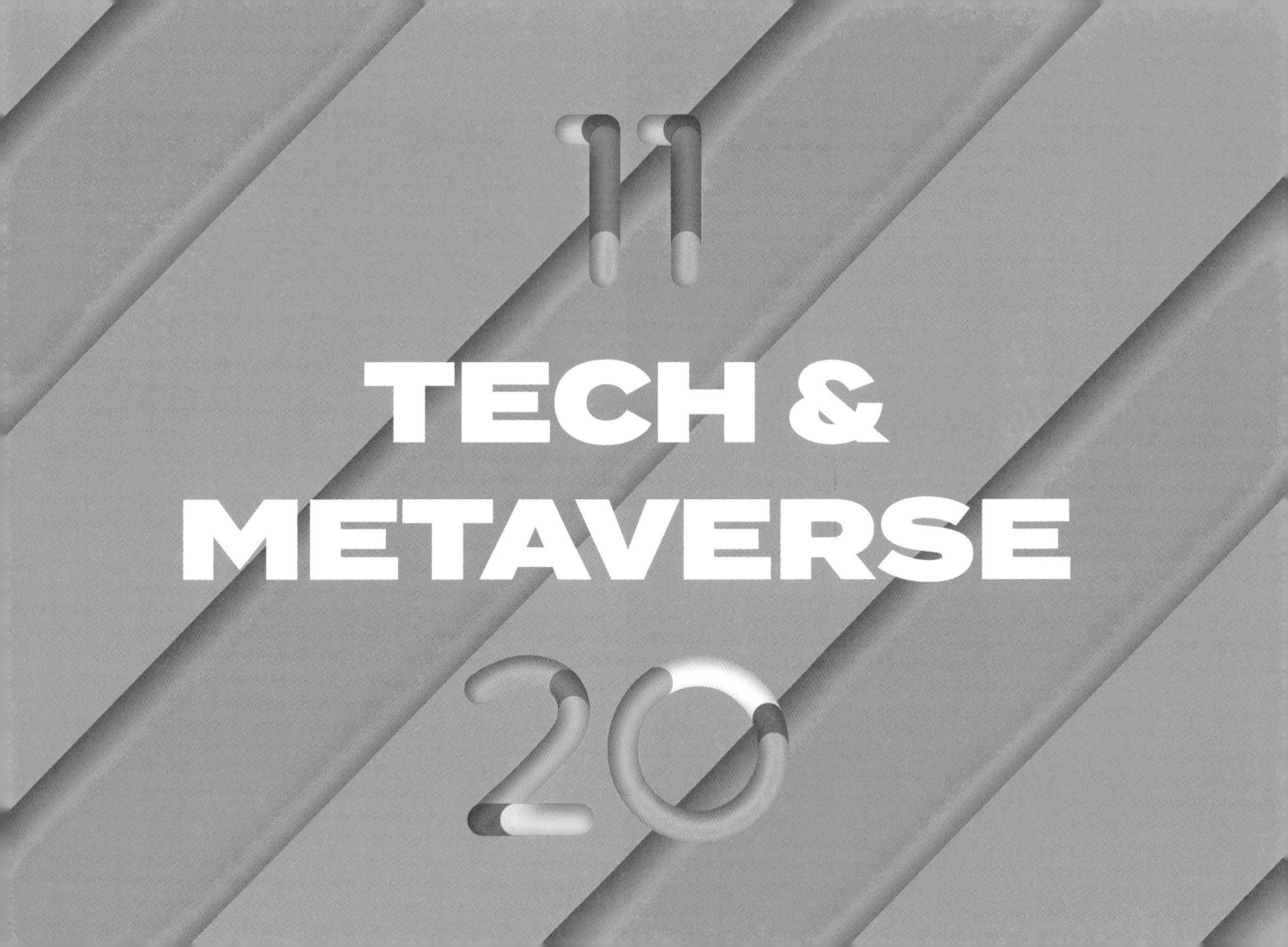

11

TECH & METAVERSE

20

TECHCESSIBILITY

Companies are redesigning their digital environments for greater accessibility.

Designing for accessibility and inclusion is not just the right thing to do, it's also big business, especially when it comes to technology. With more than 1 billion people worldwide estimated to experience disability and over 5 billion internet users, there's a major opportunity for brands to upgrade their devices, platforms, and experiences to be more accessible. As Josh Loebner, global head of inclusive design at Wunderman Thompson, tells Wunderman Thompson Intelligence, "Inclusive design is better design, and these technology considerations have the potential to be just as useful to both disabled and non-disabled people."

Big Tech is already at work. In September 2022, Twitter announced it had completed the rollout of a new alt text tool, designed to help those who use screen readers enjoy image content on the platform. Google is making widgets larger on Android devices to improve the experience for those with reduced vision, while Instagram is making accessible features the standard—as of March 2022, auto-generated captions on video are now the default for creators.

Innovative devices are also helping to shape more accessible experiences. Software company XRAI Glass has partnered with manufacturer Nreal on augmented reality (AR) glasses powered by speech-to-text recognition technology. The concept glasses use AR to project real-time subtitles into the wearer's field of vision, allowing those who are deaf or hard of hearing to understand and participate in conversations. The glasses build on an existing design by Nreal and connect to a smartphone, which handles the speech-to-text conversion.

WHY IT'S INTERESTING

Accessible design doesn't end with the physical world. When designing digital experiences and environments, brands will need to consider how to best reach audiences of all abilities. As Loebner says, "Accessible technologies have the power to invite and immerse marginalized groups into welcoming environments, communities, and experiences."

WUNDERMAN
THOMPSON   XRAI Glass AR glasses (both images)

12

DIGITAL IDENTITIES

People are bringing more of themselves into the virtual realm.

WUNDERMAN THOMPSON   Alex Box

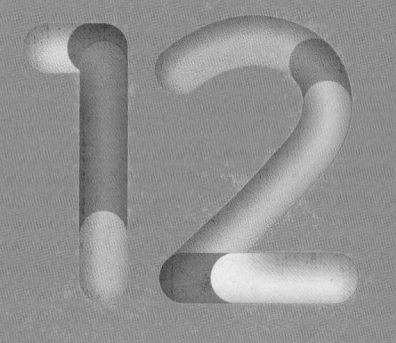

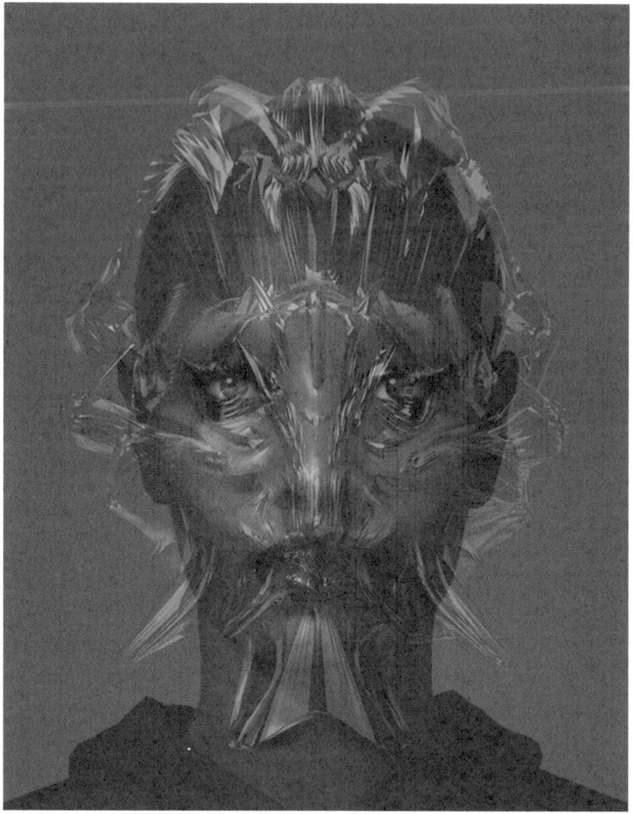

As the metaverse begins to take shape, how are users thinking about their virtual identities? According to Wunderman Thompson Intelligence's "New Realities: Into the Metaverse and Beyond" report, 76% of people familiar with the metaverse across the United States, United Kingdom, and China want their avatar to express their individuality in ways that they can't in the physical or offline world. And 51% feel it would be easier for them to be their true, authentic self in the metaverse or digital worlds.

Liam Young, a speculative architect and cofounder of urban futures think tank Tomorrow's Thoughts Today, predicts that

the distinction between online and offline lives will disappear. "We use words like 'digital' and 'physical,' but I think that these are outmoded terms," he tells Wunderman Thompson Intelligence. "We all live mediated lives that are extensions of our digital selves, and our screens have huge consequence in the physical world. To talk about them as being isolated, independent things is really problematic."

Identity designer and beauty futurist Alex Box, whose work centers on thinking creatively about how we communicate our identities and exploring how technology can elevate one's expression of self, agrees. "Identity traverses both the physical and digital," she tells Wunderman Thompson Intelligence. "I see identity design as the next important step to how we communicate and interpret multiple selves in the metaverse."

"We already have multiple identities living autonomously in our own metaverse of self, parkouring between our social media self, work self, home self, mindful self, and many more," she says. "One way of imagining identity as we move into Web3 is that our multiple selves will acquire a physicality, presence, or essence; an emotional and thinking 'texture' that will develop and regenerate autonomously through AI learning."

WHY IT'S INTERESTING
As digital lifestyles mature, people are thinking more deeply about preserving and translating their identity in virtual worlds. Expect to see an increasingly nuanced expression of identity that holds shape in both physical and virtual environments.

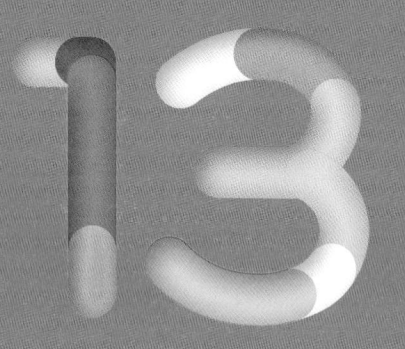

13

RITUALISTIC APPS

The next generation of social media apps are ritualizing engagement— turning it into something to be savored.

For years, social media apps, driven by powerful and intricately crafted algorithms, have been designed with maximum stickiness that demands constant engagement from consumers. But a new generation of apps is challenging this always-on approach with a focus on less frequent experiences that are more rewarding for users.

This new movement is spearheaded by French startup BeReal, the App Store's top social media download in the United States, United Kingdom, and Australia in August 2022. In contrast to the endless scrolling that underpins most social apps, BeReal is built around a simple and authentic daily ritual. At a random time every day, all users are asked to upload their daily contribution of a composite picture made up of a capture from both their forward-facing and selfie cameras at that moment. There are no filters, so users share a genuine reflection of what they and their surroundings look like at that time, which only their friends can see.

Many incumbent social media apps have responded to the success of BeReal by cloning its functionality. TikTok Now urges users to instantly share a short video or photo at an unscheduled time, while Instagram is said to be internally testing a similar function called Candid Challenges. Wordle, the successful daily word game, and dating app Thursday, which only allows singles to match and chat on one day each week, are built upon a similar dynamic. By limiting engagement, rather than overwhelming users, they build anticipation and provide fun rituals that allow people to connect with others in more authentic ways.

WHY IT'S INTERESTING

What started as a push for authenticity on social media and the rise of finite social networks is evolving, encouraging users to ceremonialize the everyday.

14

METAVERSE FOR GOOD

Brands are leveraging the metaverse to advance global humanitarian efforts.

Digital purchases in the metaverse are elevating global support for humanitarian causes around the world.

Humanitarian organization Built With Bitcoin Foundation puts 100% of its proceeds from the Built With NFT Collection toward providing clean water, building schools, sustainable farming, and humanitarian support for sponsored communities in Africa, Asia, and Latin America. The foundation is powered by Bitcoin, and the Built With NFT Collection consists of artwork by students in the sponsored communities minted on the Bitcoin network by STXNFT. "Bitcoin has been a force for good, bringing economic freedom to billions globally," STXNFT founder Jamil Dhanani said. "Projects like Built With NFT showcase that perfectly, by cutting through the hype to deliver on a meaningful cause."

Digital brand offerings are reaching beyond entertainment to benefit the physical world.

In April 2022, Epic Games and Xbox announced they had raised $144 million to support humanitarian efforts in Ukraine. In March, Epic Games pledged to donate all in-game sales to the efforts until April 3, with Xbox similarly stating it would donate the fee it normally collects for items bought by users in Fortnite. Epic Games said the proceeds would be donated to "Direct Relief, UNICEF, UN World Food Program, United Nations High Commissioner for Refugees, and World Central Kitchen in support of their humanitarian relief efforts for people affected by the war in Ukraine."

Ukraine itself sold a collection of NFTs on Twitter to raise funds for its army and civilians. Initially made up of 54 news items and photographs, the Meta History: Museum of War collection traces the timeline of Russia's invasion.

WHY IT'S INTERESTING

Digital brand offerings are reaching beyond entertainment to benefit the physical world. Companies taking advantage of flexibility, speed, and international yield in the metaverse can aid and support social causes with ease—harnessing the power to turn the metaverse into a force for social good.

15

AUGMENTED ENTERTAINMENT

AR technology is spurring on a new formula for entertainment.

Brands are elevating cinematic experiences with tools to make viewing more interactive.

Disney's first AR-enabled short film, *Remembering*, was released in September 2022. Viewers can scan codes from the film on their iOS devices for an extended version made for the small screen. Disney told *TechCrunch* that this is the first AR app to connect directly to content on the Disney+ platform, testing AR's ability to enhance films and storytelling from the comfort of home.

Disney's *Marvel World of Heroes*, an AR mobile game, will release in 2023. Players will be able to create superheroes, fight villains, and team up with friends from their own devices. In-game experiences will reflect each player's physical location and setting, similar to *Pokémon Go* game settings.

At a Goldman Sachs conference in September 2022, Electronic Arts (EA) CEO Andrew Wilson stated that the company plans to "lean more into really engaging and investing in creation." He went on to say that EA has a "very, very unique and special opportunity to deliver the future of entertainment," expressing confidence in the company's 20% gamer-created content, which is used by 50% of its player base.

A new reality show joined the cinematic universe last year, starring characters from NFT projects Bored Ape Yacht Club, Doodles, World of Women, and Cool Cat. In *The R3al Metaverse*, by animation studio Invisible Universe, the characters suddenly find themselves in the physical world, and

fans can interact with the scripted characters as they carry out the plot, helping to shape the show's content. With an NFT Producer Pass, viewers can contribute to the show's content, and avatar owners from the featured projects may have the chance to appear as their own characters in the show.

WHY IT'S INTERESTING
AR technology is changing how viewers participate with traditionally passive entertainment, adding an interactive layer to the viewing experience.

FEEL-GOOD FEEDS

Social media feeds are turning into a place to find emotional uplift.

App designers are reformulating new platforms to foster positivity.

The number one free download in the app store for several weeks in 2022, Gas is the ultimate compliment app. Users are asked multiple-choice questions that are positive and oriented to compliment their classmates and peers. Aimed at teens, the app requires users to designate their school and distributes compliments across its platform while motivating users to continue to compliment others, fostering a positive and cooperative app environment.

The Niche app is a new concept in social media: creator-owned content, rather than user-targeted content. The decentralized Web3 application consists of members, not users, who engage in communities fostered within the app based on interests and genuine connection. They are incentivized by posting content for positive, like-minded engagement rather than likes and digital promotion.

"We see social media getting smaller, more intimate. People are moving towards these networks with like-minded shared interests, backgrounds, or identity," Christopher Gulczynski, cofounder and CEO of Niche, tells Wunderman Thompson Intelligence. The future of social media, according to Niche cofounder and CTO Zaven Nahapetyan, is a place where "people have options, control, and power in their social interactions online the way they do in person. People don't see the stuff they don't want to see; they're able to connect to people that help them with what they enjoy spending time with."

WHY IT'S INTERESTING

Consumers are looking for positive modes of engagement and emotional support online. Emerging social media platforms are tapping into user desires for change, reformulating feeds around positivity and uplift.

Emerging social media platforms are reformulating feeds around positivity and uplift.

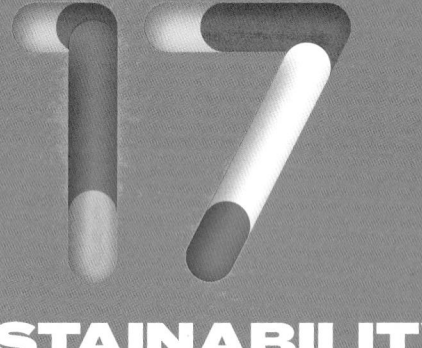

17

SUSTAINABILITY IN THE METAVERSE

How does sustainable action in the metaverse look?

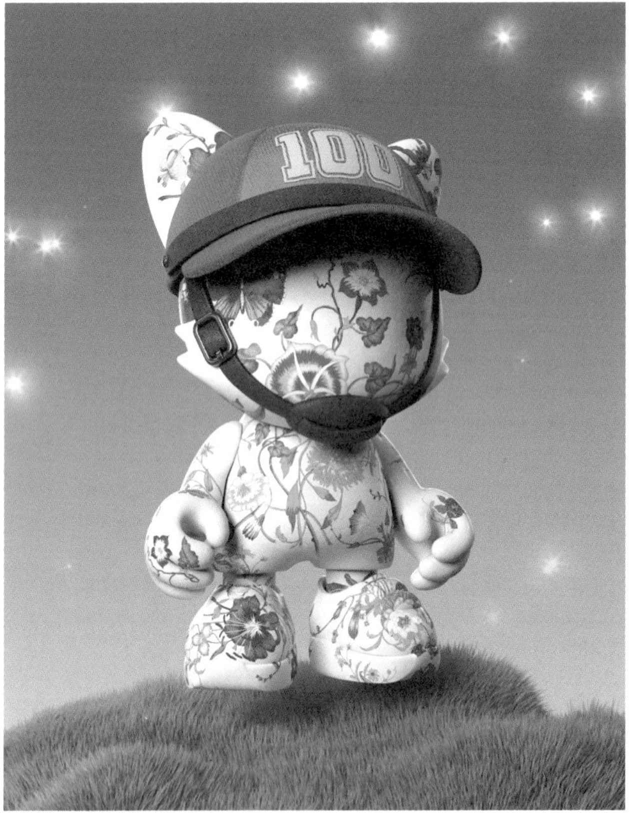

WUNDERMAN THOMPSON Superplastic x Gucci

Brands are extending their sustainable practices into the digital realm to maintain eco-friendly platforms and meet sustainable goals. According to Wunderman Thompson Intelligence's "New Realities: Into the Metaverse and Beyond" report, 71% of people who know what the metaverse is say brands need to be thinking about its environmental impact.

In September 2022, the Ethereum cryptocurrency completed a software update that reduced its carbon emissions by 99%. The merge, as the company called it, is a shift away from the validation method known as "proof of work" towards a more energy-efficient method called "proof of stake" (PoS), which effectively drops the crypto's electricity footprint from 8.5GW to less than 85MW.

Some platforms are prioritizing green practices from the get-go. Tezos is an energy-efficient PoS blockchain that offers an environmentally friendly alternative to standard blockchains through shorter NFT transaction times and reduced carbon footprints. Offering carbon-neutral minting, eco-friendly blockchain EOSIO runs on an energy-efficient PoS algorithm that doesn't encourage server farms to mine constantly. Consumers looking for a sustainable NFT marketplace or gallery can turn to Abris.io and KodaDot, respectively.

According to Wunderman Thompson Intelligence's "Regeneration Rising: Sustainability Futures" report, 86% of respondents expect businesses to play a part in solving big challenges such as climate change; 88% believe that sustainability should be a standard business practice; and 89% believe brands should do a lot more to reduce their carbon impact. Consumer payment service

Ripple, whose leaders are cofounders and active members of the Crypto Climate Accord and WEF's Crypto Impact and Sustainability Initiative, aims to achieve carbon net-zero by 2030.

Gucci accepts payments from a sustainable crypto solution built on the XRP Ledger: the world's first major global carbon-neutral blockchain. The brand also created an NFT collection with Superplastic, a carbon-neutral digital collectibles creation platform. Burberry dropped its second NFT collection on Blankos Block Party in June 2022, which does not require any crypto mining.

WHY IT'S INTERESTING
Whether companies decide to use eco-friendly blockchains or balance their carbon footprint with greener platforms, there are many approaches brands can take to enter the metaverse sustainably.

Consumers can now purchase crypto and use traditional banking services without leaving the digital realm.

In August 2022, Decentraland launched the first ATM in the metaverse in partnership with Metaverse Architects studio and Transak payment gateway. Players can use it to purchase cryptocurrency in the same way they would take out cash in the physical world, and property holders on the platform can add an ATM to their virtual land for easy access to crypto.

JPMorgan Chase was the first bank to open a lounge and an office in the metaverse. Onyx, JPMorgan's blockchain arm, released a report alongside the lounge launch to describe the opportunities offered by the metaverse, including that the metaverse will "infiltrate every sector in some way in the coming years." The bank has also invested in payments fintech Tilia, which provides payments services in the metaverse for game, virtual world, and mobile applications. that "As

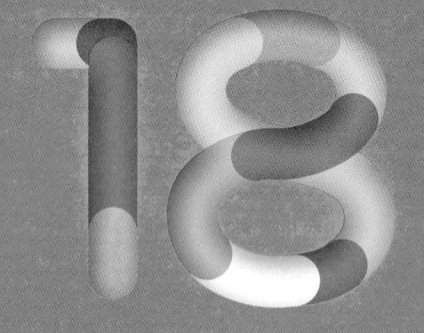

18

ATM (ETAVERSE)

Banks are rethinking digital finance.

consumers spend a greater portion of their time in video games and seek ways to gain ownership of the in-world items, new monetization models are emerging and require the right solutions," JPMorgan Chase tells Wunderman Thompson Intelligence.

In March 2022, American Express filed trademarks for a virtual marketplace and cryptocurrency services in the metaverse including card payment services, an ATM, banking, and fraud detection services as well as entertainment, travel, and concierge services for its virtual clientele.

Adaptive digital bank Quontic offers banking services in its virtual offices and a debit card with Bitcoin reward checking accounts, in addition to cash and high-interest checking accounts. Digital bank Cogni purchased a collection of NFTs

> "As consumers spend a greater portion of their time in video games and seek ways to gain ownership of the in-world items, new monetization models are emerging."

JPMorgan Chase

from Bored Ape Yacht Club in summer 2022, and is creating a Bored Ape debit card for future Web3 customer experiences.

The Sandbox will host several major financial institutions in the near future: HSBC plans to open a digital office, Siam Commercial Bank plans to launch a virtual headquarters, and DBS will create "DBS BetterWorld" on the platform. The interactive experience will show consumers the importance of sustainable practices and prove the metaverse can be a force for good.

WHY IT'S INTERESTING
Banking institutions are offering consumers one-stop shops for virtual commerce, advice, meta-banking, and crypto-purchases. Banking practices may soon be commonplace in the digital realm.

MAPPING REALITY

Why navigation tech is a linchpin of Web3 futures.

Some of the world's leading tech brands are devoting themselves to what may seem like a basic task: mapping the physical world. "When we look at the most valuable and/or impactful technology companies in the world, they are working on mapping, reading, and understanding the physical world through sensors and computer vision," Ryan Mullins, CEO and founder of Aglet, tells Wunderman Thompson Intelligence, pointing to tech giants such as Tesla, Instagram, Apple, and Snapchat.

Meta, Microsoft, Amazon Web Services (AWS), and Dutch mapping company TomTom joined forces in December 2022 to develop interoperable open map data. Called the Overture Maps Foundation, the partnership aims to power new map products through openly available datasets that can be used and reused across applications and businesses.

At CES 2023, BMW showcased the UniMap by Here Technologies automated mapping technology, which will allow users to generate their own digital maps and location tools.

Newer brands are also zeroing in on this burgeoning sector. Unveiled at CES 2023, Loovic's wearable navigation device is designed to be worn around the neck so that users don't have to look at their phone screen for directions, and can bolster spatial awareness for the visually impaired. Another innovation launched at CES 2023, Ashirase introduced a device that attaches to shoes and uses a combination of voice assistance (through a connected phone) and haptic indicators to direct the wearer.

Why the focus on maps? "The real revolution isn't simply mapping but a new opportunity for UI and how we will interface with the internet," Mullins explains. "Mappings and computer vision are the start of a new spatial internet where reality is a first-person experience of movement and participation in a world."

WHY IT'S INTERESTING

Mullins positions mapping "as the latest phase of internet evolution," which is moving digital engagement "from pages and scrolling to places and movement." The significance of Web3, then, is much bigger than just blockchain and crypto—it is in creating "a spatial, place-based internet. It's not only pages and people but reality itself that is made machine-readable."

20

VR DATING

Could virtual reality be the next dominant force in matchmaking?

It's over 10 years since Tinder profoundly altered the landscape of online dating. Now the metaverse is ushering in a new era of romance where relationships flourish in virtual worlds.

Metaverse dating centers around interacting with avatars, and virtual reality (VR) dating app Nevermet has a strict rule— no profile photos. In a world where people have become accustomed to judging others by their online dating photo this is a radical move, but it's giving users the opportunity to explore other means of connection. "Nevermet is a personality-first dating app that lets people explore personality and compatibility first, before knowing what the other person looks like in the physical world," Cam Mullen, CEO and cofounder of Nevermet, tells Wunderman Thompson Intelligence.

From unoriginal conversation starters to formulaic venues, first dates often carry a lack of surprise, but the VR dating app Flirtual is shaking things up by offering spectacular dates only

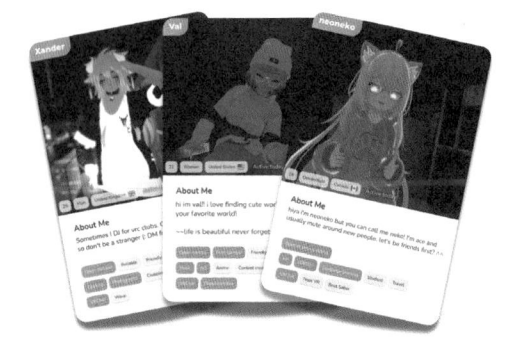

possible in virtual worlds. Launched in March 2022, the app offers tens of thousands of possible dates, from swimming with sharks to observing a black hole.

With the help of VR, Planet Theta is hoping to make catfishing a thing of the past. The app is set to revolutionize identity verification, with a feature that "is able to determine if your identity is fraudulent with a high degree of certainty," as Chris Crew, CEO of Planet Theta, tells Wunderman Thompson Intelligence. "It uses government records, online databases, past data breaches, and other resources to see if your name and account email are associated."

WHY IT'S INTERESTING
In the future, relationships might blossom first in the metaverse. "It's easier to fall in love through VR than any other digital medium," says Flirtual CEO and cofounder Anthony Tan. VR can deliver a fresh take on intimacy while tackling some of the downsides of existing online dating platforms and apps.

"It's easier to fall in love through VR than any other digital medium."

Anthony Tan, CEO and cofounder, Flirtual

21

TRAVEL & HOSPITALITY

30

21

DEEPSEA TOURISM

Travelers are venturing to the bottom of the sea in search of extreme adventure.

OceanGate Expeditions is taking travelers to new depths. The company, which describes itself as "a team of explorers, scientists, and filmmakers dedicated to exploring the deep," led the first civilian expedition to the Titanic in 2022. Guests paid $250,000 to travel nearly two and a half miles below the surface of the ocean to view the wreckage.

The dive was a holy grail trip for many. "I'm not a millionaire," banker Renata Rojas told the BBC. "I've been saving money for a long, long time. I made a lot of sacrifices in my life to be able to get to Titanic."

The travelers, called "mission specialists," must meet certain physical criteria, including basic strength, balance, mobility, and flexibility. OceanGate Expeditions gives examples such as climbing a six-foot ladder or carrying 20 pounds.

The company has another dive planned for 2023, and CEO and founder Stockton Rush anticipates growing demand. "There will be a time when people will go to space for less cost and very regularly," Rush told the BBC. "I think the same thing is going to happen going under water."

WHY IT'S INTERESTING

We charted the rise of elite academic adventures curated by scientific experts in "The Future 100: 2022." One year later, as the travel industry continues to stabilize post-lockdowns, people are still looking for once-in-a-lifetime travel experiences—and they're venturing into the unknown to get them.

21

22

ABSURDIST STAYS

The weird and the wonderful take center stage as travelers opt for one-of-a-kind stays.

By summer 2023, travelers will get the chance to stay in a floating avocado in Chile, a giant flowerpot in the United States, or a blooming pink flower in Mexico. These are a few of the projects that have been selected by Airbnb as part of its 2022 OMG! Fund.

In October, Airbnb injected $10 million to help realize 100 fantastical guest experiences around the world. The projects will sit within the site's OMG! category, which already features unusual short-stay rentals ranging from a converted Spice Bus from the original *Spice World* movie in the United Kingdom to a guitar house in Korea.

The investment from Airbnb shows demand for strange and uncommon stays, while the tens of thousands of entries around the world demonstrate the creative thirst of aspiring designers, architects, and builders. One recipient, Pablo C from Mexico, took inspiration from sci-fi movies for his organic-form spaceship. "The idea was to do something out of the ordinary, never seen before; something rare and beautiful that would impress any human being."

WHY IT'S INTERESTING

Travelers are seeking novel and memorable stays that are equal parts quirky and fun, and have an OMG factor.

> "The idea was to do something out of the ordinary, never seen before; something rare and beautiful that would impress any human being."
>
> **Pablo C,
> Airbnb OMG! Fund recipient**

23

TEMPERATE TRAVEL

Rising temperatures will prompt travelers to seek out cooler destinations.

Climate change is already impacting the tourism industry. The headline-making heat of summer 2022 saw planes grounded and rail journeys canceled. With the crisis set to continue, cooler destinations are playing up their advantage, seeking to attract visitors who want to avoid prolonged and intense heat, while hotter spots face a battle to retain tourists.

During the UK's July 2022 heatwave, Promote Shetland, the marketing organization for the Shetland Islands, tweeted it was "officially the coolest place in the UK." Located in the middle of the North Sea, the islands have average highs of 58°F in the summer months. The tweet aimed to entice travelers seeking more comfortable temperatures and appeal to those who would not previously have considered Shetland a must-see summer destination.

In the future, climate change is likely to be a key factor in planning travel.

In the United States, San Francisco could soon lure tourists from heat-trapped cities further inland. The city stands to benefit from its coastal location as cold winds sweeping in from the ocean make for a moderate climate in the summer months. Joe D'Alessandro, CEO of the San Francisco Travel Association, told the *New York Times* that he was "considering marketing the summer shivers with tourist slogans along the lines of 'Come cool down'."

For hot spots, the battle is on to keep tourists coming. The city of London launched the third iteration of its Cool Spaces map in 2022, which highlights indoor and outdoor locations where visitors and residents alike can retreat from the heat.

WHY IT'S INTERESTING

In the future, climate change is likely to be a key factor in planning travel. Prepare to see the concept of a summer vacation evolve as tourists reimagine travel over the coming years.

24

METAMOBILITY

Automotive brands are reimagining mobility for the metaverse.

Car brands and automakers are bringing their mobility solutions to the metaverse. Renault is partnering with The Sandbox to offer virtual automotive experiences in the metaverse. Renault Korea Motors inked a deal with the virtual platform in September 2022 to bring its cars into the virtual realm and "to introduce new types of experiences that combine automobiles and digital assets in The Sandbox," says Cindy Lee, CEO of The Sandbox Korea.

Volvo launched its latest electric vehicle in the metaverse in summer 2022. Conceptualized by a consortium of WPP agencies, Volvoverse hosted Volvo India's launch event for the rechargeable XC40. The event took place in the metaverse as a way to highlight Volvo's sustainable ethos. "The metaverse launch also contributes to our sustainability mission as it leaves a negligible carbon footprint as compared to conventional launches," explains Jyoti Malhotra, managing director of Volvo Car India.

The metaverse market for the automotive industry is projected to grow from $1.9 billion in 2022 to $16.5 billion by 2030.

Also in India, Hyundai took to Roblox in August the same year to launch its latest SUV. The event included educational spaces such as virtual test drives, a virtual showroom, and a virtual service center, alongside social gaming elements including a mini game, photo booth, and treasure hunt.

Ford is preparing to enter the metaverse with the filing of 19 trademarks across its brands that cover virtual cars, trucks, vans, SUVs, and clothing, and also cover a proposed online marketplace for NFTs.

WHY IT'S INTERESTING

The metaverse market for the automotive industry is projected to grow from $1.9 billion in 2022 to $16.5 billion by 2030, according to a report by MarketsandMarkets. Innovative leaders in the auto industry are looking to capitalize on this growth—rethinking metamobility and traditional consumer touchpoints along the way.

25

SEXUAL WELLNESS RETREATS

A new class of retreat is promoting sexual wellness.

In 2022, the Global Wellness Institute predicted that global wellness tourism would be worth $1.3 trillion by 2025, with sexual wellness the fastest growing sector in the market. Sexual intimacy and literacy programming are already on the rise at wellness-focused resorts.

Guests at the St Regis Punta Mita can partake in the resort's latest offering: a sexual wellness retreat. A first for the luxury brand, the stay is led by a sex educator who invites participants to explore their mental and physical sexuality in a private, intimate setting. Couples and singles are encouraged to attend.

Located in the Hamptons in New York, Shou Sugi Ban House offers a private 90-minute sexual workshop for women. The Sensual Lover workshop costs spa guests $350 and aims to "encourage guests to explore health through a more intimate lens," the hotel's creative director Jodie Webber told *Travel and Leisure Southeast Asia*. The W Brisbane hotel in Australia also has a resident sexologist for its own workshops and retreat offerings.

WHY IT'S INTERESTING

Wellness offerings in the travel and hospitality industries are embracing sexual wellness as consumers look to deepen their understanding of their bodies, their minds, and the connection between the two, during their travels.

26

TOP THREE DESTINATIONS

Morocco is the next affordable travel hotspot for remote workers.

With its mild climate, rich history, desert, beaches, and relative affordability compared to nearby Europe, Morocco is attracting the next wave of remote workers.

In 2022, remote working and coliving company Outsite took over a traditional-style riad in Marrakesh. It offers rooms built around a central courtyard, with coworking staples such as a shared kitchen and working spaces alongside a pool, hammam, and rooftop terrace. New York Stock Exchange-listed Selina opened luxury Bedouin-style tents in Agafay in May 2022, the first of what the brand says will be a big portfolio in the North African kingdom. While Morocco doesn't yet have a digital nomad visa, many visit on a 90-day tourist visa.

Kyoto wants tourists back—but with less Instagram chasing and more small, curated tours.

Pre-pandemic, Kyoto attracted nine million visitors a year, drawn by its temples, gardens, geishas, and cuisine. There were traffic jams and crowds.

Now as Kyoto reopens, it wants to offer a more meaningful experience through smaller, tailored itineraries. Hotel The Mitsui Kyoto runs private tours of nearby Nijō Castle, originally built in 1603 as the residence of Tokugawa Ieyasu, the first

shogun of the Edo Period. In spring 2023, Danish chef René Redzepi's Noma is opening a 10-week pop-up in the city, featuring celebrated local ingredients during cherry blossom season. New venture Manabi Japan (or Study Japan) is starting small tours in 2023 just outside Kyoto city, with day trips to the center. There will be guest speakers on topics such as Noh theater or indigo dyeing, aimed at "helping people get below the surface," founder Lucinda Ping Cowing tells Wunderman Thompson Intelligence.

Tanzania is fast becoming known as the go-to destination for solo travelers.

Famous for adventure and family travel, Tanzania is now starting to draw solo travelers as well.

It is a place of superlatives: Mount Kilimanjaro, the highest peak in Africa; Ngorongoro Crater, the world's largest intact volcanic caldera; and the Olduvai Gorge, one of the most important paleoanthropological sites on the planet. Then there's Serengeti National Park, known for the largest annual migration in the world of wildebeest and zebra, and home to the largest lion population in Africa. Chanice "Queenie" Williams, who runs travel planning site Fly with Queenie, described her solo trip to Tanzania as "perfect for solo travelers, particularly women who may not feel comfortable alone," in an interview in the *Washington Post*.

27

URBAN SANCTUARIES

Hospitality brands are designing luxury oases for the heart of the city.

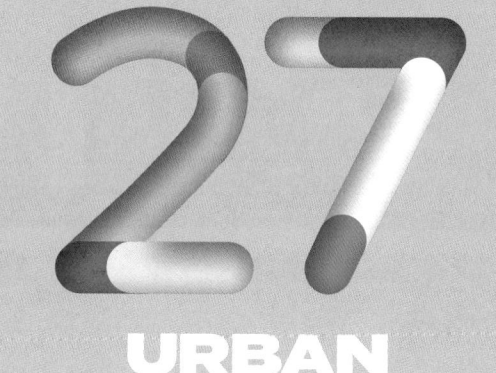

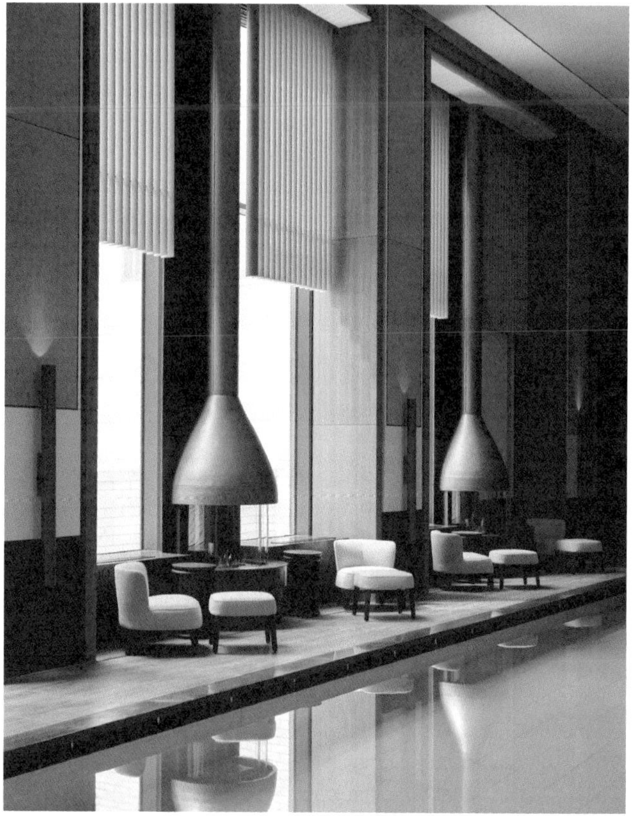

Aman New York

Peace and tranquility can be hard to find in the city, but new hospitality locations are solving that. From hotels that offer guests serene retreats to eateries where diners can sit back, relax, and recharge, places of sanctuary are popping up in cities around the world. These pockets of calm offer an escape from the hectic pace of urban life.

Aman Beverly Hills, due to open in 2026, describes itself as "a serene oasis in a legendary city." The resort aims to celebrate the power of nature, with Californian foliage and palm trees integrated into the architecture and landscaping, guaranteeing that guests feel cocooned from the frenzy of Los Angeles. Multinational hospitality company Aman also opened a New York hotel in 2022.

Here, a sense of calm is anchored in composed and harmonious design, juxtaposing the concrete jungle that surrounds it.

Similarly in Europe, Six Senses is launching a new resort in Rome. This latest addition to its global portfolio is set to open in early 2023 and is within walking distance of the Trevi Fountain. Inspired by ancient Roman traditions, it invites guests to discover the art of bathing at the resort's spa, a wellness retreat within urban surroundings, while the rooftop conceals a restful secret garden where guests can unwind. Both Aman and Six Senses ensure their guests can recharge and are revitalized when they choose to enter the city again.

Edition hotels tapped Japanese architect Kengo Kuma to design a plant-filled refuge in the heart of Tokyo. "I wanted to prove that it was possible to create a real oasis at the heart of the big city," Kuma told *Dezeen*. The hotel, which first opened its doors in October 2020, began welcoming international travelers in 2022.

It's not just hotels offering escape from the hustle and bustle. In Melbourne, the Au79 café is a haven of tranquility within the busy Chadstone Shopping Centre. The coffee destination, created by interior design studio Mim Design, mimics a botanical greenhouse, with its arched structure and hanging greenery making it the ideal location for passers-by to take a breather from shopping.

WHY IT'S INTERESTING

The future of ultra-luxe travel is to offer visitors the best of both worlds: seclusion and quiet mixed with urban culture and excitement.

27

The Tokyo Edition hotel, Toranomon. Photography by Nikolas Koenig

28

METATRAVEL

Hospitality is being reimagined for the metaverse.

The metaverse is revolutionizing travel experiences, as physical destinations begin to blur with fantastical virtual worlds.

After opening its first real-world hotel in Manchester in the United Kingdom in 2021, design-led hotel brand Leven announced in 2022 that its second location would be in Decentraland. The Levenverse is a digital amenity space offering activities, networking, and wellness events. "By integrating the real-world hospitality experience with the virtual world through brand collaborations, art, design, and activations, travelers in both spaces will be able to experience unique social and game experiences IRL and AFRL (away from real life)," Timothy Griffin, Leven cofounder and principal at Wellbrook Hospitality, tells Wunderman Thompson Intelligence.

Tapping into the world of augmented reality (AR), Moxy Hotels, part of Marriott International, launched the Moxy Universe, Play Beyond AR experience in July 2022. The experience allowed

visitors to create their own avatars in the Moxy Universe, which transcended the digital into the physical hotels as a series of AR challenges. Avatars could join visitors while they had a drink in the hotel bar, in their private hotel rooms, or even during an exercise session at the gym. The experience was available at 12 Moxy Hotels across the Asia-Pacific region from July to December 2022.

Luxury travel company Brown & Hudson is already delivering meta travel experiences for its high-net-worth clientele. A new metaverse collection includes Capo, where virtual reality capabilities in the metaverse allow clients to re-experience trips they have already enjoyed in the real world. With a videographer capturing the action IRL, holidaymakers are able to retrace their steps in a more immersive way than through photos alone, reliving happy memories and continuing to explore long after they've arrived home.

WHY IT'S INTERESTING

Hospitality brands are stepping in to act as home bases and guides for a rising class of metatourists. Joshua Senior, cofounder of Leven and director at Branco Capital, predicts that "as the metaverse evolves from a sci-fi concept into a reality, every industry disrupted by the digital era will feel its impact. We believe the potential for creative hospitality brands is limitless."

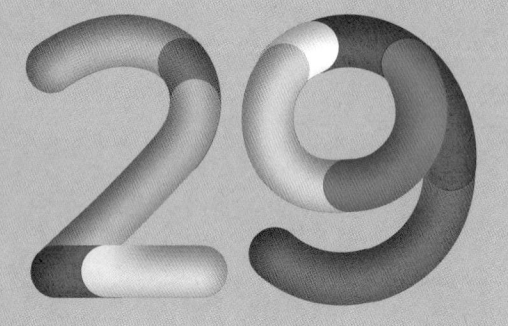

29

HIDDEN DESTINATIONS

Hoping to lure new travelers, sites that were once off-limits are opening up.

Saudi Arabia, which has only allowed foreign tourists to visit for non-religious reasons in the past couple of years, is investing massive sums into its tourism trade in a bid to become the region's leading destination. This includes sharing its previously hidden treasures with the world, opening ancient heritage sites for the very first time. Previously off-limits ancient pagan sites such as the tomb of Qasr al-Farid (which means "lonely castle") are now open to visitors, indicating a relaxing of the kingdom's previously strict social codes. In September 2022, the government announced further plans to streamline visas for foreign tourists to make travel easier.

Other destinations are going below ground. In Rome, the Catacomb of Commodilla, constructed in the fourth century, is set to open to visitors for the first time in 2025 after being restored by the Vatican's Pontifical Commission for Sacred Archaeology. In London, old tube stations and tunnels are also being opened to the public for the first time in 100 years. Through its Hidden London series, the London Transport Museum is launching a tour of the original Shepherd's Bush Underground station, unseen since 1924.

WHY IT'S INTERESTING

While the past several years have seen travel hotspots attempting to curb crowds or even closing off monuments for preservation reasons, a growing number of destinations are using previously inaccessible areas to attract travelers seeking unique experiences.

WUNDERMAN
THOMPSON London Transport Museum Hidden London tour of
Shepherd's Bush Underground station

30

DARK ZONES

Adventurous travelers pursuing grit and history are turning to dark destinations.

Not for travelers seeking to soak up the sun and relax, dark tourism takes visitors to hard-hitting locations that are often associated with death, war, and disaster. Places such as Japan's "suicide forest" Aokigahara, Auschwitz in Poland, and Cambodia's Killing Fields are considered dark travel destinations. The market value of dark tourism is expected to reach $36.5 billion by 2032, according to an October 2022 survey by Future Market Insights.

Visit Ukraine has launched guided tours including "Kyiv is Unbeatable," which it describes as "very popular among foreign tourists." Since September 2022, it has been offering tours to de-occupied and demined cities, including Romanivka, Bucha, Irpin, Hostomel, and Borodyanka. "We realized that caring people have a demand to see the traces of war with their own eyes," says Anton Taranenko, CEO of Visit Ukraine. The tours are not intended for profit and all funds are donated

towards people and cities affected by the ongoing war. As well as witnessing the effects of war, Taranenko explained to CNN that he also wants tourists to experience Ukrainian bravery and the defiant spirit of the people.

Nuclear disaster zone Chernobyl became a popular destination after the eponymous HBO television series took to the screens in 2019, but in 2020, the COVID-19 pandemic brought travel to a halt. Now, as travel continues to reopen, 73% of travelers are looking forward to experiencing "out of comfort zone" travel that pushes them to their limits in 2023, according to a global survey by Booking.com.

WHY IT'S INTERESTING

The allure of dark travel is to offer perspective. "People are trying to understand dark things, trying to understand things like the realities of death, dying, and violence," Jeffrey Podoshen, professor of marketing at Franklin and Marshall College, told the *New York Times*. "They look at this type of tourism as a way to prepare themselves."

73% of travelers are looking forward to experiencing "out of comfort zone" travel that pushes them to their limits in 2023.

31

BRANDS & MARKETING

40

31

WEB3 BRANDS

Brands are taking on Web3.

YSL Beauté debuted its Web3 and NFT initiative in June 2022, aiming to create a new loyalty experience. YSL NFT holders will gain access to additional content, launches, drops, and more throughout the year on the brand's token-gated page. The same month, Prada dropped its first Timecapsule collection of NFTs, which allow consumers to access exclusive experiences—the monthly Timecapsule issues have sold out ever since. The Prada Crypted community on Discord also launched as part of the initial drop, to expand the brand's digital reach and community.

Niche is a new form of social media for Web3 that aims to democratize data and expand opportunities for growth for its consumers, users, and brands. Cofounder Zaven Nahapetyan tells Wunderman Thompson Intelligence that his new platform "opens up a lot of opportunities that don't exist with traditional, non-decentralized social media, because—by the nature of decentralization—it makes it really easy to buy, sell, and trade content."

Even food brands are taking advantage. Starbucks will soon offer a Web3-based rewards program in which collectible coffee-themed NFTs will serve as tokens for owners to gain access to additional drops, membership, and events. McDonald's has filed trademarks to deliver food digitally and in person from a virtual restaurant. Both McDonald's and McCafé are included in the trademark applications, with language outlining details for "operating a virtual restaurant online featuring home delivery," indicating that fast-food fans may have the chance to order a future Big Mac in the digital realm.

WHY IT'S INTERESTING

Web3 is inevitable. To prepare for its arrival, brands are arming themselves with updated digital strategies.

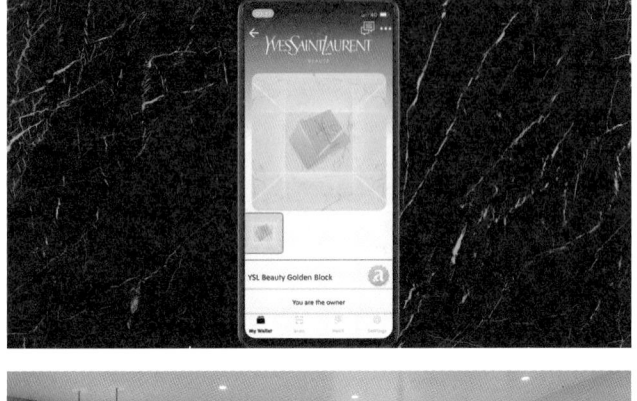

Web3 is inevitable. To prepare for its arrival, brands are arming themselves with updated digital strategies.

Above top: YSL Beauté
Above: Starbucks

32

VIRTUAL AMBASSADORS

Brand representatives are getting a digital upgrade.

Soul Machines pairs photo-realistic digital humans with artificial intelligence (AI) to offer a more intimate virtual engagement. "AI and, more broadly, Autonomous Animation can help brands connect with their audience through the ability to provide empathy and personalization at scale," Shantenu Agarwal, vice president of Soul Machines, tells Wunderman Thompson Intelligence. The company is currently working to create personalized customer experiences for clients such as Nestlé, Twitch, and the World Health Organization.

"We are seeing many brands use this new platform as an opportunity to rethink how they want to represent themselves, with some realizing that the power of digital technologies allows them to easily provide multiple looks and personalities," explains Agarwal. "This in effect empowers their audience to choose who they speak with and customize their experience, which has not been possible until today."

The metaverse is set to enhance social interactions in three-dimensional virtual worlds and the roles of avatars are gaining

"As our world gets increasingly digital, brands need a new way to be more human."

Dentsu

brand value. During the VivaTech June 2020 conference in Paris, the LVMH luxury group introduced Livi, a digital representative showcasing its new innovations. Qatar Airways unveiled a "metahuman" cabin crew member, Sama, to guide guests through its QVerse digital flight. And Dermalogica has created Natalia as a training tool. "We can now use metaverse technology to train millions of consumers and hundreds of thousands of therapists about changing skin condition," says Aurelian Lis, global CEO of Dermalogica.

In addition, brand adoption of virtual ambassadors has prompted Japanese marketing agency Dentsu to launch a division dedicated to creating virtual identities. "As our world gets increasingly digital, brands need a new way to be more human," Dentsu states.

WHY IT'S INTERESTING

As the metaverse evolves, the advanced avatars tracked in "The Future 100: 2022" are now being leveraged by brands to better connect with people. "The future for brands is more connected, and authentic relationships are possible due to these more immersive, engaging, and interactive experiences," says Agarwal.

33

EARTH AS STAKEHOLDER

Our planet is taking its rightful place at the corporate table—as a stakeholder.

In September 2022, Yvon Chouinard, the billionaire founder of Patagonia, gave the company away to a trust designed to funnel all profits to fight environmental devastation. In doing so, Chouinard set a new bar for environmental corporate leadership.

"As of now, Earth is our only shareholder," the cult outdoor gear company declared. "All profits, in perpetuity, will go to our mission to save our home planet."

Patagonia's headline-grabbing move stands in stark contrast to the usual path of going public with a stock market listing. "Instead of going public, you could say we're 'going purpose'," said Chouinard. "Instead of extracting value from nature and transforming it into wealth for investors, we'll use the wealth Patagonia creates to protect the source of all wealth."

The move contrasts with the approaches of Elon Musk and Jeff Bezos, also billionaires, who have chosen to train their sights on life beyond Earth.

Patagonia's move is jaw-dropping and unsurprising at the same time. The California-based company has long donated 1% of its sales to environmental groups and is known for generous employee benefits, from on-site nurseries to surfing afternoons off.

Also in September 2022, Edinburgh-based Faith In Nature, an eco beauty company, appointed a "nature guardian"—a director to represent nature—to its board. Brontie Ansell, a director of Lawyers for Nature and a lecturer at Essex Law School, is the first to be appointed to the role. She told the *Guardian* her role was akin to a

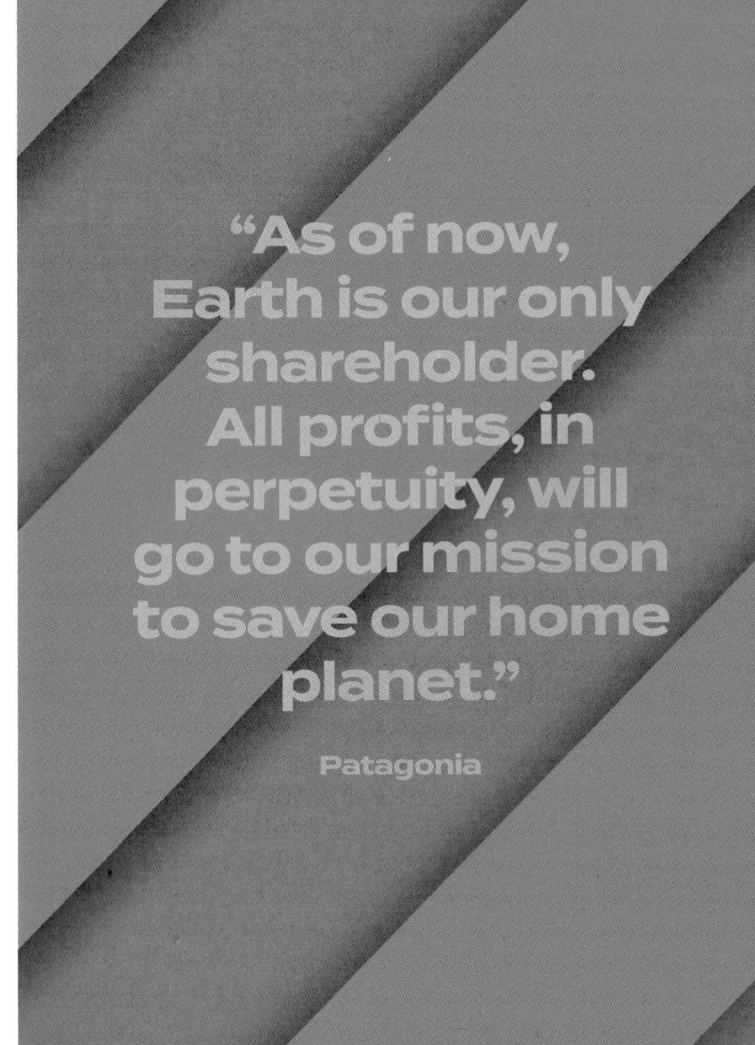

Earth is now our only shareholder.

guardian acting on behalf of a child in court.

Other businesses taking sustainable strides include the British high-street retailer Selfridges, which has pledged that by 2030, 45% of transactions will come from circular products, whether resale, rental, refill, repair, or recycled.

WHY IT'S INTERESTING

Despite years of shrinking forests, species extinction, and increasingly severe weather, most for-profit businesses have taken only baby steps towards sustainable practices, citing profit-thirsty shareholders. By designating Earth as a shareholder, Patagonia and others are reframing the debate— and radically raising the bar.

"As of now, Earth is our only shareholder. All profits, in perpetuity, will go to our mission to save our home planet."

Patagonia

34

META-INCLUSIVITY

Brands and creators are bringing inclusive values to the metaverse.

Wunderman Thompson Intelligence's "New Realities: Into the Metaverse and Beyond" report finds that 65% of people who have heard of the metaverse think it will be more inclusive than the real world. Now a host of brands are working on initiatives that could deliver on that promise.

In 2022, the World Economic Forum announced an initiative with Microsoft, Sony, Lego, Meta, and others to collectively work towards an "ethical and inclusive metaverse."

Beauty brand Clinique has launched "Metaverse More Like Us," an NFT beauty campaign that stakes a claim for equitable representation in the metaverse. The brand partnered with Daz 3D, creator of one of the world's most inclusive avatar collections, Non-Fungible People, and commissioned three makeup artists from underrepresented communities to create signature looks—one virtual, one real-life—that were then released to the Daz 3D community.

While some projects tackle inclusion with a broad brush, others are zeroing in on the needs of specific marginalized communities.

Also in 2022, the NFTY Collective launched Unhidden, an NFT collection to represent people with seen and unseen disabilities. Creator Giselle Mota wants to give disabled people "a choice to take on a virtual identity that reflects their true physical selves if they so choose." She tells Wunderman Thompson Intelligence that "a truly inclusive metaverse looks as diverse as the people it intends to have as users."

Catering to Islamic values, MetaKawn is an emerging metaverse platform whose Huffaz NFT collection highlights themes of tolerance, multi-ethnicity, and gender equality. Idiat Shiole of Hadeeart, a Muslim virtual fashion designer, creates designs for gaming platforms like Decentraland with a distinct Nigerian aesthetic, such as hijabs, tribal markings, and hair braids.

For the LGBTQ+ community, Meta and Mastercard recently collaborated with creators RhondaX and Skitter on True Self World, a social experience in Horizon Worlds where members and allies

can meet and connect.

Yiran Shu, a digital creator and metaverse designer, sums up the collective motivation for all of these initiatives, explaining to Wunderman Thompson Intelligence: "In the metaverse, it's more of a matter of representation. We want to make people feel welcome, to feel that you are not ignored, you're not just another avatar. We acknowledge your superpower in this world. I think that's the difference: it's a step we choose to take—to represent."

WHY IT'S INTERESTING

Brands have a responsibility to create an inclusive metaverse by ensuring avatars, spaces, and narratives offer full-spectrum representation.

35

MULTIVERSAL BRANDS

Established brands are dropping limited-edition products cloaked in the mystique of futuristic technology.

The Into the Multiverse trend that Wunderman Thompson Intelligence reported in "The Future 100: 2020" first explored the idea that consumers, tired of the mundanity of modern life, are seeking portals of escapism and adventure that offer a glimpse of a more captivating and engaging reality. Brands are now using this insight as the catalyst to create intriguing, otherworldly products. Rather than relying on traditional product cues based on ingredients, provenance, scent, and flavor, this new generation of experiential products embraces futuristic technology and the language of the metaverse.

Coca-Cola's Creations platform, launched in 2022, "aims to surprise, delight, and engage global audiences through magical and unexpected tastes, moments, and collaborations." The inaugural product, the outer-space-themed beverage Starlight, was described as a taste "reminiscent of stargazing around a campfire, as well as a cooling sensation that evokes the feeling of a cold journey to space." Subsequent products have included Byte and Dreamworld that, in place of standard flavor descriptions, are said to taste like pixels and dreams respectively. Coca-Cola trademark president Selman Careaga told the *Drum* these Creations products received twice the engagement of any other program in 2022.

Unilever-owned deodorant brand Lynx also eschewed the conventions of its category with the launch of Lynx AI body spray, which it created with Swiss fragrance specialist Firmenich. The launch includes no scent or fragrance notes, but taps into the allure of futuristic technology, proclaiming the limited-edition product is "powered by artificial intelligence" using "46 terabytes of data, 6,000 ingredients, 3.5 million possible combinations." Lynx stated that the product launch aims to drive growth in the deodorant category by "tapping into Generation Z's fascination with the world of tech and crypto."

WHY IT'S INTERESTING

Brands are pushing the boundaries of reality, blurring the lines between what is real and what is not. As creativity becomes unbounded, brands are transporting consumers to other worlds (see 61, Multiversal design, page 144, and 74, Intergalactic luxe, page 172).

As creativity becomes unbounded, brands are transporting consumers to other worlds.

36

VIP NFTS

NFTs are changing the game
for brand loyalty.

Brands are leveraging NFTs to unlock consumer loyalty for the next era of metaverse engagement, offering consumers exclusive access to products and services.

The first NFT restaurant in New York City is in the works. NFTs will serve as the key to entry for diners at the Flyfish Club, a members-only upscale seafood restaurant set to open its (physical) doors in 2023. The membership will potentially stand as a true "asset": buyers may be able to lease, sell, or use their membership on a monthly basis.

Coachella has launched the Coachella Keys Collection, a group of 10 NFTs providing each buyer a lifetime pass to the festival. Purchases made in the NFT marketplace included exclusive perks for the 2022 festival, such as a celebrity chef dinner and front-row access to events. A first in exclusive NFT entertainment, Mila Kunis and Ashton Kutcher sold NFT tokens to allow access to their gated NFT web series Stoner Cats.

Consumers who bought an NFT from Hennessy received a physical and digital version of the first and last limited-edition bottles of Hennessy 8. Buyers could request that the physical asset—which includes a commemorative sculpture, an engraved Baccarat-blown carafe, a pipette, a cork holder, a chest, and an authentication plate—be delivered at whim.

Patrón tequila has also launched its first NFT collection: 150 one-of-a-kind editions of the brand's Chairman's Reserve, accompanied by one physical and one digital bottle. The crypto purchase is secured by BlockBar with a digital record of authenticity and

ownership, and the physical product can be delivered, traded, or gifted via the BlockBar.com marketplace.

"When we look at a virtual shoe, we don't just see the shoe," said Ron Faris, VP/GM of Nike Virtual Studios, which is exploring new Web3-enabled loyalty formulas with its .Swoosh platform (see 62, Cocreative commerce, page 146). "This is a shoe that one day could unlock a preorder for a physical product, or another day it unlocks access to a secret chat room with our designers, helping to cocreate. We're learning that buying a virtual product isn't the end of a purchase journey, it's the beginning of it."

WHY IT'S INTERESTING

NFTs are changing the future of loyalty, giving buyers exclusive access to select brand experiences.

37

AMPLIFYING DIVERSE CREATORS

Growing calls for authentic representation in advertising are driving a wave of brand collaborations with marginalized creative talents.

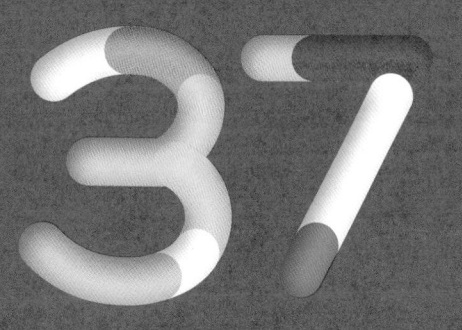

Globally, 86% of people believe that to support disadvantaged groups, brands need to work with them, not just for them, according to data compiled for Wunderman Thompson Intelligence's 2022 report "Inclusion's Next Wave." Companies are upping their collaborations with creators, artists, and influencers from marginalized backgrounds in a bid to deliver more inclusive and authentic brand communications.

Diversity in Design, a US-based consortium of big-name brands such as Herman Miller Group, Gap, and Airbnb, launched in 2021 with the aim of helping young Black creatives enter the design and creative industries. The General Excellence winner of Fast Company's 2022 Innovation by Design Awards, the organization focuses on reaching potential creatives in high school, college, and early careers to help them get a foot on the ladder. Also focusing on early-stage career

development, Snap launched a creative accelerator for Black creatives in June 2022. The program provides mentorship and financial support to emerging Black creators, to help them get established on the platform.

Brands that need support finding potential collaborators can turn to the growing number of talent collectives that focus on those traditionally underrepresented within the creative industries. TripleC, a UK-based organization that aims to increase access to the arts and media industry for those who are deaf, disabled, and/or neurodivergent, is working on a talent finder initiative to connect disabled artists and creatives with potential employers.

In similar vein, the Asian Creators Index was launched in May 2022 by the Anak design practice, to showcase the myriad Asian creative talent and artists. The index highlights multidisciplinary talent in a visual and searchable format, making it easy for brands to locate diverse collaborators.

WHY IT'S INTERESTING

Consumers will support the efforts of truly inclusive brands and 66% are more inclined to buy from brands that speak out on issues of equality and inclusion. By passing the mic and engaging with marginalized communities, brands can deliver authenticity while upping representation, empowerment, and equality of opportunity.

38

BRAND SAFETY IN THE METAVERSE

How can brands stay protected in the metaverse?

Gartner predicts that one in four people will spend at least one hour a day in the metaverse by 2026, so it makes sense for brands to become part of the metaverse. Navigating the evolving metaverse landscape is becoming increasingly important for law firms and in-house legal departments, as more brands roll out new digital strategies.

A number of brands have filed trademarks protecting them in the metaverse. Hermès, CVS, Coca-Cola, Nike, and Mastercard are among the companies that have trademarked their name, logo, virtual goods, and digital assets in the metaverse. Rolex has filed trademark applications with the United States Patent and Trademark Office covering "online auction services for virtual objects" and "online spaces for buyers and sellers of virtual products such as watches and watch parts."

Beyond patenting, Gareth Burkhill-Howarth, global data protection officer at WPP, has extra tips to share with Wunderman Thompson Intelligence. These include utilizing the technology that comes with the metaverse, such as "smart contracts" for transactions, ownership, and access in virtual worlds; observing what other brands are doing by learning from their wins and fails; and not forgetting about existing brand safety measures. "The metaverse may seem like a completely new space, but learnings from Web 2.0 and the real world should still be applied," says Burkhill-Howarth.

Burkhill-Howarth believes the metaverse is here to stay. "But don't necessarily expect engagement to be how it is now, " he says. The metaverse will be largely defined by users, who will be shaping experiences for virtual worlds, digital assets, and ownership. Tracking behaviors in the metaverse will be critical for brands to future-proof their strategies as this digital space evolves.

WHY IT'S INTERESTING

It's time for brands to become metaverse-ready, or risk falling behind. "I would recommend that brands bring together their legal, treasury, finance, compliance, and cyber-security teams with their brand and marketing teams to ensure that they understand the opportunity, risks, and challenges and are ready to execute their metaverse activities," says Burkhill-Howarth. "Don't end up playing catch-up."

"Don't end up playing catch-up."

Gareth Burkhill-Howarth, global data protection officer, WPP

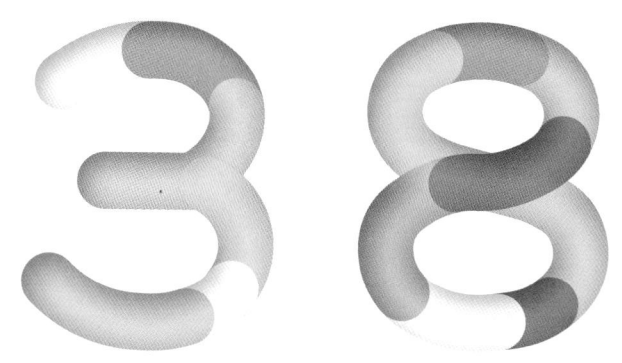

39

MASS INCLUSIVE BRANDS

Businesses are bringing inclusive products into the mainstream.

"When we design for accessibility, it ends up benefiting a much broader group of people," according to Kat Holmes, author of *Mismatch: How Inclusion Shapes Design*. It's also something consumers think brands should do; 72% of global respondents agree that we don't need to fix disabilities, we need to fix the world for disabled people, according to data from Wunderman Thompson Intelligence's "Inclusion's Next Wave" report. Realizing the potential business opportunity, more brands are now looking to bring accessible products to the masses.

In July 2022, US-based furniture retailer Pottery Barn launched a new range of adaptive furniture based on its 150 best-selling styles. The pieces were designed with support from the Disability Education and Advocacy Network and are more accessible for people with mobility issues. The range is available online and in stores, at the same price as the original designs.

American clothing retailer Kohl's is also expanding its ranges of adult clothing with adaptable options. In September 2022, it announced it will be adding adaptive products to its own-label Sonoma Goods for Life and Tek Gear brands, as well as introducing adaptive items from other brands to its online store.

Packaged goods are also getting an overhaul. Strauss, one of Israel's largest food manufacturers, announced in February 2022 that it will adapt its snack packaging to make it easier to open for people with disabilities. In Europe, Kellogg's has added NaviLens codes to all of its cereal boxes, allowing those with sight impairments to use their phone to scan the package for nutritional and other information.

WHY IT'S INTERESTING

People with disabilities and their families have an estimated $13 trillion in spending power, according to the "Global Economics of Disability 2020" report from Return on Disability. By considering the various needs of a wider audience, brands are able to tap into the opportunity that inclusive design brings, creating better, more accessible products for all.

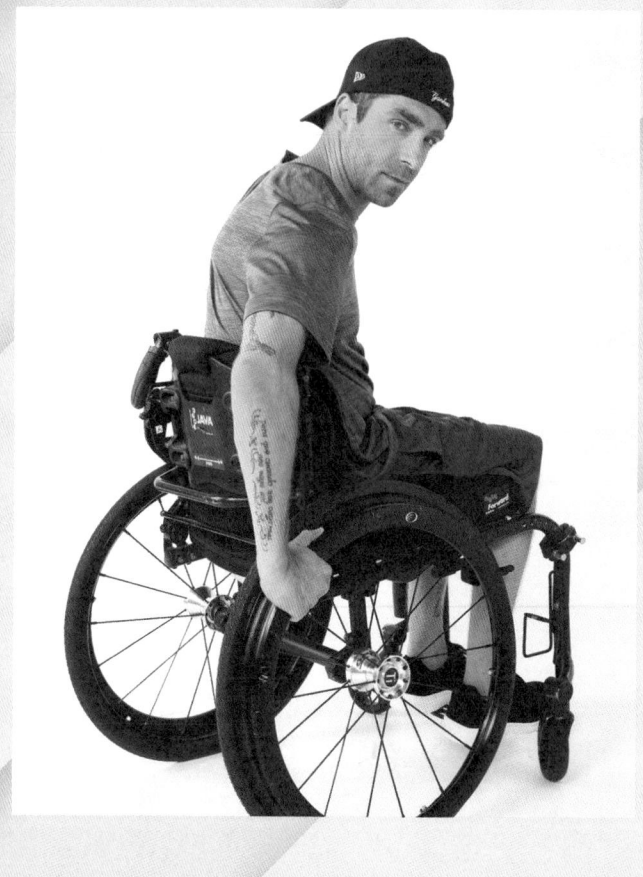

40
AGELESS PLAY

Brands are encouraging play for consumers of all ages.

McDonald's wants to help people recapture the playfulness and joy of childhood. The fast-food chain introduced Happy Meals for adults in October 2022, serving up a toy with popular menu items. "Everyone remembers their first Happy Meal as a kid ... and the can't-sit-still feeling as you dug in to see what was inside," the company says. "That little red box could turn a regular Tuesday into the best. day. ever. And now, we're reimagining that experience in a whole new way—this time, for adults."

Moxy Hotels is offering travelers "playful stays." Moxy describes its latest location, opened in the Lower East Side of Manhattan in November 2022, as a "playful haven" with a design "inspired by the circuses and old-time menageries that once lined the Bowery." The hotel offers "endless amusements enlivened with the spirit of the absurd," inviting guests to "Play On #atthemoxy." The hospitality brand further channeled its "Play On" spirit with an augmented reality campaign in Asia Pacific, "Moxy Universe, Play Beyond," launched in July (see 28, Metatravel, page 69).

Canadian cannabis company Houseplant is injecting a dose of playfulness into its product experience. The brand unveiled new packaging in April 2022 that takes inspiration from Lego blocks. "We wanted to leverage Houseplant's playful identity and design into something that could be collected and reused over time," Javier Arizu, cofounder of Pràctica design studio, a collaborator on the redesign, told *Dezeen*.

WHY IT'S INTERESTING

After an unpredictable few years, people are looking for moments of emotional release. Brands are tapping into the cultural desire for optimism and childlike abandon by redesigning their offerings to encourage joy and play.

Brands are tapping into the cultural desire for optimism and childlike abandon by redesigning their offerings to encourage joy and play.

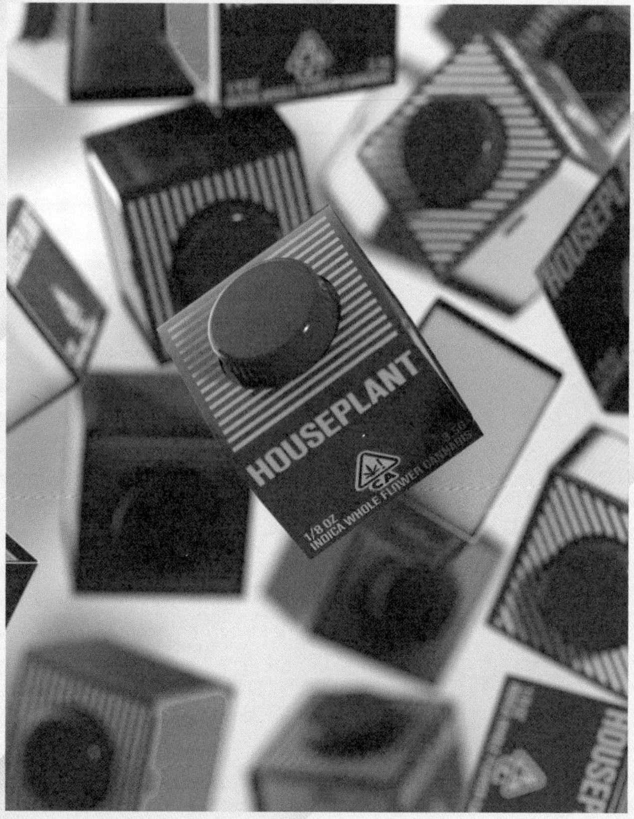

Above: Moxy Hotels
Right: Houseplant

FOOD & DRINK

41

INTREPID DINING

Pioneering diners are indulging in otherworldly meals.

Diners are embracing extraordinary culinary experiences that offer inventive menus, theatrical preparation, and extreme locations.

Bompas & Parr, a London-based design studio known for its multisensory experiences, served dishes cooked over molten lava at a dinner hosted in February 2022 in Saudi Arabia's historic AlUla region, renowned for its distinctive sandstone canyons and black lunar volcanic plateaus. Lava technicians poured out the molten rock in a performance spectacle, with expert chefs then searing local produce across a stream of lava heated to a staggering 1,350 degrees Celsius.

OceanSky Cruises is offering fine dining on its airship expeditions to the North Pole, set to take flight in 2024. As well as gourmet meals served in the air, travelers can also enjoy an element of alfresco dining in the snow as part of the 38-hour adventure.

Wine aged in space tastes out of this world, auction house Christie's reports. Last year, connoisseurs bid on a bottle of Petrus 2000 that had spent 14 months in orbit aboard the International Space Station, matured in zero-gravity conditions, and survived almost 180 million miles of travel.

WHY IT'S INTERESTING

Consumers are embracing extreme dining for a unique escape from everyday life, relishing memorable experiences that take them beyond the usual restaurant setup.

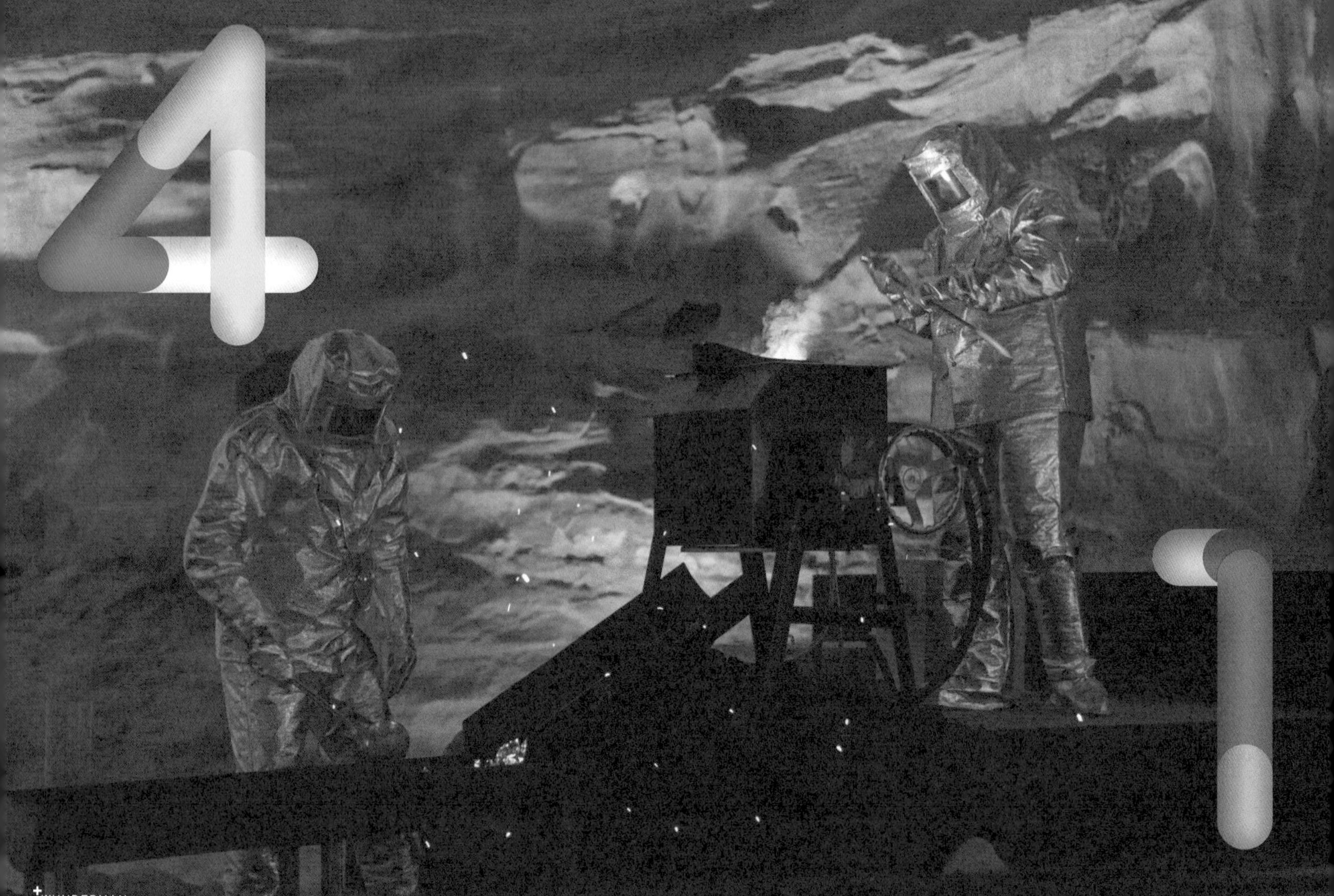

WUNDERMAN THOMPSON Bompas & Parr

42

VIRTUAL FLAVORS

What does the metaverse taste like?

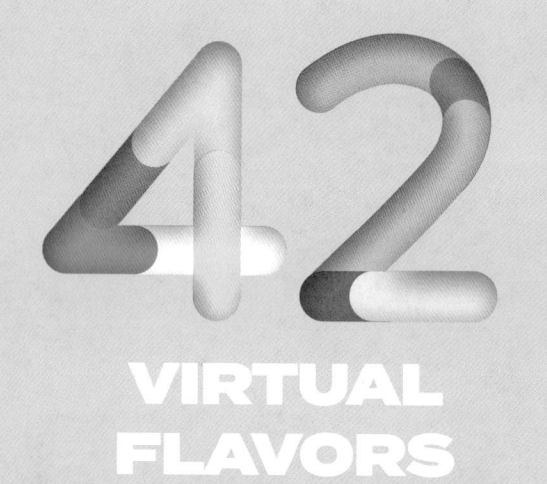

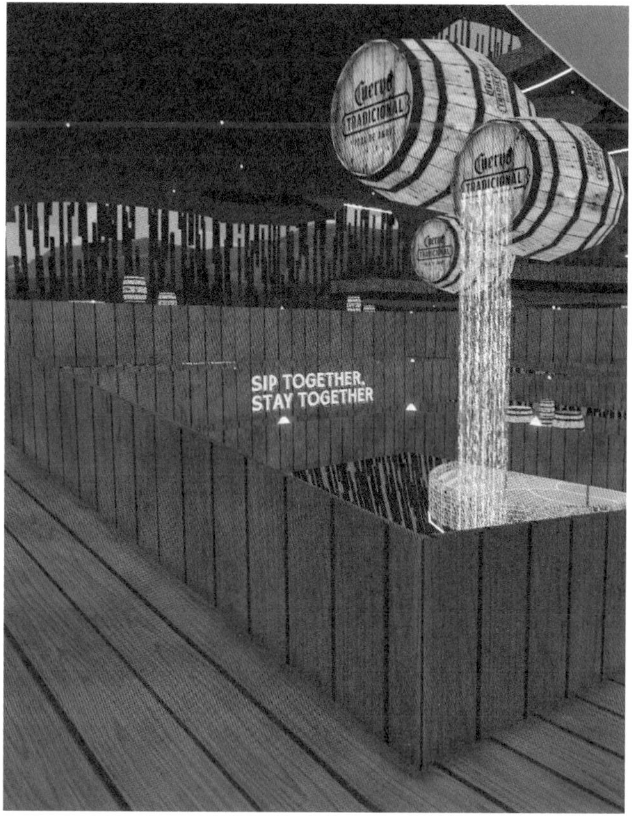

SIP TOGETHER,
STAY TOGETHER

The metaverse is influencing the food and drink industry, inspiring new flavor profiles and reimagining the dining experience.

In May 2022, Coca-Cola released a new soda flavor with an unusual inspiration: the metaverse. Coca-Cola Zero Sugar Byte, which first launched in Fortnite, was designed to taste like pixels. "We wanted to create an innovative taste inspired by the playfulness of pixels, rooted in the experiences that gaming makes possible," said Oana Vlad, the brand's senior director of global strategy. "Just as pixels power digital connection, Coca-Cola Zero Sugar Byte brings people together."

Other brands are also picking up on the theme of togetherness to reimagine eating and drinking for the metaverse. Mexico-based architect Rojkind Arquitectos and experimental design studio Bompas & Parr created a virtual distillery for Jose Cuervo on the Decentraland platform, "bringing the polysensory experience of the real world into the limitless world of Decentraland," said the studio's cofounder Harry Parr.

The design firm is reinterpreting the role that food and drink can play in the future of digital living, focusing on its connective power. "The structure's form was inspired by the roots of the agave, a plant nucleus that, when observed, evokes feelings of protection and consolidation," said the architect. "The Jose Cuervo Meta-Distillery aspires to be the center around which all individuals can forge stronger bonds, building an inclusive community."

WHY IT'S INTERESTING

Eating and drinking is a distinctly physical experience—but brands are starting to explore how this translates into the virtual realm, and how virtual experiences inform physical food and drink products. As virtual lifestyles evolve, expect to see more creative reinterpretations of food and drink for the future of metaliving.

43

ZERO-PROOF LIFESTYLES

A rising sober generation wants to experience the buzz without the alcohol.

Alcohol has "lost its cool," according to a September 2022 article by *Vice*, which notes the growing non-alcoholic options at bars and restaurants, and some consumers ditching alcohol completely. This trend stems from more people, particularly gen Zers, choosing a zero-proof lifestyle. The *Guardian* reports British 16-24-year-olds are the driving generation shunning alcohol, with 26% fully teetotal.

"There is a heightened awareness around health and wellbeing, which means many are recognizing the negative impacts alcohol has," Jay Richards, cofounder of gen Z research agency Imagen Insights, tells Wunderman Thompson. Richards adds, "society is also becoming more accepting of those who opt not to consume alcohol."

Temperance bars elevating the drinking-out experience minus the alcohol are on the rise. NoLo is Dubai's first non-alcoholic bar, soft launched in July 2022, serving artisanal cocktails that have a health-conscious twist. In the same year, Temperance Bar opened in San Francisco as an invitation-only speakeasy, offering over 100 non-alcoholic spirits, mixers, and drinks. In Melbourne, Brunswick Aces Bar, which launched in April 2021, is Australia's first non-alcoholic bar.

It's not just bars that are focusing on a sober-curious clientele; bottle shops are also displaying the wide range of alcohol-free choices. The Zero Co is Atlanta's first non-alcoholic store. Opened in December 2022, the shop caters to a growing demand for low-alcohol to zero-proof lifestyles. It stocks over 300 bottles of alcohol-free spirits, wines, and beers, and has a space for tastings too. In September 2022, pop-up Sèchey opened its permanent store in New York City's West Village.

Founder Emily Heintz is committed to introducing people to healthy alternatives that forgo the hangover the next day, while still challenging taste buds with a tasting counter. In Singapore, Free Spirit opened in 2020 as the country's first zero-proof bottle shop.

WHY IT'S INTERESTING

Zero-proofing is the new cool. The past few years have seen a steady rise in people wanting low- or no-alcohol options, as beverage brands started producing more refined non-alcoholic alternatives. Now these products are being integrated into social settings, thanks to modern bottle stores with tasting counters, and chic bars going completely teetotal.

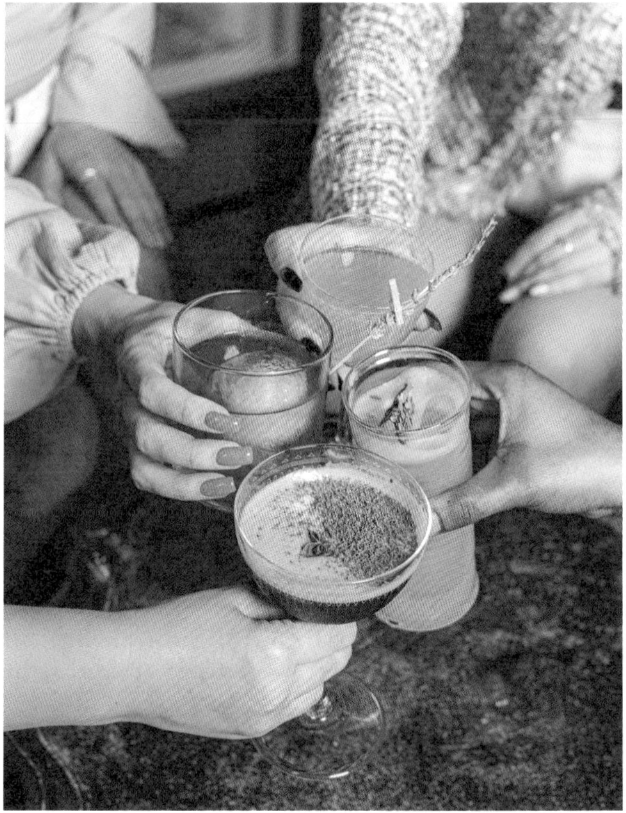

Zero-proofing is the new cool.

NoLo bar at Dusit Thani Dubai

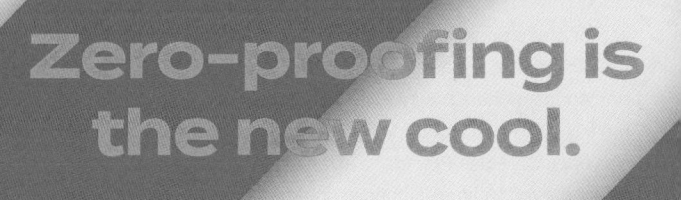

SURVIVALIST DINING

Gathered, wild-grown ingredients are informing a new class of survivalist diets.

People are tasting the thrill of a scavenger's menu. *Chefs vs. Wild* is a new show on Hulu that, each episode, follows two world-class chefs who are dropped into remote locations to scavenge for wild ingredients in order to make a meal worthy of a fine-dining experience. The series was first aired in September 2022, and each chef is paired with an outdoor expert and survivalist to ensure they don't accidentally ingest any poisonous flora or fauna, or injure themselves.

To apply, the chefs must have experience or knowledge in areas such as foraging and butchery, and, once selected, they have to forage, hunt, and fish for their produce. Using their wild-harvested ingredients, they're led to a "wilderness kitchen" to prepare an exceptional meal for the show's two hosts: adventurer and professional chef Kiran Jethwa, and wild-food expert Valerie Segrest.

WHY IT'S INTERESTING

The series reflects a growing cultural interest in nature-inspired, foraged diets and lifestyles. In an evolution from foraged cocktails (trend 41 in "The Future 100: 2022") consumers are combining their desire to be sustainable with a growing interest in rewilding in daily life.

Chefs vs. Wild, season 1, courtesy of Hulu

45

CLUBSTAURANTS

Exclusive eating clubs are the new
ultra-elite dining experience.

Private members' clubs are being hybridized with restaurants, offering highly personalized concierge service and top-quality food in "behind the paywall" restaurants only open to members.

Haiku in Miami is an invitation-only restaurant for members, who pay an annual fee and must also commit to at least four reservations per year for a lavish 12-course omakase feast. ZZ's Club, which also launched initially in Miami, has taken the clubstaurant concept to New York with a three-story, 25,000-square-foot location in Hudson Yards. It houses the latest incarnation of popular Italian eatery Carbone as well as a Japanese restaurant and several bars, all of which are only open to members paying an annual fee that is only revealed upon application. Flyfish Club, set to open in Manhattan in early 2023, puts a tech-enhanced spin on this approach to court the crypto elite. The seafood-inspired offering from hospitality and restaurant group VCR includes two restaurants where membership is purchased on the blockchain through a Flyfish NFT.

Premium London restaurant Casa Cruz's four-story New York establishment hybridizes the clubstaurant approach even further. The main restaurant and lounges are open to the public, but only investors paying upward of $250,000 to join have access to the dining room and roof terrace on the fourth floor.

WHY IT'S INTERESTING

Fine dining is offering a new tier of elite eating experiences for the upper echelons: one that prioritizes membership and exclusivity, and caters to the crypto elite.

Fine dining is offering a new tier of elite eating experiences.

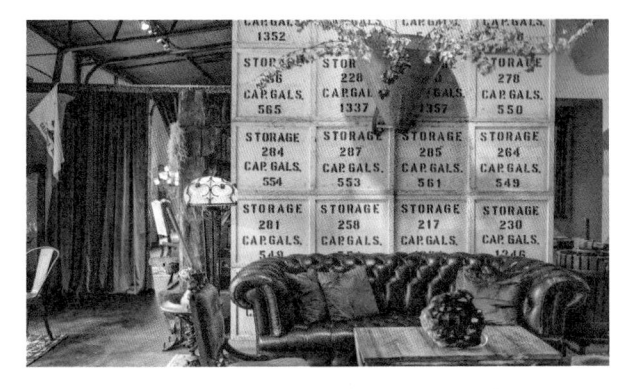

46

WEB3 WINERIES

The traditional winery is getting a Web3 upgrade.

The wine industry is ripe for disruption—and new players are starting to explore Web3-enabled reinvention.

Evinco is a California-based wine company that has taken inspiration from cryptocurrency and the metaverse to set up as a decentralized autonomous organization, or DAO. This distributed leadership model spreads ownership and decision-making power throughout the winery's community, meaning everyone with an NFT has equal voting rights over the future direction of the venture.

"Wineries have not had any disruption outside of manufacturing and direct to consumers in a generation," Evinco cofounder Joy Pathak tells Wunderman Thompson Intelligence. "Gamification of the wine and spirits world has never been done. Making people feel they have ownership with the brands they support has never been done. We are taking brand loyalty and community to a whole new level."

"Gamification of the wine and spirits world has never been done."

Joy Pathak, cofounder, Evinco

Evinco NFT holders also receive access to exclusive products and events, and this idea of using NFTs to provide extra benefits, seamlessness, and transparency is something other wine companies are also exploring. Cuvée Collective is an NFT-based wine club that offers token holders access to VIP experiences and concierge services in California's wine country. Luxury NFT marketplace BlockBar and WiV, which claims to be the world's first blockchain-based wine investment club, both sell NFTs that are digital clones of real-life bottles and cases of wine. The blockchain-backed NFTs verify the authenticity and provenance of the real product, while also allowing frictionless digital trading between wine connoisseurs.

WHY IT'S INTERESTING

We predicted the rise of DAOs in "The Future 100: 2022," looking at how the Web3 economy is providing an alternative to corporate employment. Now they're extending beyond that, being used to restructure traditional industries using decentralization, democratization, transparency, and community ownership.

47

TOP THREE INGREDIENTS

Indigenous palates and authentic cuisine will determine the top ingredients for the year ahead.

Achiote

Achiote, popular in Mexican cooking, comes in many forms. The word "achiote" comes from "achiotl" in Nahuatl, the ancient Aztec language. Described as earthy and tangy, the ingredient brings an orange to red color as well as flavor to chicken al pastor and fish dishes. Though its origin is disputed, it is produced primarily in Latin America as well as countries in the Caribbean, Asia, and Africa.

Its recent popularity reflects a growing interest in indigenous dishes and cuisine, marked by several rising chefs and restaurant owners intentionally incorporating cuisines into their menus based on their heritage and traditional dishes. In August 2022, Chipotle announced that it would introduce a new chicken al pastor dish featuring achiote as one of its star ingredients for a new level of spice.

Sansho peppercorn

Sansho peppercorn is a popular ingredient in Japanese cuisine. Zesty and versatile, it can be used in a range of dishes for all levels of cooking. New condiment brand Cabi launched its range of Japanese-inspired toppings and flavors in September 2022. Its trio of products includes Zesty Sansho Peppercorn Miso, which can be used with salmon and minced meat based on recipes from the brand's website.

As gen Z—the most diverse generation to date—fuels a rise in multicultural dining, new-age formulations made from ingredients with history and cultural significance will continue to grace menus and kitchens.

Yaupon

Made from a holly bush native to the United States, yaupon is the continent's only naturally caffeinated plant. Known for its sweet and earthy flavor profile, it was used by Indigenous Americans in herbal teas and purification rituals.

It's brewed by tea crafters including Florida's Yaupon Brothers, North Carolina's Yaupon Tea Co, and Texas's CatSpring Yaupon. BBQ Ramen Tatsu-ya, a new restaurant that opened in Austin, Texas in October 2022, incorporates yaupon tea into its Melo-Byrd cocktail alongside sotol, umeshu, aperitivo, and plum salt. Expect to see yaupon featured on many shelves and menus in 2023.

48

CELL-CULTURED DISHES

As cell-cultured food moves from lab to grocery store, luxury dining may be the first beneficiary.

Cell-cultured meat or dairy is a promising way to produce animal protein without the twin evils of animal suffering and environmental degradation. But until very recently, it's been very expensive to do so.

The process involves taking cells from a living animal and placing those starter cells in a growth medium inside a bioreactor, so they can grow into fat and muscle. The first lab-grown hamburger in 2013 cost over €200,000 to produce; the cost has now fallen to under €10. In 2021, almost a billion dollars was invested in cell-cultured meat startups around the world, according to Crunchbase.

With investors pouring money into exploring lab-grown alternative proteins, it makes sense that some see their first applications in high-end dining. In 2021, scientists at Osaka University created wagyu beef—complete with streaky fat—using 3D printing, while Dutch scientists were experimenting with lab-grown caviar.

In September 2022, cell-based milk startup TurtleTree hired chef Dominique Crenn, the star of Netflix's *Chef's Table* series, as its food innovation advisor.

Crenn's flagship restaurant Atelier Crenn in San Francisco has three Michelin stars and is known for pescatarian dishes chosen for their minimal impact on the environment, as well as for presenting its menus in the form of poems.

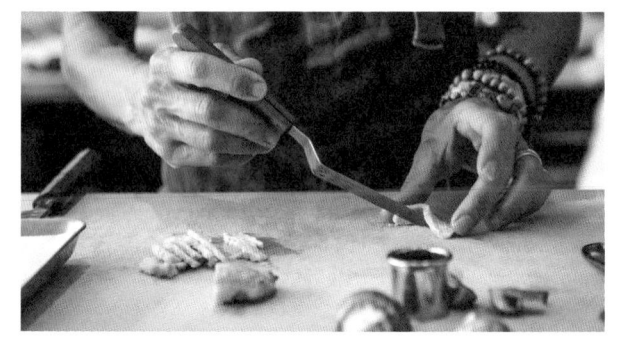

"I sincerely believe we will make food that thrills, delights, and tantalizes again—and then the revolution can truly begin," TurtleTree founder and CEO Fengru Lin told the *Sacramento Bee*. TurtleTree has a facility in Sacramento and headquarters in Singapore.

In early 2022, California-based Upside Foods, known for its cell-cultured chicken, moved upmarket by buying Wisconsin-based Cultured Decadence, which develops cultured seafood including lobster. Upside Foods has also partnered with Crenn to add its cultivated chicken to her menu once regulators approve it for sale to the public.

WHY IT'S INTERESTING

Cell-cultured proteins are still on the cusp of commercialization, with Singapore the only country that currently allows cell-cultured chicken for sale. For some consumers, the first mouthfuls could come from white-tablecloth restaurants rather than from the grocery aisle.

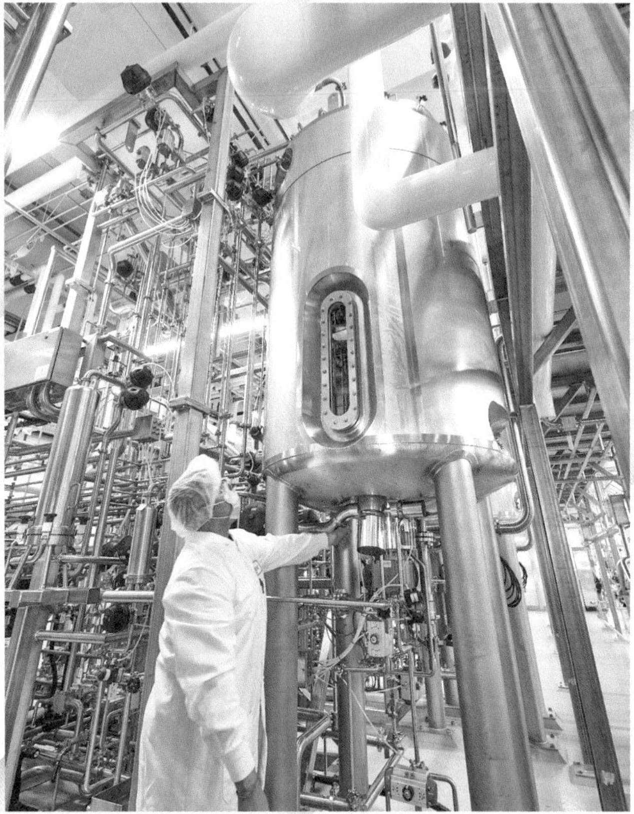

Upside Foods (both images)

48

49

SURREALIST DINING

The food and drink industry is innovating in the face of the energy crisis.

As energy prices soar in Brussels, chefs and restauranteurs are experimenting with stoveless, gasless cuisine served using little to no electricity. Brasserie Surrealiste serves cold and lightly grilled dishes to its guests, using only a flaming charcoal grill for cooking and candles on each table for light. Its menu includes raw white tuna, grilled pork with beans, focaccia cooked on a wood fire, and a brioche with anchovies.

"The idea is to go back to the cave age," said Francesco Cury, owner of Racines, whose employees serve and cook at the brasserie. "We prepared a whole series of dishes that just need to be grilled for a few seconds."

In the United Kingdom in October 2022, a restaurant in Frodsham opened without mains power, serving guests a nine-course tasting menu by candlelight as a protest against rising energy costs. Next Door used charcoal, smoking, curing, and fermentation techniques to prepare the dishes, with fire to heat tea and warm drinks and food. Instead of fridges, the cellar was used to store ingredients, and the site was cash only. Head chef Richard Nuttall used innovative practices to prepare each dish and maintain every ingredient. "We've got onions and carrots roasted in coals, and we're dehydrating herbs next to the fire," he told the BBC.

WHY IT'S INTERESTING

The dining industry is feeling the financial effects of the energy crisis in Europe. Chefs are taking extreme measures to innovate the dining experience while conserving money and reducing energy costs.

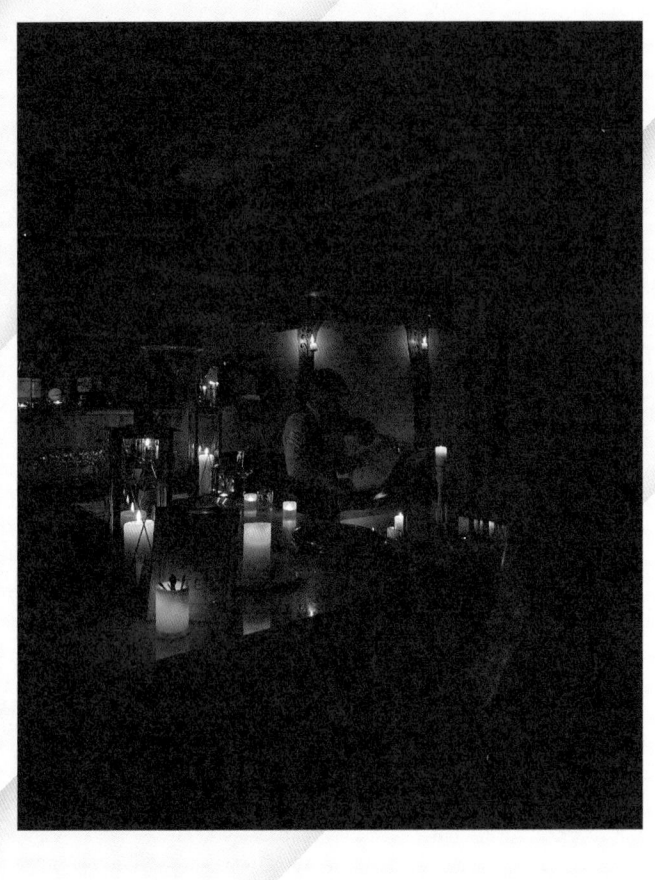

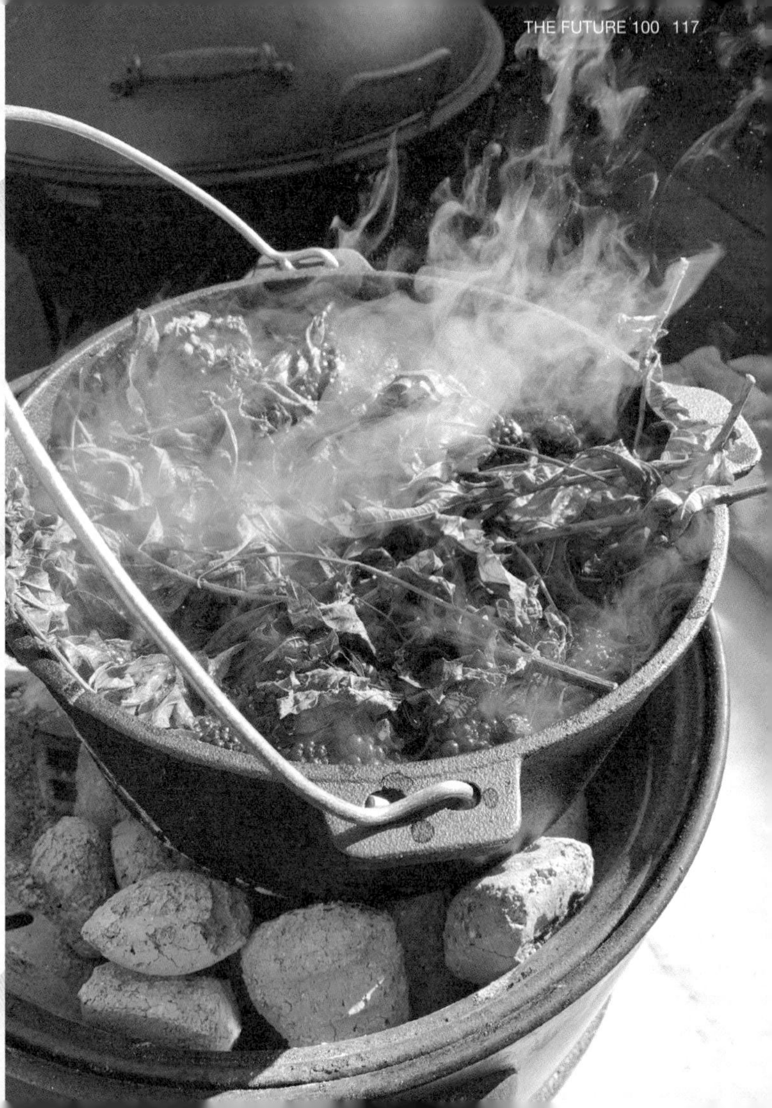

Next Door restaurant (both images)

50

SUPER-CIRCULAR DESIGN

Restaurants are getting
a circular redesign.

Vrå restaurant. Photography by Emma Thurr

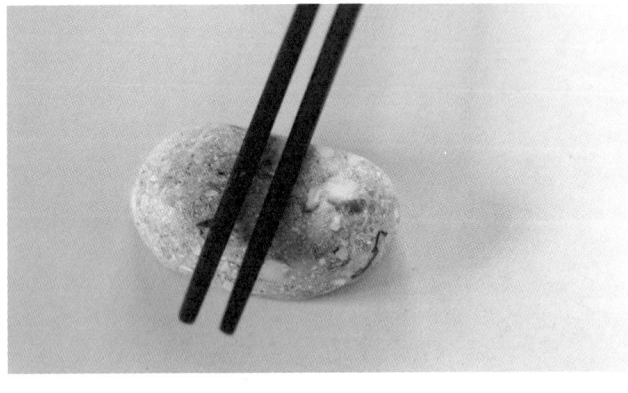

Future dining settings will do more than reduce food waste or use biodegradable materials: the entire environment will be designed in an eco-friendly fashion.

Vrå, a restaurant in Gothenburg, Sweden, uses furniture made from food waste and biproducts. Created by local designer Carolina Härdh, the pieces aim to help guests visualize the value food waste can have if reused properly.

Härdh's stool and side-table combo is made from crushed seashells, rice starch, and fish bones, and resembles terrazzo—although it is bio-based rather than cement-based. Leftover biomaterial is used to make fertilizer for the restaurant's rooftop garden or chopstick rests for the Japanese-inspired cuisine.

Härdh told *Dezeen* that the materials she decided to use "were picked based on an investigation I did of the restaurant's waste bin." She hopes that sitting on and witnessing the furniture "may add something to the guest's experience, to follow the ingredients from being food on their plate to becoming waste material and interior object."

WHY IT'S INTERESTING

Sustainable practices in the food industry are evolving, allowing brands to do more than reduce their food waste. Circular design in restaurants and social environments is the next iteration of eco-dining.

51

BEAUTY

60

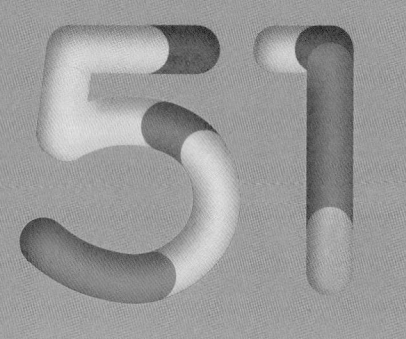

51

CIRCADIAN SKINCARE

Skincare regimens are harnessing the body's circadian rhythm.

Beauty sleep is inspiring new formulations as brands embrace the skin's natural circadian rhythm in their newest products.

The Chronobiology Sleep Mask by science-based skincare label Noble Panacea, launched in February 2022, "precisely delivers active ingredients into skin in a pre-programmed sequence synchronized with skin's natural circadian rhythm," the brand states. Three stages of activation occur throughout the night: during the Detox stage, from 11 p.m. to 4 a.m., the sleep mask releases PHA and pre-, pro-, and post-biotics; the mask then delivers retinol and peptides during the Repair stage; and, finally, ceramides and hyaluronic acid are released during the Nourish stage, when skin is at its maximum absorption.

A serum by 4AM skincare and an oil by La Prairie also claim to maintain and work with the skin's natural circadian rhythm in order to reduce typical signs of aging.

Beauty brand Mutha coined the term Circadian Dermablend in reference to its luxurious Cream Extreme, designed to complement the body's circadian rhythm each night. Launched in June 2021, its formulation of botanicals repairs and stimulates the skin as it heals from daily aggravators during the night, leaving it smooth and rejuvenated.

WHY IT'S INTERESTING
Beauty consumers are hacking their biology to uplevel skincare.

Beauty sleep is inspiring new formulations as brands embrace the skin's natural circadian rhythm.

52

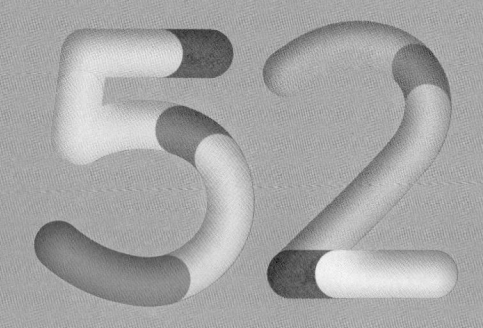

PSYCHO-DERMATOLOGY

Beauty brands are tapping into ingredients that not only nourish the skin but also feed the mind.

WUNDERMAN THOMPSON Selfmade

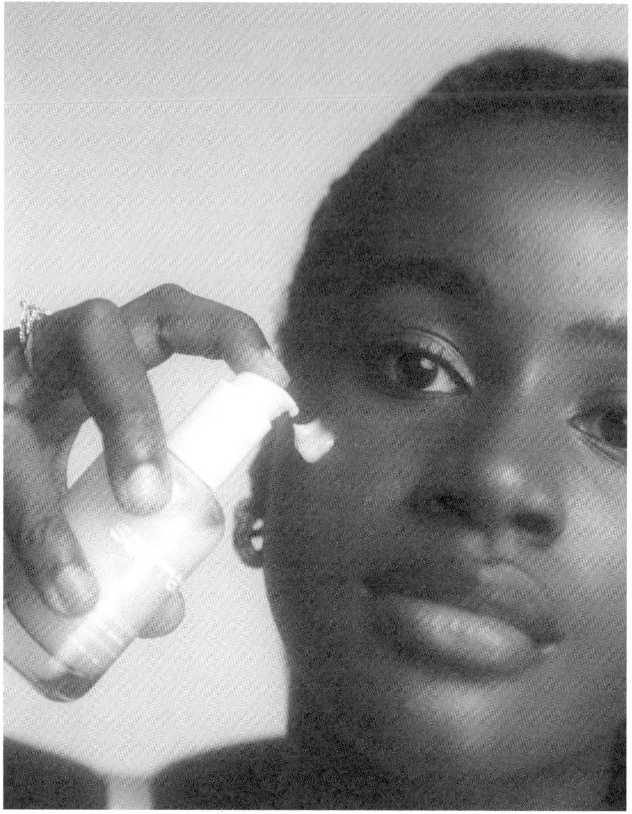

Japanese skincare brand Tatcha aims to harness the skin-mind connection with psychodermatology, by promoting intentional ritualization and ingredients that benefit the psychosomatic network, such as sweet fennel to boost focus and hinoki oil for relaxation. In a summer 2022 survey conducted by the Unilever-owned brand, 69% of respondents reported feeling burned out in the past 12 months and 70% noticed negative changes in their skin because of stress. This further supports the need for ingredients and rituals around promoting the health of the mind as well as the skin.

Launched in 2020, Selfmade is "the first emotionally intelligent personal care brand" with psychodermatology and emotional wellbeing as core pillars. The company works with mental health experts and a junior advisory board of gen Zers—who

"Psychodermatology is a discipline that explores the relationship between the brain and skin."

Stephanie Lee, founder and CEO, Selfmade

are passionate about tackling mental health issues—to ensure the brand "is rooted in credible mental health sciences, that shows up in how we speak about our stakeholder and our products," Stephanie Lee, founder and CEO of Selfmade, tells Wunderman Thompson Intelligence.

"We are overstressed without effective tools that help us explore and meet our own human needs," explains Lee. "Psychodermatology is a discipline that explores the relationship between the brain and skin." Selfmade's products, which include the Self Disclosure Intimacy Serum and True Grit Resilience Scrub, reflect that. In September 2022, the brand launched the Corrective Experience Comfort Cream, which has self-soothing properties and uses Cortinib G as a key ingredient to lower cortisol and offer stress relief.

WHY IT'S INTERESTING
Seventy-four percent of people sense their mental state and their skin are connected, according to Tatcha's survey. Beauty brands are offering products that actively help tackle stress, with psychodermatology rituals and functional ingredients to benefit the skin and soothe the mind.

53

RESURRECTED INGREDIENTS

Brands are bringing back extinct and forgotten sensory ingredients.

Brands are resurrecting extinct flora for their latest scents, using ingredients as gateways to the past and preserving sensory experiences for future generations.

A recent collaboration between Haeckels and Tetsuo Lin, an MA Material Futures graduate from London's Central Saint Martins, is resurrecting scents for the beauty industry. The project aims to revive lost scents by engineering fragrances using small amounts of DNA from floral samples, marking a new milestone in Haeckels' sustainability efforts. Lab-grown scents bypass the use of physical flora and essential oils, ultimately eliminating the intensive resource impacts of farmed ingredients.

In Europe, research project Odeuropa is using artificial intelligence (AI) to recreate lost smells from the past. Researchers are applying AI techniques to archived imagery and literature from the 16th to early 20th century, to identify "how 'smell' was expressed in different languages, with what places it was associated, what kinds of events and practices it characterized, and to what emotions it was linked," according to Odeuropa. The project hopes to highlight Europe's rich olfactory heritage.

WHY IT'S INTERESTING

Bringing back extinct ingredients is more than just an attention-grabbing narrative. Resurrected ingredients will simultaneously help preserve nature today while securing its history for future generations.

WUNDERMAN THOMPSON

Above: Haeckels
Right: Odeuropa

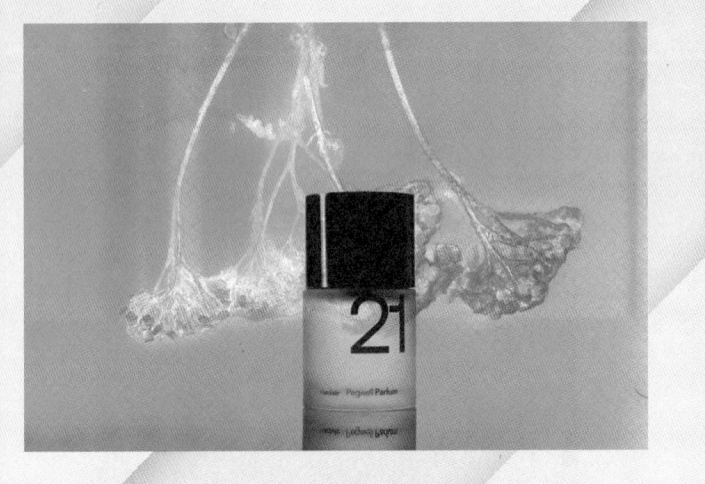

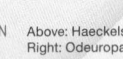

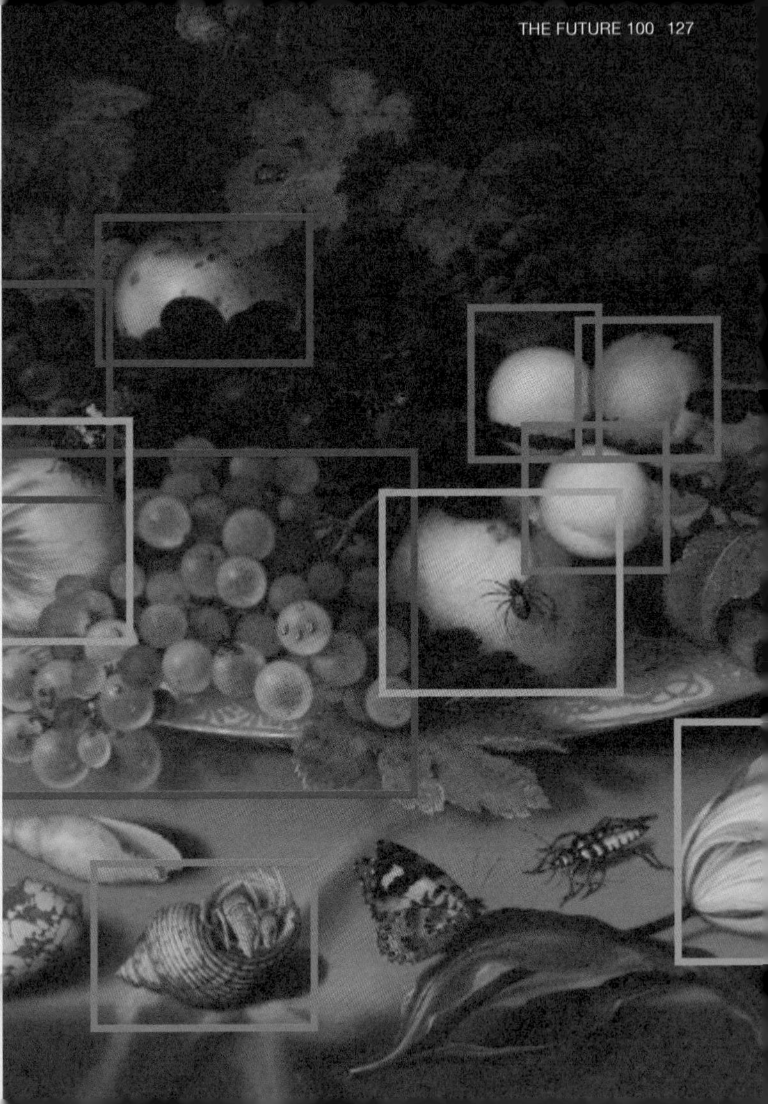

54

ADAPTOGENIC BEAUTY

Functional wellness makes its way into skincare formulations.

Herbar, a new adaptogenic beauty brand, launched in August 2022 with the premise that "beauty can be healing." Herbar defines adaptogens as "non-toxic, non-harmful, life-enhancing plants that are often used due to their abilities to help the body resist physical, biological, or chemical stressors." The new line features ingredients derived from "fauna, flora, and fungi only"—all of which have dual benefits for internal and external healing properties.

The brand's inaugural Face Oil product features three key adaptogenic ingredients: tremella, which is known for detoxifying and hydrating properties; reishi, which is used to reduce skin inflammation, puffiness, signs of aging, and free-radical damage; and da zao (or Chinese jujube date), which is rich in iron and vitamin C, and is proven to treat acne, blemishes, and scars.

Allies of Skin launched its Advanced Brightening Serum in 2022, which includes an adaptogenic complex with reishi and shiitake mushrooms to strengthen and hydrate the skin. And Hydrafacial x JLo Beauty launched a booster in October 2022 that features a fermented adaptogenic blend.

WHY IT'S INTERESTING

Skincare is increasingly becoming synonymous with health care—shifting skincare brands from the beauty category into the health and wellness sector.

55

VIRTUAL PERFUME

Beauty and fragrance brands are redefining scent for the metaverse.

Gucci launched its Gucci Flora virtual perfume on Roblox in August 2022. With no smell, the fragrance instead includes a range of experiences, including challenges, games, and interactive learning experiences, as well as a digital backpack inspired by the perfume bottle that Roblox users can wear.

Byredo and RTFKT took a different approach to their virtual fragrance. Announced in June 2022, Alphameta interprets scent as a wearable aura. Each of the 26 auras represents a different emotion, like "acuity" or "naivety." Users are encouraged to alchemize their own personalized auras by combining multiple emotions. The scents are available as limited collectible "elements" for what RTFKT calls its "avatar ecosystem."

Altra, a self-titled "profuture" perfumery, is also linking scent with emotion in virtual environments, and launched its virtual scentscapes in February 2022. "I'm fascinated by how something as sensorial as scent can cross over into the virtual world," Altra cofounder Beckielou Brown told *Harper's Bazaar*. Brown described the scentscapes as "immersive digital scent moods offering a new way to imagine the experience of scent and evoke emotions for the viewer in an increasingly digital landscape."

WHY IT'S INTERESTING

To date, digital environments have been very visually driven. These early metaverse plays show how the future of digital engagement is shaping up to be truly immersive—reimaging sensory experiences for virtual environments.

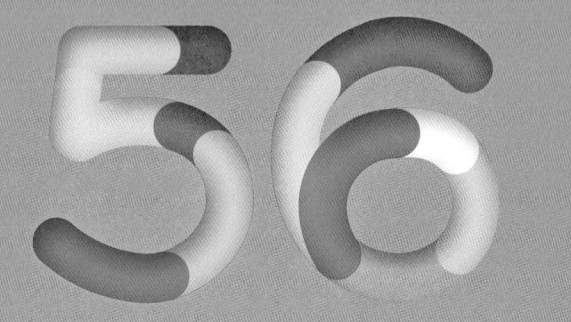

56

SKIN CYCLING

The latest sensation in at-home skincare involves minimizing products and alternating application days.

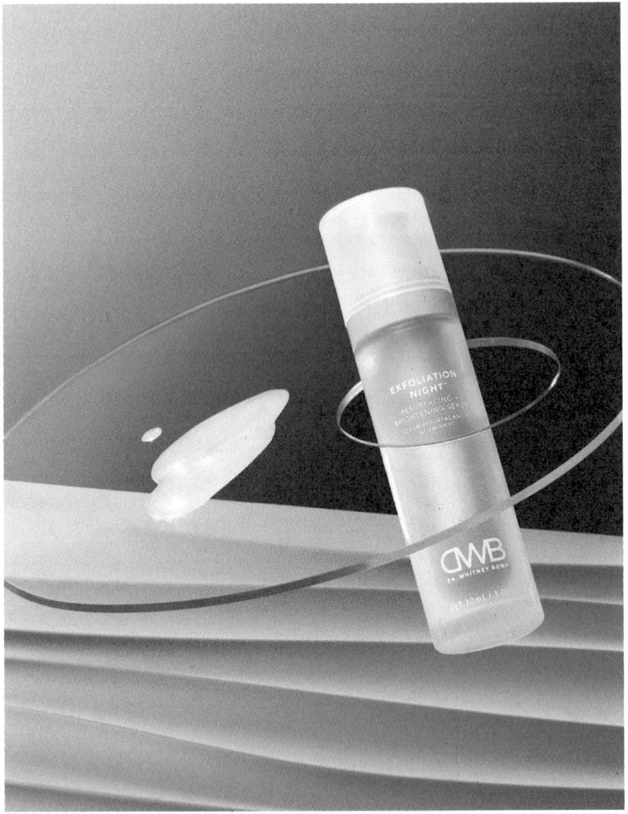

Dr Whitney Bowe

Beauty consumers are bringing their mental health habits to their skincare regimens

TikTok users have a habit of spawning beauty trends, and among the latest to take over the app is skin cycling. With an impressive 3.5 billion hashtag views as of January 2023, skin cycling clips educate viewers about the benefits of rotating their skincare products and taking recovery days. While TikTokers' routines vary, a typical approach might involve a four-day cycle, with active ingredients such as acids and retinol applied on a maximum of two days, followed by two further days when skin can rest.

While skincare specialists have long lauded the benefits of rotating active ingredients, New York board-certified dermatologist Dr Whitney Bowe is credited with coining the term skin cycling. In a 2022 guest appearance on *The Art of Being Well* podcast, Bowe said, "The way to get optimal skin health is to cycle through your night-time routine" before going on to highlight that giving skin a much-needed break provides an opportunity to "restore the skin barrier" and "recover the microbiome."

Brands are tapping into this trend by curating skin cycling kits that give beauty consumers everything they need to reset their skincare routine. The Skin Cycling Kit from By Beauty Bay consists of four serums and instructions for nightly product rotation. Nip & Fab's Skin Cycling Kit includes hydrating creams alongside active products glycolic acid and retinol, plus a four-day usage guide to make the cycle easy to follow.

WHY IT'S INTERESTING

Beauty consumers are bringing their mental health habits to their skincare regimens—embracing the benefits of rest days and listening to the body's needs, rather than constantly chasing results or accomplishments.

57

LAB-GROWN BEAUTY

New ingredient formulations are utilizing biotech to improve the sustainability, functionality, and production time of beauty products.

Estée Lauder-backed English beauty brand Haeckels launched Haeckels 2.0 in September 2022. This range of laboratory-grown skincare products is made with fully sustainable, compostable packaging and lowered carbon emissions, and cuts previous production times by half. The launch is the latest in the brand's revolutionary sustainable beauty formulations.

Unilever has pledged to invest $120 million in plant-based alternatives for its home care, beauty, and personal care products in partnership with the San Diego-based biotechnology group Geno. Unilever chief research and development officer Richard Slater says that by creating an alternative option to palm oil or fossil fuel for its products, the investment "will sit right at the intersection of science

Genomatica lab, courtesy of Unilever

and sustainability," and will position the brand as a "future-fit business for consumers, shareholders, and the planet."

Lab-grown formulations are improving product functionality as well. UK-based skincare brand Cellular Goods launched lab-made cannabinoid skincare in February 2022. Ourself, a biotech beauty brand that launched the same year, aims to mimic in-office procedures with a line of biotechnologically created beauty ingredients.

Cosmetic chemist Jen Novakovich told *Allure* that biotech ingredients can be manipulated to "produce whatever you want. You can turn up a part of it that makes a certain effect." Using biotechnology to produce ingredients can even improve sustainability, according to Novakovich: "Many life cycle analyses [tracking ingredients' environmental impacts based, in part, on land and water use] show favorable results for sustainability for biotech."

WHY IT'S INTERESTING
Beauty brands are embracing lab-grown ingredients to elevate product sustainability and precision.

58

THREE NEW INGREDIENTS

Mental health and natural formulations are leading this year's top three ingredients.

Hinoki

In September 2022, Japanese beauty brand Tatcha released a new line of bodycare products designed to soothe the mind and body. Hinoki, the key ingredient, is a cypress plant naturally found in Japan with a relaxing, forest-inspired scent. It is often referred to as "King of the Woods," and reflects the Japanese practice of forest bathing—walking through the woods and nature for relaxation. Cofounder and COO of Credo Beauty Annie Jackson told *Well+Good* that "brands are adapting medicinal ingredients that you'd find in a forest to boost your skin's immunity and promote stress relief."

Rambutan

This tropical Southeast Asian fruit is making waves in skincare as a forest-derived alternative to retinol, which fights blemishes and fine lines. Proven to be very effective on crow's feet—fine lines around the eye area—rambutan promotes production of collagen and elastin in the skin, provides antioxidants, and is much less irritating to the skin than many retinol products and derivatives. The whole fruit provides benefits to the skin according to board-certified dermatologist Hadley King. "The peel, pulp, and seed are rich in sugars, tannins, and flavonoids, which have antioxidant properties," she told *Well+Good*. Brands such as Dr Loretta, Alpyn Beauty, Indie Lee, and HoliFrog released new serums and creams with rambutan as the star ingredient in 2022.

Plant-based milks

Rice, coconut, and nut-based milks are becoming increasingly popular across skincare and haircare due to their moisturizing and exfoliating properties. From our coffee cups to our countertops, plant-based milks are appearing in top skincare brand formulations: Dermalogica's Daily Milkfoliant uses dehydrated coconut milk and ground oats as an exfoliant, Fresh's Milk Body Collection is a 2022 plant-based version of its dairy-inspired line from 1996, and Sol de Janeiro released its Brazilian Joia Milky Leavẹ-In Conditioner that features Brazil nut, cupuaçu, and babaçu to nourish the hair.

58

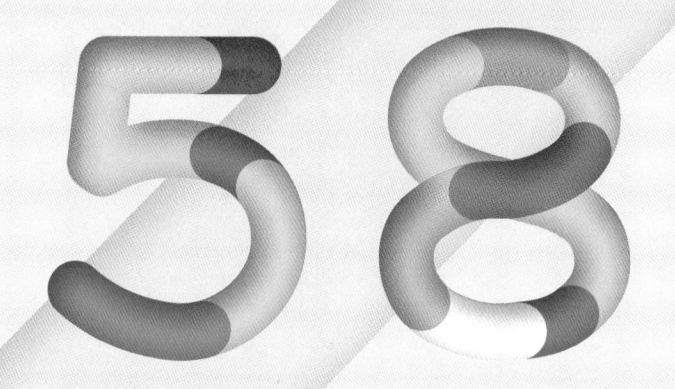

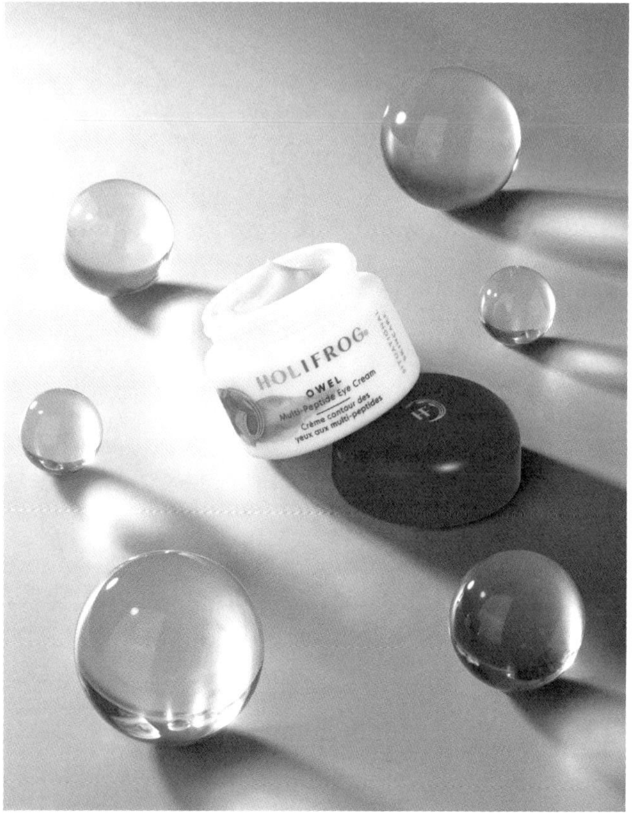

+WUNDERMAN THOMPSON HoliFrog

SUPERCHARGING HAIR HEALTH

Hair health for women is moving from treatment to prevention.

Hair health products are flooding the market, as a range of factors from pandemic stress to genetics to simply wearing a hijab can result in hair loss and breakage.

The issue of women's hair loss is popping up everywhere from glossy magazines to NBC's *Today Show*, which in May 2022 featured hair-raising footage of a doctor in New York City injecting "platelet-rich plasma injections" into a patient's scalp. More commonly, women with thinning hair are turning to a combination of oral nutritional supplements and topical creams, serums, and shampoos that contain ingredients like hyaluronic acid. Drugstore brands from L'Oréal to Rejoice have introduced "anti-hairfall" ranges.

The global haircare product market will reach more than $150 billion by 2028, according to Coherent Market Insights, and the hair-loss-prevention product market specifically is projected to reach over $31 million by 2028, according to a report by The Insight Partners.

Cult hair and beauty brand Ouai launched a scalp serum and vegan supplement capsules for thinning hair in May 2022. The Scalp Serum and Thick & Full Supplements utilize well-known haircare ingredients including peptides, biotin, hyaluronic acid, and pea sprout extracts to nourish hair strength and promote growth. "Every product we launch is born from our community's feedback," says Ouai CEO Colin Walsh. "We constantly received requests for products that address concerns like scalp dryness, dull strands, and breakage."

UK-based Nue Co launched two products for hair growth and density in January 2022. Growth Phase, an oral supplement, aids with hair growth and reduces shedding, and Supa Thick is a topical pre-wash product that exfoliates the scalp while also aiding hair growth and preventing loss. Nue Co founder Jules Miller told *Glossy* that the products are for "the women who are shedding more hair than they usually do. Statistically, that's one in three of us."

Salon-linked luxury hair brand Oribe launched its Hair Alchemy range in February 2022 to target hair breakage. Product development manager Gabriella Raccuia told *Harper's Bazaar*: "Prevention has always been a main category in skincare, and now is starting to make its way into haircare as consumers become increasingly savvy."

WHY IT'S INTERESTING
Prevention is moving beyond the realm of skincare and bodycare to include hair health.

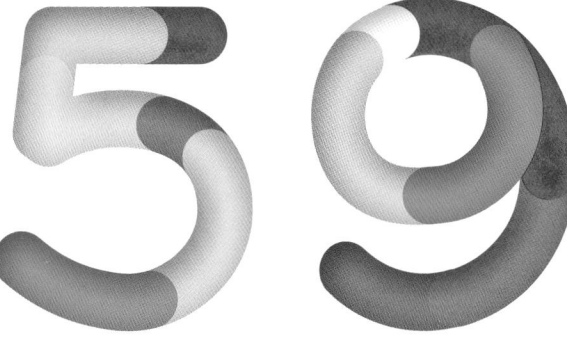

"Prevention has always been a main category in skincare, and now is starting to make its way into haircare as consumers become increasingly savvy."

Gabriella Raccuia, product development manager, Oribe

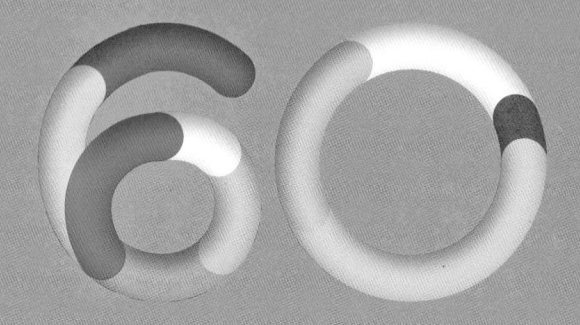

60

AFFIRMATIONAL BEAUTY

Beauty is merging with identity exploration and play, elevating makeup into an act of self-affirmation.

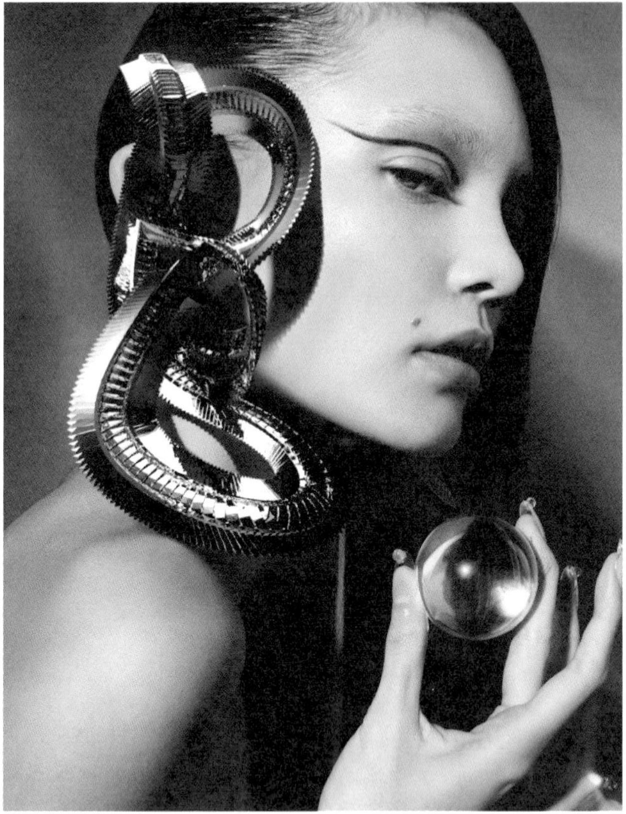

WUNDERMAN THOMPSON

The Fabricant Xxories

Isamaya Ffrench is reframing makeup as an exploration of identity and alter-egos. The artist's eponymous makeup line, Isamaya, launched in June 2022 and has served as a master class in character building. Each of her two drops to date has channeled a distinct identity. The inaugural drop, Industrial, espoused a "hardcore" aesthetic taking cues from "leather and latex, piercings and rubber, flesh, strength, and self-possession."

The latest collection, Wild Star, "pays homage to our inner cowgirl," and personifies someone who "is tenacious, feisty, and holds her own," Ffrench says. "She knows who she is and she never compromises. She's completely in tune with her desire to feel glamorous yet powerful. She's wild at heart."

Donni Davy, the makeup artist behind television show *Euphoria*'s iconic looks, launched her own line in May 2022, riding the wave of euphoric beauty (see 51, Euphoric makeovers, in "The Future 100: 2020") that the show spawned. The Half Magic range is backed by an entertainment company, further enmeshing beauty and dramatis personae. "Half Magic grew out of the global beauty cultural phenomenon created by *Euphoria* fans around the world," Michelle Liu, general manager of Half Magic, told *Allure*. "Creators behind the show came together to continue evolving the conversation around self-exploration and self-expression."

The Fabricant is bringing this concept into the virtual realm. The digital-only fashion house launched Xxories, a line of virtual facial accessories, in October 2022. "Digital beauty has the potential to let us extend our identity into places we haven't seen before," said The Fabricant creative director Amber Slooten. It lets beauty

enthusiasts "explore identities beyond this realm and discover new sides of ourselves."

WHY IT'S INTERESTING

Beauty is moving "beyond being a pleasing visual expression towards something that communicates our beliefs, feelings, or personal point of view," Michaela Larosse, head of content at The Fabricant, told *Vogue Singapore*. In the digital world, beauty will become a reflection of users' shifting emotional states—opening the door to infinite identities. "We will have many different virtual selves available to us," Larosse continued, "allowing us to express how we feel at any given moment, switching between these personas at a click."

RETAIL & COMMERCE

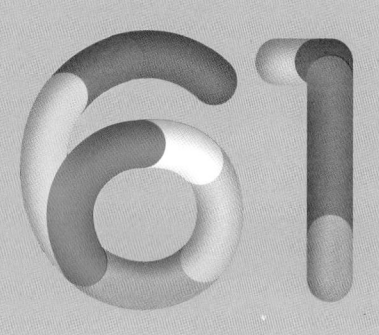

MULTIVERSAL DESIGN

Dreamlike, otherworldly design is reimagining physical spaces for a new era of creativity.

Physical spaces are getting dreamy, absurdist redesigns—transporting visitors to imaginary worlds and alternate realities. As digital environments and virtual worlds evolve, they're ushering in a new modern creative vernacular—one marked by a boundless creativity that surpasses the constraints of physical reality.

Balenciaga wrapped its London store entirely in pink faux fur in April 2022—covering the walls, floors, and shelves in the fluffy material, and giving visitors the sense of stepping into a playfully absurd alternate world.

In May 2022, fashion designer Simon Jacquemus launched a series of pop-up installations for Selfridges, which were designed as a "surrealist reimagining" of a bathroom, Selfridges said. "I wanted to create crazy and unrealistic installations, all related to water and bathroom imagery," said Jacquemus.

Louis Vuitton created a life-size toy racetrack at the Louvre in Paris for the backdrop of its spring/summer 2023 show in June 2022. "A giant children's toy racetrack becomes a yellow-brick road for the imagination," the brand said. "An evolutionary path for the mind where childlike fantasies come to life."

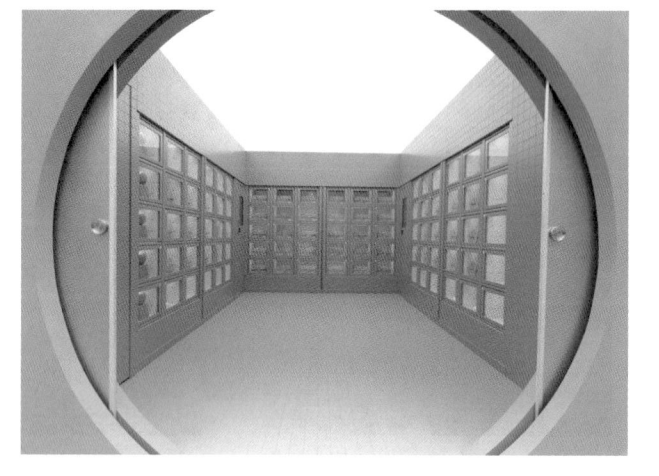

The Taste of Dadong restaurant in Shanghai was conceived "to deliver an emotional, dream-like dining experience." Sculptural partitions, dark surfaces illuminated by otherworldly blue and purple lighting, a "psychedelic" soundtrack, and mirrored panels covering the ceilings, showing warped and inverted reflections of diners and staff, all contribute to the "dreamy quality of the space."

WHY IT'S INTERESTING

We are on the cusp of a new golden age of creativity, catalyzed by the dawn of the metaverse. As digital design gets more sophisticated, it's untethering creativity from the bounds of the physical world—opening the door to multiversal design, both on and off screens.

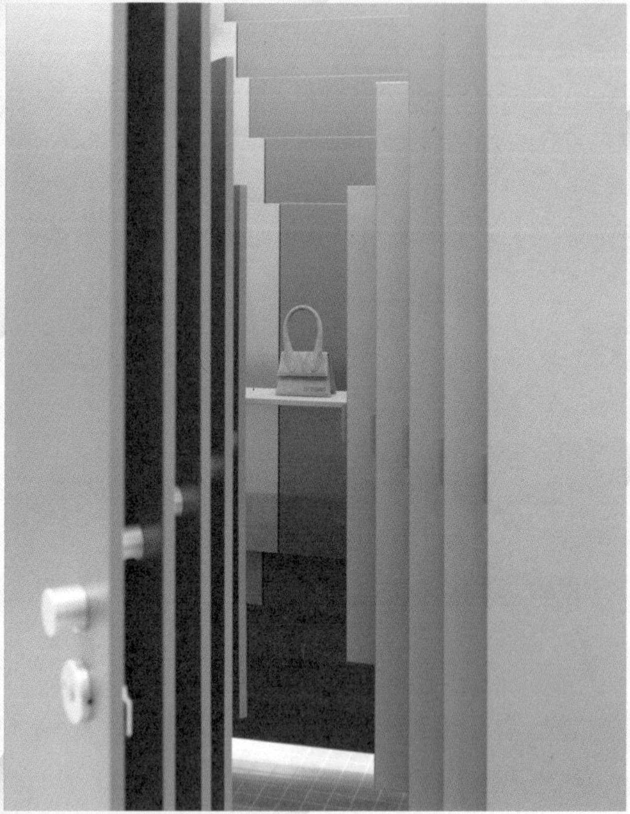

Selfridges (both images)

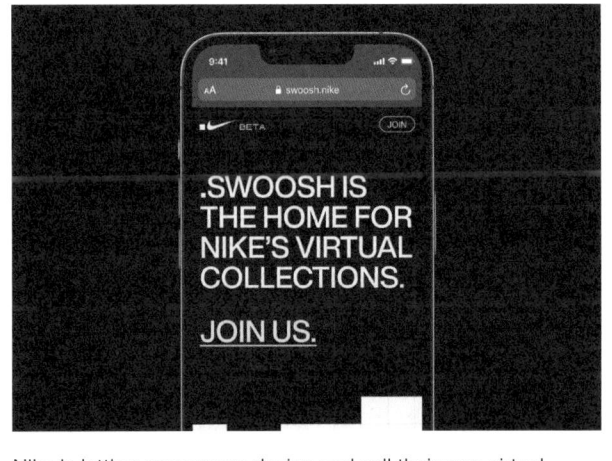

62

COCREATIVE COMMERCE

Could the next era of retail see users cocreating brands' virtual products and storefronts?

Nike is letting consumers design and sell their own virtual sneakers as part of Dot Swoosh, its new Web3-enabled platform. Nike describes the platform, which launched in beta in November 2022, as part virtual marketplace, part VIP loyalty community, and part creator economy. The platform will be a place to buy and trade Nike's virtual goods, participate in community challenges to unlock exclusive access to events and products, and cocreate Nike gear.

Nike has teased that .Swoosh's community challenges will expand next year to include competitions in which members can win a chance to codesign virtual Nike products with the brand's designers, even earning royalties on their sales. "We want to redefine what it means to be a creator," said Ron Faris, VP/GM of Nike Virtual Studios.

Forever21 is inviting shoppers to curate and operate their own virtual storefronts on Roblox. Announced in December 2021, Forever 21 Shop City introduces a new user-generated retail format. Users build, stock, and operate their own virtual Forever 21 franchises—managing everything from stocking inventory to assisting customers, operating the cash register, hiring employees, and decorating their storefront windows. Users fully customize their store design, picking furniture, art, lighting, and music that suit their style. They even curate the Forever21 products they want to sell, hand-picking pieces from the brand's latest collections, which are updated on Roblox with each new physical release.

Metaverse commerce is growing—and bringing with it a new set of retail formats. According to Bloomberg, the metaverse market is expected to reach $783 billion in 2024, up from

$479 billion in 2020. Nike Digital is the brand's fastest growing segment, now comprising over a quarter (26%) of the brand's total revenue. Its virtual Nikeland experience on Roblox—which lets users customize their own Nike sneakers—had attracted 26 million people as of November 2022, and its Web3 products had generated $185 million in revenue as of August 2022.

WHY IT'S INTERESTING

The future of virtual retail will be cocreative. Creativity is becoming the new status symbol for the dawning Web3 era (see 2, Creator communities, page 12) and brands are adjusting their virtual activations to trade in creativity and cocreation alongside traditional products. Expect to see more brands democratizing vcommerce by offering creative control to their consumers.

63

TWILIGHT STORES

Hybrid fulfillment locations are adding a sense of community to the dark store model.

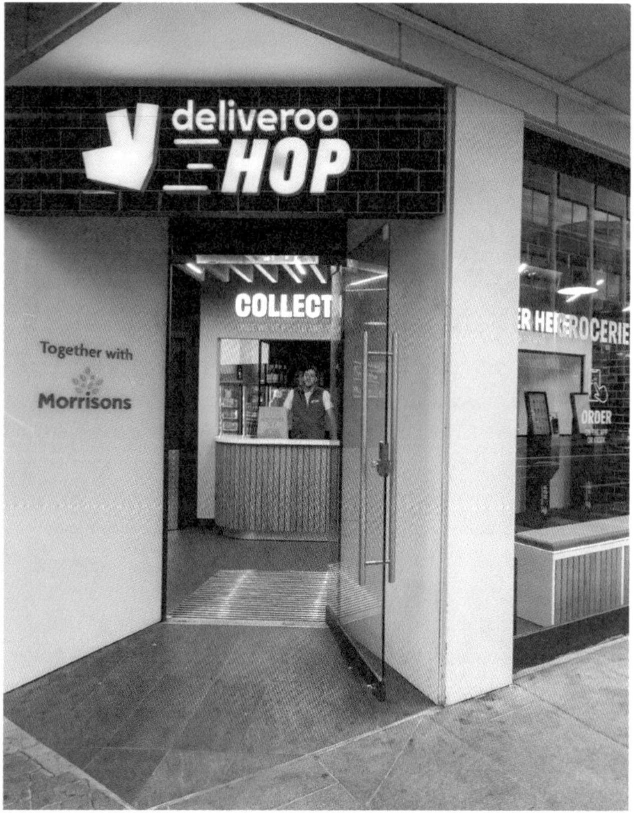

The pandemic ushered in a rapid acceleration of the ultra-fast delivery trend, with dozens of on-demand logistics companies offering product delivery in as little as 10 minutes in global cities, using networks of hyper-local dark stores. However, more recently dark store and kitchen operators have been receiving backlash from city dwellers for taking up valuable community space, leading to some countries taking steps to ban them. For example, in France dark stores have been reclassified as warehouses, rather than as shops, giving local authorities the power to remove them from urban centers. At the same time, big players like Gorillas, Getir, and Zapp have been scaling back their operations in some countries as supply has outweighed demand.

As the long-term viability of dark locations comes into question for the first time, a new hybrid approach has emerged that brings elements of community back into the mix. These twilight stores add a customer-facing element to the previously private format,

Twilight stores add a customer-facing element to the previously private format.

allowing operators to both engage with locals and benefit from walk-in customers.

German courier service DPD has opened a dual-purpose twilight store in Berlin that is a micro-depot from which local deliveries are made via ebikes, while also operating as a store that removes the pain points of sending and receiving parcels. Similarly, on-demand delivery company Deliveroo's Hop location is a grocery delivery hub for the surrounding London neighborhood, but also includes a reception area where customers can pick up their groceries and where passers-by can place orders.

Taster, which says it runs "delivery-first restaurants" rather than dark kitchens, has launched British chef Jamie Oliver's new delivery brand Pasta Dreams via two pop-up locations in London. The strength of the hybrid approach, according to Taster CEO Anton Soulier, is that it optimizes efficiency while allowing the brand to "create direct relationships with customers."

WHY IT'S INTERESTING
The convenience of dark stores is still attractive, but they aren't a good use of space in densely populated areas—leading to a new hybrid retail format that capitalizes on space, convenience, and community.

64

CRYPTOLITERACY

Financial institutions and fintech brands want to demystify the metaeconomy.

In March 2022, the US Treasury launched a campaign to educate the public about crypto risks. The Treasury's Financial Literacy Education Commission is responsible for creating educational materials and organizing outreach to inform the public about how crypto assets work and how they differ from other forms of payment.

Nellie Liang, US Treasury undersecretary for domestic finance, said that the initiative aims to raise awareness about the risks of investing in cryptocurrencies as the digital asset moves from the fringes of the financial system to the mainstream, *Reuters* reported. "We're hearing more and more about investors and households who are purchasing crypto assets, and we recognize the complexity of how some of these assets operate," Liang said. "It felt like this is an area also where more education (and) more awareness could be helpful."

Finance brands are also stepping in to fill the gap in crypto education. Fidelity Investments launched a financial education center in the metaverse in April 2022. The eight-floor virtual learning center, located in Decentraland, helps educate visitors on investing basics, the metaverse, and Fidelity's new metaverse exchange-traded fund. The center was created to "inform a new generation of investors," the brand said.

In February 2022, Mastercard expanded its consultancy services to cover cryptocurrency, NFTs, and open banking. The new suite of services will help banks and businesses adopt digital assets like cryptocurrency and NFTs, address risk assessment for digital currencies and NFTs, and advise on the

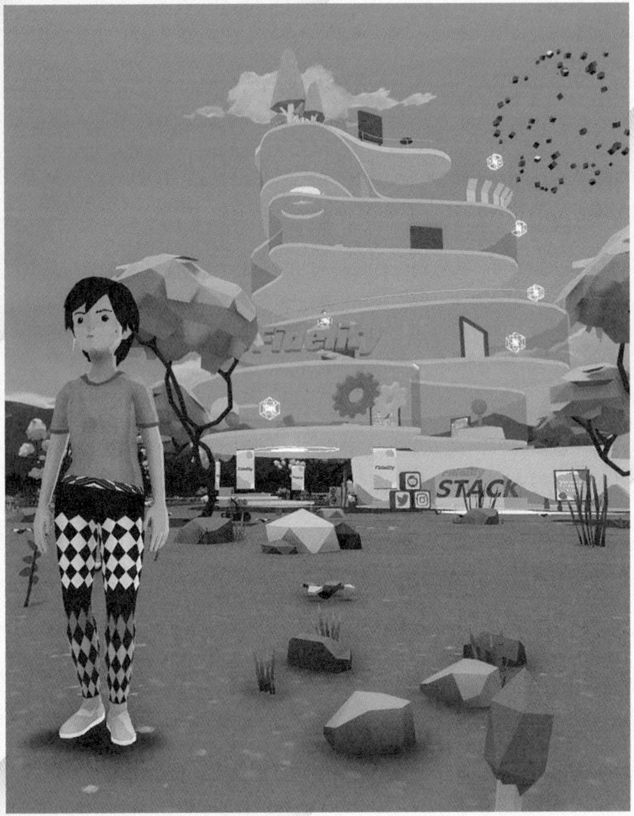

WUNDERMAN THOMPSON Fidelity

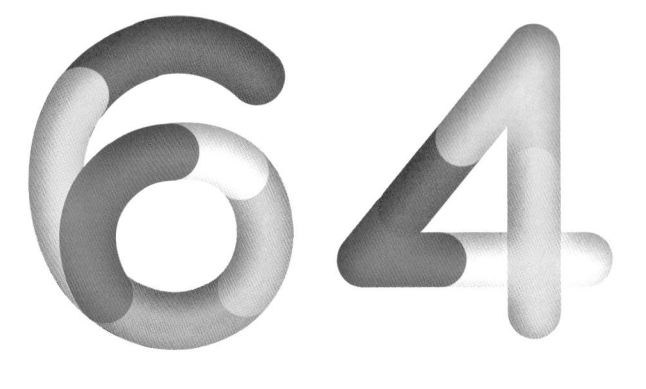

64

development of digital wallets, crypto credit cards, and crypto loyalty programs.

Visa launched a crypto advisory service for financial institutions and merchants in December 2021. The service is aimed at financial institutions eager to attract or retain customers with crypto offerings, retailers looking to delve into NFTs, or central banks exploring digital currencies, the company said.

WHY IT'S INTERESTING

The metaverse and Web3 are giving rise to new retail avenues and a nascent digital goods economy—all of which will inform spending patterns and are leading to the creation of a new cryptonomic ecosystem. But first, education needs to take place; the future of Web3 commerce hinges not only on adoption but also on education—for both consumers and brands.

65

ACCESSIBLE COMMERCE

Brands are tapping into advances in voice-recognition technology to make physical and digital spaces accessible to all.

Tech giants including Amazon, Apple, Google, Meta, and Microsoft have all joined forces with the University of Illinois Speech Accessibility Project, which aims to make voice-recognition technology more effective at understanding people with conditions that alter their speech pattern. The project will create a dataset of representative speech samples of people with amyotrophic lateral sclerosis (Lou Gehrig's disease), Parkinson's disease, cerebral palsy, and Down syndrome. This will be used to train the machine-learning models that power voice-recognition technology so that it will be better equipped to respond to the needs of people with these conditions.

Developments in voice-recognition technology like this are supplying physical retailers and ecommerce players alike with the tools to create more inclusive and accessible retail channels. Alibaba's online marketplace Taobao is expanding its use of voice search to make China's leading ecommerce platform more accessible to elderly users who live outside tier one cities. Previously only accessible to those speaking Mandarin, the search function will now recognize regional dialects used in places including Tianjin, Shandong, Henan, and Hebei.

As part of its commitment to "design, test, and scale more inclusive design standards and experiences across its store portfolio," Starbucks has announced it is trialing speech-to-text technology in its locations. This will allow both customers and staff to see a live visual display of all conversations during the ordering process, making its cafés more approachable for the deaf and hard-of-hearing community.

WHY IT'S INTERESTING

Brands are leaving money on the table by failing to make their spaces and services universally accessible. Voice-recognition and speech-to-text technologies play a key role in making physical and online retail inclusive for all.

66

CRISIS RETAIL

As the financial crisis bites, brands are stepping up to help their most vulnerable consumers.

At the height of the pandemic, many brands started taking a proactive role in their communities to ensure their customers had access to essentials. As the cost-of-living crisis takes its toll on consumers' spending power globally, companies are once again stepping up.

Retailers are making a strong commitment to reduce prices or release value alternatives for those most in need. On-demand rapid delivery platform Getir has rolled back the prices of key grocery staples to 1990s levels, allowing customers to get hold of items such as bread, pasta, chocolate, toothpaste, and washing-up liquid at up to 80% below the current retail price. With inflation hitting a 41-year high of 11.4% in Canada in September 2022, grocer Loblaws also froze the prices on 1,500 products in its affordable No Name range. In Japan, Muji has pivoted to make home essentials affordable. Its new dollar-store-inspired Muji 500 format sells home goods for less than 500 yen (about $3.30).

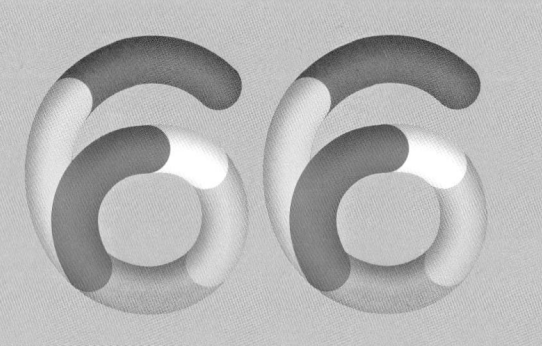

Consumers are looking for frugal life hacks to make their budgets stretch.

UK supermarket Sainsbury's is taking a different approach by educating its shoppers and nudging them towards more frugal behavior. Its Recipe Scrapbook website shows how to make family meals for less than £5 (about $6), while its Sainsfreeze pop-up in London hosted tutorials about how surplus fresh ingredients can be frozen and used later, helping customers to get the most out of each purchase. Value supermarket Iceland is also taking on an advisory role via its Shop Smart Cook Savvy partnership with energy supplier Utilita, which includes in-store and on-pack instructions about the most energy-efficient and cost-effective way to cook its food.

WHY IT'S INTERESTING

As the cost-of-living crisis intensifies, consumers are looking for frugal life hacks to make their budgets stretch. Brands can play a key role here to show their community values and drive long-term loyalty.

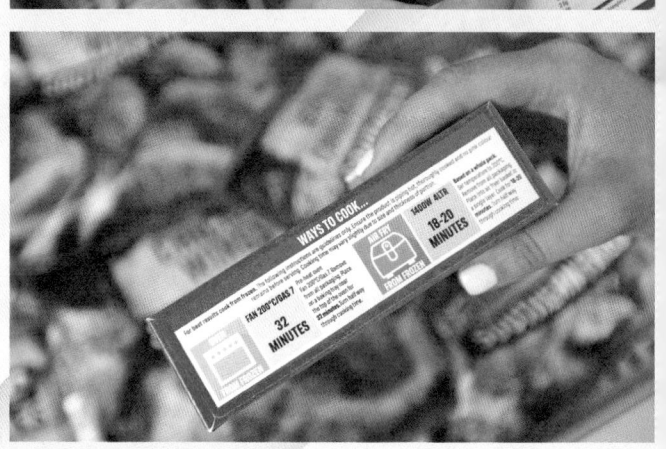

67

WEB3 MARKETPLACES

Newly minted marketplaces are transforming ecommerce.

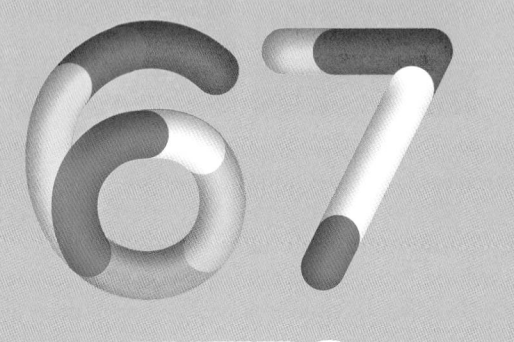

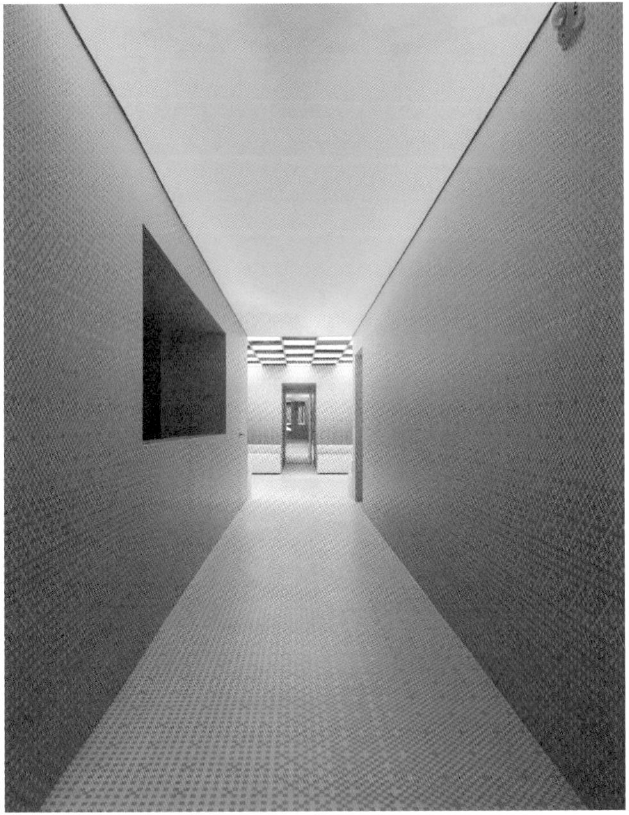

WUNDERMAN THOMPSON Zero10

Consumer shopping habits are changing, and new platforms for digital retail and commerce are meeting a need for more immersive and engaging purchasing experiences.

Draup, an upcoming digital fashion platform, is building out a marketplace where digital fashion can be sold, bought, traded, and showcased. Draup will be a place where "digital fashion can be curated, displayed, and ported into off-platform virtual environments," wrote Daniella Loftus, founder and chief executive officer of Draup, in a paper published in January 2022. With $1.5 million in seed funding, Draup aims to "curate a community of digitally native creators and consumers, providing them with the access and education they need to maximize the value they get from digital fashion."

In New York City's SoHo neighborhood, Zero10, in collaboration with the Crosby Studios creative practice, is bringing digital fashion to the popular shopping district. Zero10

is an augmented reality (AR) retail pop-up that customers can visit and try on virtual clothing in a physical, store-like setting.

George Yashin, CEO and cofounder of Zero10, tells Wunderman Thompson Intelligence that with "a wider adoption of AR technology by the fashion industry, it will become more sustainable and more interactive. Getting back to offline stores, shoppers—including gen-Z customers—are looking for a new immersive experience that AR provides." By incorporating an AR mirror or AR try-on apps like the one Zero10 has created, Yashin predicts that retailers will be able to "sell items that are not stocked in store, but available for preorder. Instead of producing more clothing, people can try its virtual prototypes through augmented reality."

WHY IT'S INTERESTING

These activations offer a first glance into the future of Web3 shopping.

SHARIA FINTECH

Fintech apps are transforming
Islamic banking.

A wave of sharia-compliant fintech apps are coming on the market, with founders who left the conventional banking world and are bringing their financial and tech expertise together with religious beliefs.

The main difference between *sharia*-compliant and conventional finance is that *sharia* shuns the concept of *riba* (interest), which is *haram* (forbidden) in Islam, and instead uses a profit-sharing model. Speculation and gambling are also forbidden.

Globally, Islamic financial assets stood at $3.6 trillion in 2021, up 7.8% from a year earlier, according to DinarStandard, a New York-based research consultancy.

In Southeast Asia, the biggest ecommerce firms are exploring *sharia*-compliant financial products: Indonesia's GoPay, which is part of ride-hailing and ecommerce giant GoTo, has partnered with the Indonesian Mosque Council to enable digital donations, including *zakat* compulsory alms, across thousands of mosques. Bukalapak, another top ecommerce firm, offers a *sharia*-compliant investment app called BMoney in partnership with PT Ashmore Asset Management, with investments starting at amounts as low as 1,000 rupiah (around 60 cents).

There's also Alami, which has provided peer-to-peer business financing for small and medium-sized businesses since 2018. Its cofounder and CEO is Dima Djani, formerly of Citi and Société Générale in Jakarta.

As of August 2022, Alami had amassed 95,000 users on its

platform—which includes an app, a website, and live chat—and distributed over 3 trillion rupiah ($201 million) with zero non-performing or bad loans. Business grew even in the pandemic. In 2021, it acquired BPRS Cempaka Al-Amin, which it relaunched in 2022 as Hijra Bank, a digital *sharia* banking app.

"Whatever your profession, if your intention is *ibadah* (a form of worship), *insya Allah* (God willing), there will be a good pathway for you until *akhirat* (the afterlife)," Dima, Alami's CEO, tells Wunderman Thompson Intelligence. "For all Muslims, all activities that you do must be done within the corridors of *sharia*."

WHY IT'S INTERESTING

Governments in Muslim majority countries are actively encouraging a robust *sharia* financial sector as an economic driver and export sector. *Sharia* fintech is the latest iteration of that wave.

Globally, Islamic financial assets stood at $3.6 trillion in 2021, up 7.8% from a year earlier.

69
DIGITAL NESTING

Mass retailers are helping avatars design their virtual homes.

west elm

Lifestyle design retailers are tapping into gaming with a new avenue for Web3 commerce.

Robin Games, a mobile gaming startup, is adding Playhouse, an interior design-focused game, to its "lifestyle gaming" offering. Playhouse combines gaming with shopping. Consumers can add and drop furniture and décor to digital interiors to create their own spaces and room designs, adding sofas, wall art, plants, and tables, and resizing and layering items as they wish.

People are nesting in their digital spaces, making cozy and comfortable homes in the metaverse.

While other games, including CrowdStar's Design Home and Playtika's Redecor, have similar capabilities, Playhouse is taking lifestyle gaming into the future by teaming up with physical design and furniture brands, to make purchasing products for players' physical homes possible direct from the app. Partnering with brands including Article, Lulu & Georgia, Jenni Kayne, and Society6, the game makes its creative outlet a reality to consumers, who can further redesign their homes and physical spaces with the touch of a button.

West Elm Home Design is the furniture brand's first metaverse experience, introduced on Roblox in October 2022. Users can customize their homes with over 150 digital replicas of physical products by the brand, visit the virtual store and coffee shop in the West Elm Hub, and collect wearable West Elm accessories for their avatars.

WHY IT'S INTERESTING

People are nesting in their digital spaces, making cozy and comfortable homes in the metaverse.

MENDING GOES MAINSTREAM

High-street brands are bringing repairs to the mass market via fresh in-store options.

Inflationary pressures added to eco-aspirations are driving a resurgence of the make-do-and-mend mentality. Retail repair services, once the preserve of luxury brands, are proliferating on the high street.

Uniqlo recently expanded its repair service at its London Regent Street store after struggling to keep up with customer demand for patches, piping, and embroidery as well as basic repairs. The Japanese retailer plans to roll out the service across Europe, adding to existing services in Berlin and New York.

H&M is also an advocate of mending. The global fast-fashion giant's Kalverstraat store in Amsterdam hosts a Repair & Remake workshop that will revamp items from H&M or other brands.

Nike is taking a high-tech approach. In its London store in late 2022, the brand piloted its Bot Initiated Longevity Lab, known as BILL, a "robot-augmented system" that can repair and clean customers' sneakers. The in-store robot identifies areas of wear and tear during a 3D scan, which can then be repaired with a patch of the shopper's choice.

In December, Apple rolled out its self-repair service in Europe. The service, which first launched in the United States earlier in 2022, gives iPhone 12 and 13 and some MacBook owners access to repair manuals plus more than 200 individual parts and tools to fix their own devices.

While consumers were already making efforts to curb consumption (see Anti-excess consumerism in our "Future 100: 2020" report),

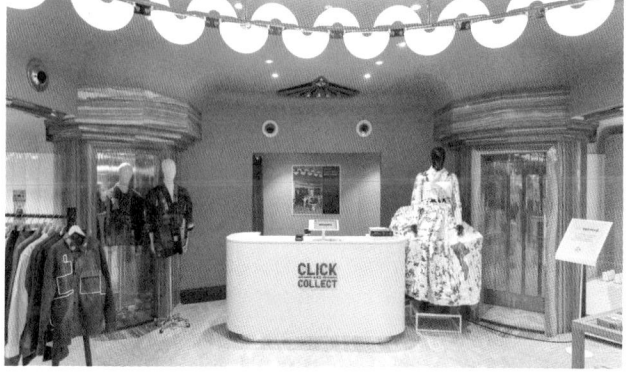

the cost-of-living crisis is adding further impetus. July 2022 research from Penneys (Primark's brand in Ireland) finds that 62% are motivated to repair items by saving money, rising to 95% among generation Z.

Madeline Michell, social conscience communications officer at British retailer Toast, which has offered a mending service since 2018, tells Wunderman Thompson Intelligence: "It may seem counterintuitive to be advocating for our customers to stop spending and start mending. Our hope is to reshape buying habits, advocate for quality and longevity, and shift the thinking of those who value novelty above durability."

WHY IT'S INTERESTING

Repair services are no longer just for luxury brands. The make-do-and-mend approach is becoming the smart and conscious choice for everyday consumers under pressure to save money and the planet.

Above: Uniqlo
Right: Apple

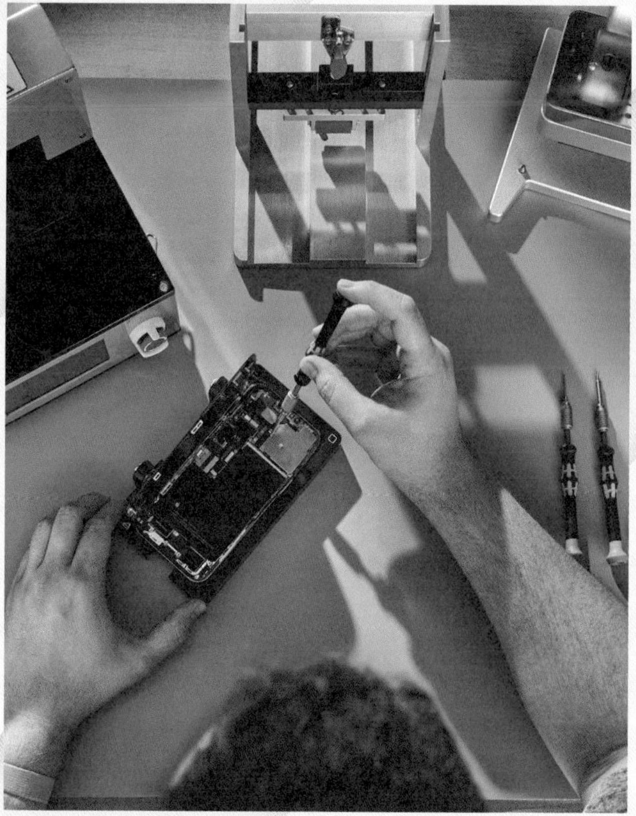

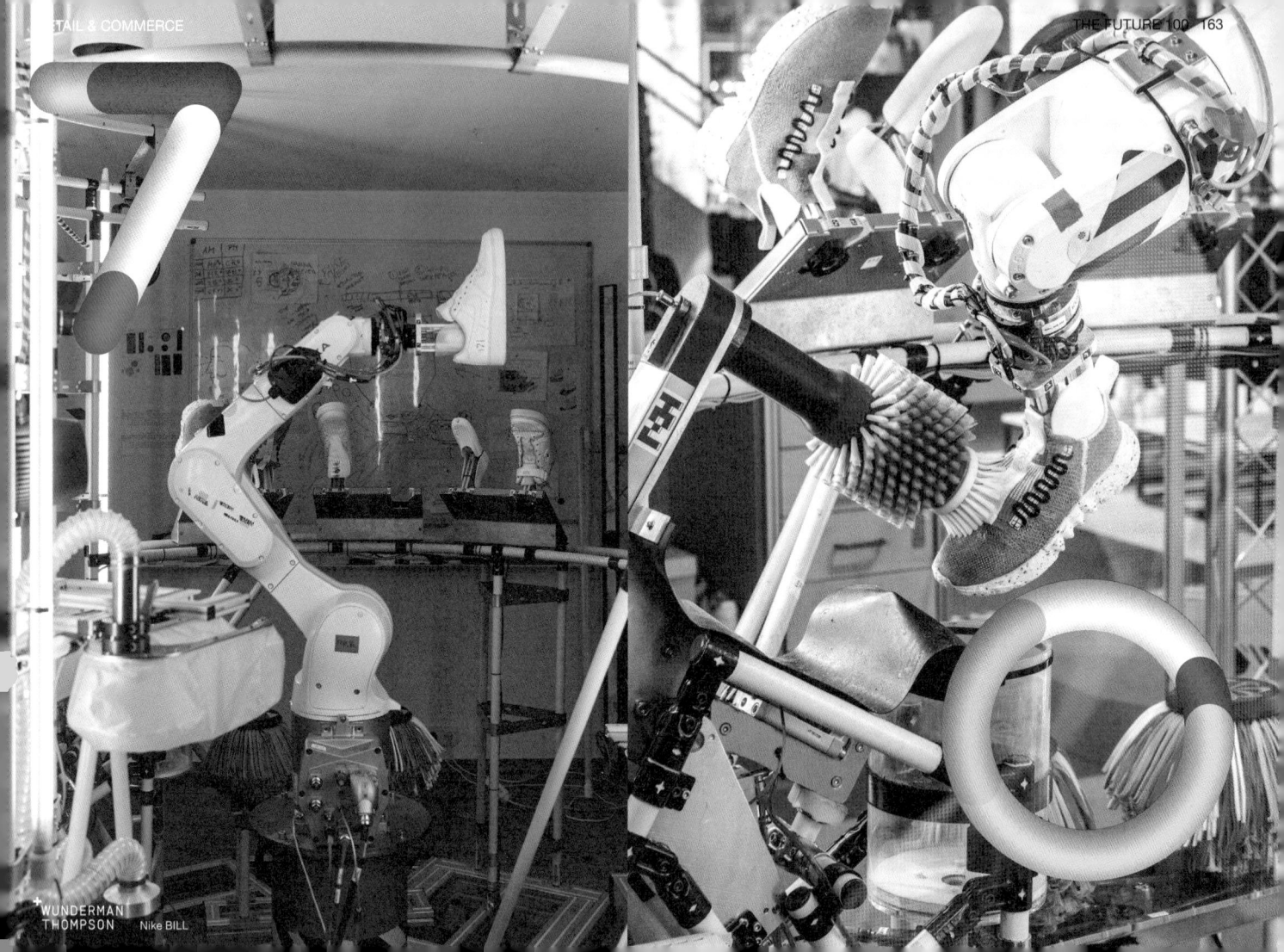

71

LUXURY

80

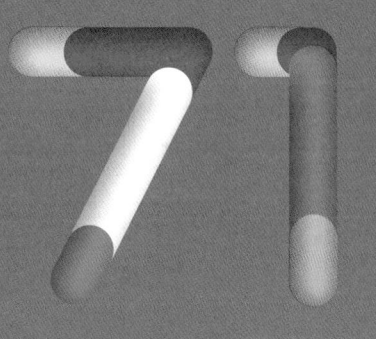

71
CRYPTO CLUBS

What does a members-only social club look like in the age of decentralization?

Friends With Benefits (FWB) has been called a "decentralized Soho House" and a "VIP lounge for crypto's creative class." An informal Discord chat room turned exclusive digital members' club, its valuation reached $100 million in 2022. Admittance requires a minimum buy-in of $FWB tokens, the club's proprietary cryptocurrency, which unlocks access to exclusive benefits and services. Members with at least one $FWB token can read the group's newsletter and blog posts, the New York Times reported. Those with at least five tokens have limited access to FWB chat rooms on Discord and entry to offline events. Global membership costs 75 $FBW tokens (around $4,000 as of November 2022) and grants access to all Discord chat rooms.

For crypto investors with a case of wanderlust, the Lucky Ape Travel Club's travel-inspired NFT collection offers a range of benefits to each buyer: a room key at an exclusive resort, an access pass to an invite-only event, or a ticket to an exotic destination. Essentially, the club turns NFTs into virtual tickets for physical travel perks, and ownership of any of the NFT collectibles provides a free stay at participating clubs. Ownership unlocks access to a luxurious, members-based community centered around a passion for travel and cultural exploration.

High-end brands are courting a new class of cryptoluxe consumers by introducing crypto payment options for shoppers. Gucci announced in May 2022 that it would accept crypto payments for goods at North American stores. That year Equinox also began accepting cryptocurrencies as membership payments for any of its New York City flagship locations. The luxury gym reportedly has plans to expand crypto payments to other locations in the future.

WHY IT'S INTERESTING
According to Morgan Stanley, the metaverse is a $50 billion revenue opportunity for the luxury market. Members clubs are being virtualized to serve a rising crypto elite.

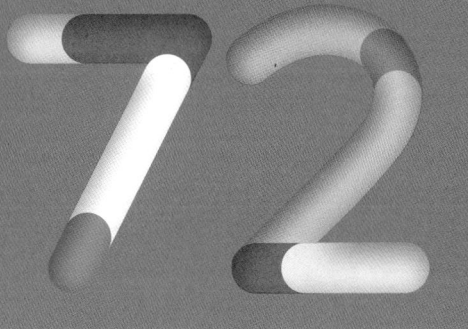

72

SUPER-RARE PALATES

Rarity is its own form of luxury.

From Amazon-foraged ants to hand-harvested wild rice to 15-year-matured champagne, businesses are standing out with hard-to-find ingredients and infusions.

The celebrated Minneapolis restaurant Owamni by The Sioux Chef is known for its "decolonized" menu, which eschews any ingredients brought by European colonizers from wheat flour to dairy, as well as modern-day farm animals like chickens and pigs. It was named Best New Restaurant in the US by the James Beard Foundation in 2022. Owamni serves Native American food such as blue corn, elk, and bison and also the rare hand-harvested wild rice called manoomin. Manoomin only grows around the Great Lakes and is linked to the origin story of the Ojibwe people, who moved inland from the East Coast centuries ago, to find "the food that grows in water,"

according to a *New Yorker* profile of the restaurant. Manoomin harvesters still use the age-old method of traveling by canoe to knock the grains from the heads of the rice stalks, which grow on the edges of lakes.

In Baltimore, rare ingredients foraged from the Amazon are a bar highlight at Alma Cocina Latina, a restaurant run by a Venezuelan native. Ingredients such as lemon ants add a citrusy flavor to cocktails, while murupí peppers give heat when infused in rum. Alma Cocina Latina sources its ingredients from an organization that works to preserve ancestral ingredients and cuisines by building a profitable business for communities who produce them, while offering an alternative livelihood to illegal mining, *Forbes* reported.

While Owammi and Alma Cocina Latina are driven in part by issues of social justice and identity, others are simply looking for rarity as a pairing to luxury. Emirates, the Dubai-headquartered airline, offered a super-rare champagne—Dom Pérignon Plénitude 2—to its first-class travelers for a period in autumn 2022. Plénitude 2 is cellar-matured for 15 years and boasts lime and toasty mineral flavors, finishing with hints of dried apricots, apples, candied raspberry and fig. "Its vibrant yet generous palate, powerful and precise with great energy, leads to a persistent, spicy, and saline finish," the airline said.

WHY IT'S INTERESTING

Some businesses are holding their own—and in some cases supporting small local producers at the same time—by infusing rare ingredients into their offerings.

Rare ingredients foraged from the Amazon are a bar highlight at Alma Cocina Latina.

73
ELITE SLEEP

Upscale brands across categories are turning good sleep into the latest luxury.

Luxury brands are waking up to the potential of the sleep economy, introducing a wealth of new products and services.

Gucci partnered with the Finnish health tech company Oura to launch a sleep tracker ring in May 2022. The tracker, which retails at $950, is crafted from black synthetic corundum and embellished with 18-carat gold—and is an interesting first move for Gucci into the sleep space.

Retail and slumber collided in summer 2022 as luxury retailer Selfridges introduced its Sex & Sleep pop-up. Shoppers keen to optimize their sleeping habits could explore a range of sleep-inducing herbal blends, essential oils, and supplements. Alongside the pop-up, sleep sessions were hosted at Selfridges' in-house cinema. Customers were invited to take a power nap before hitting the shop floor again with renewed vitality.

Luxury travel brands are getting in on the act by helping their guests establish sleep habits that persist beyond their stay. Rosewood Hotels & Resorts introduced Alchemy of Sleep in January 2022, tapping into the rise of sleep tourism. Guests can enjoy a one-night Dreamscape or an immersive five-night Sleep Transformation. These breaks offer an opportunity for guests to immerse themselves in meditation and restful treatments that they can continue to implement at home.

WHY IT'S INTERESTING

"The pandemic has accelerated society's focus on prioritizing health," Oura tells Wunderman Thompson Intelligence. As we predicted at the onset of the COVID-19 pandemic, every business is now a health business. Upscale brands are looking to build out their wellness credentials for high-end consumers who see sleep as the latest luxury investment.

74

INTERGALACTIC LUXE

Luxury brands are espousing a spirit of adventure and wonder, flaunting playful mysticism in the face of pragmatism.

Burberry is venturing into the unknown with its "Night Creatures" campaign, launched in October 2022, and described as celebrating the "power of curiosity and exploration of the unknown." The campaign follows three protagonists as they encounter an otherworldly sci-fi creature. The video, which was created in collaboration with creative collective Megaforce, is reminiscent of a fairy tale, and straddles the known and the imaginary. "We wanted to express the bold attitude that it takes to dive into the unknown: the fearless and playful spirit of adventure," Megaforce said.

Gucci is also exploring the unknown. It first presented its Cosmogonie show—a "galactical" collection of looks—in May 2022. The show was inspired by "mystical encounters and mythological places," the brand said, and was hosted at what Gucci director Alessandro Michele called a "stargate between earth and sky."

The show was inspired by the "metaphor of constellations," which Michele describes as "previously unknown configurations of reality that can break the constraints of tradition." The show aimed to "draw conjunctions between fragments of worlds which would otherwise be dispersed," Michele said. "I was looking for a magical and mythical place, where I could lose myself."

WHY IT'S INTERESTING

Luxury brands are pushing the boundaries of reality, looking to the magical and mystical for inspiration. After two years of prioritizing pragmatism and taking a subdued, serious tone, luxury brands are reflecting a cultural desire for exploration and wonder. "Fashion speaks," Michele told *WWD*. "It's not a hieroglyph for an elite; it talks about life. It's a mirror."

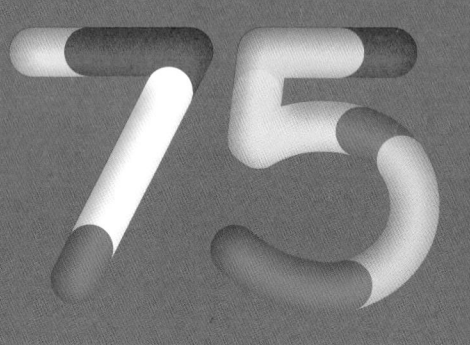

75
NEW LUXURY PLAYS

The luxury retail model is undergoing a seismic shift.

In August 2022, online luxury marketplace Farfetch struck a groundbreaking deal to build a luxury ecommerce giant by buying a big stake in its competitor, Yoox Net-a-Porter. The deal, which is expected to close by the end of 2023, points to a future of consolidation in the luxury ecommerce space. It is a step toward "building an independent, neutral online platform for the luxury industry," says Johann Rupert, chairman of Yoox Net-a-Porter owner Richemont.

A few months prior, in April 2022, Farfetch and Neiman Marcus Group (NMG)—the largest omnichannel luxury retailer in the United States, which houses luxury mainstays Neiman Marcus and Bergdorf Goodman—announced a strategic partnership "to revolutionize integrated luxury retail." José Neves, Farfetch founder, chairman, and CEO, explained the move: "This partnership is about revolutionizing the luxury landscape globally, both online and offline, by combining NMG's iconic presence in the US and Farfetch's luxury new retail vision and technology." As part of the partnership, NMG will gain access to Farfetch's ecommerce and tech toolbox, which it will use to revamp the Bergdorf Goodman website and mobile app.

The pandemic drove a rise in virtualized shopping. According to the US Census Bureau's 2022 report, ecommerce sales increased by a substantial 43% in 2020. This shift, combined with the rising competition luxury retailers face from third-party ecommerce sites like Amazon—which entered a partnership with secondhand retailer What Goes Around Comes Around in October 2022 to sell pre-owned items from many of the luxury brands that decline to sell directly on Amazon—has luxury brands rethinking their strategies.

"I believe the US luxury market is at a pivotal point," said Neves. "While the US is proving to be a long-lasting source of growth for the luxury industry, fueled by younger generations who are highly engaged with the category, businesses will have to significantly upgrade their digital capabilities—powering both online and offline customer journeys—to meet these new customer expectations and stay ahead in what is going to be a competitive space in the coming years."

WHY IT'S INTERESTING

Following the Death of the luxury department store (68 in "The Future 100: 2020") and Department stores reformatted (66 in "The Future 100: 2022"), luxury big-box retailers are pooling their resources to explore new avenues. Expect to see more fluidity and cobranded plays among luxury retailers as brands make their way into the next era of retail.

WUNDERMAN
THOMPSON

"The US luxury market is at a pivotal point."

José Neves, founder, chairman, and CEO, Farfetch

76

WELLNESS GUILDS

The newest gathering space is part high-end gym, part social club.

WUNDERMAN THOMPSON Remedy Place

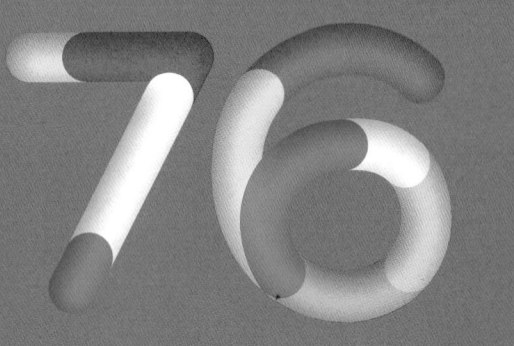

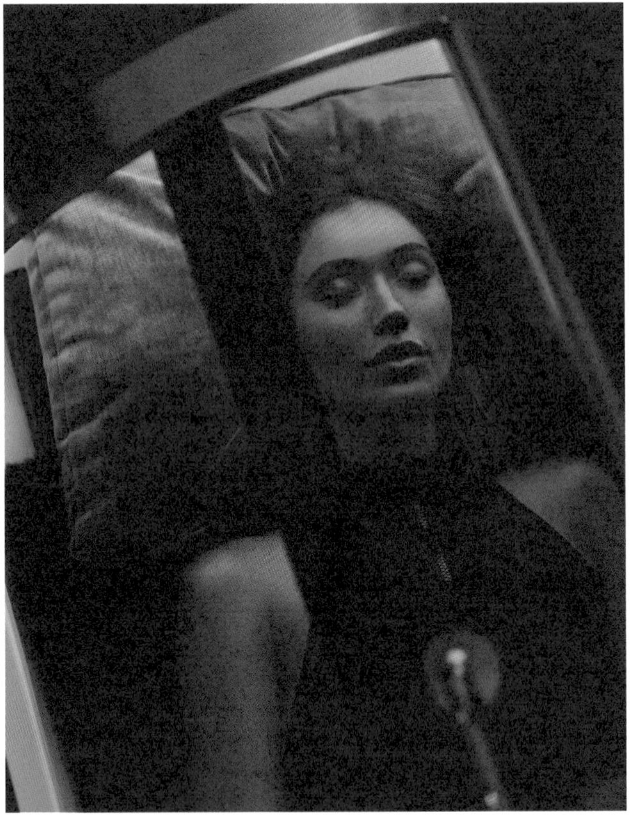

Dedicated spaces for social, mental, and physical wellbeing are opening to meet a growing consumer desire for wellness-centered community and holistic health practices.

A self-described "social wellness club," Remedy Place opened in New York City in September 2022 as a new, sober, and health-centered concept for socialization. Remedy Place is "a club that is temptation and toxin-free, that enhances health and social life at the same time," founder Dr Jonathan Leary told *Vogue*. "It needed not just to be self-care, but social self-care." The club offers ice baths and breath work, guided classes and saunas, acupuncture, vitamin IV suites, and more.

In Los Angeles, Heimat offers a new space designed for an indulgent social atmosphere. The private fitness and lifestyle club offers members a rooftop pool, a bootcamp studio, a Michelin-starred restaurant, and a spa, in addition to its gym and fitness classes. Heimat provides an intimate, luxurious setting where its wellness community can connect, relax, and rejuvenate.

Soho House, the OG social club, deepened its wellness offering in September 2022 with the launch of its vegan, cruelty-free Soho Skin skincare line. Made with science-backed ingredients for top-of-the-line beauty treatments, the products are free for guests at select Soho Houses and can be purchased at Bloomingdale's in New York City.

WHY IT'S INTERESTING

Consumers are making self-care social. "The most important part of self-care is human connection," Dr Leary told *Vogue*. "People need authentic relationships."

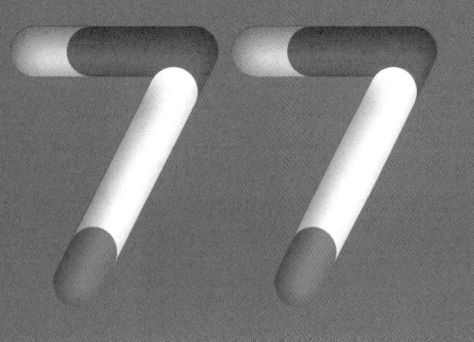

COMFORT FIRST CLASS

First-class menus are serving up lashings of feel-good food.

During the pandemic, many turned to comfort food, drawing on family recipes, and on food shows and blogs that took them back to a time of stability. As planes take to the skies again, some airlines are revamping first-class menus in the same way, introducing feel-good cuisine that invokes a sense of home.

In August 2022, Delta began serving Southern comfort food developed with chef Mashama Bailey, James Beard's 2022 Outstanding American Chef, in its premium seats. The first-class menu draws from Bailey's restaurant The Grey, located in Savannah, Georgia, and includes dishes such as a flounder

"It's for those who want something that's feel-good."

Mashama Bailey, chef

and oyster creation with fumé blanc, green apple, potato, bok choy and turnips; short ribs with kanni sauce and smoked collard greens; and vegan vegetable tagine with roasted sweet potato topped with chermoula sauce. For dessert, there's buttermilk cornmeal tres leches with candied kumquats and mandarin oranges.

"We have a few things that are going to resonate with people who are away from home," Bailey told *Food & Wine*. "It's for those who want something that's feel-good."

In premium cabins on international flights, Delta is also letting passengers build their own sundaes, with toppings such as Morello cherry compote, chocolate sauce, and cookie crumbles.

On Singapore Airlines, which recruited California's Golden Door wellness retreat to jazz up its in-flight menu, the luxury spa's executive chef Greg Frey Jr has developed a portobello mushroom "meat ball" that's served with risotto in vegetable broth—serving up comfort without heaviness. "It's so satisfying and you get all those umami flavors," Frey told CNBC. "The best part is, an hour later, you're not going: 'Ugh, I wish I didn't have the meatballs'."

WHY IT'S INTERESTING
As people start flying again, airlines are drawing on comfort, including on the menu, to lure clients into the premium seats with the biggest margins.

78

HYPER-PRIVATE LUXURY

Luxury brands are taking exclusivity to the next level with inner-sanctum access for their top customers.

Nobu Ryokan Malibu

Chanel plans to open private boutiques in Asia in 2023 to cater to its most important customers. The Paris-based luxury brand generated revenue of nearly $16 billion in 2021, up almost 50% from 2020, and close to half of that came from Asia Pacific.

The move, which sparked a social media debate over whether the brand had taken its snob factor too far, appears in line with recent moves to raise the price of handbags and limit the number of items each shopper can buy of the most coveted designs.

In the same vein, Dior invited top customers to spa cruises down the Seine in Paris in June and July 2022, overlapping fashion show season. The French fashion house already has two permanent spas in Paris, one at Hôtel Plaza Athénée and another at the Cheval Blanc. Customers could book a two-hour slot aboard the boat, including an hour's treatment, with the rest of the time devoted to enjoying river views. The idea was

inspired by the historic Bains de la Samaritaine, 19th-century floating baths along the Pont-Neuf on the edge of the Seine.

Nobu Hotels was founded by the Japanese chef Nobu Matsuhisa, with Hollywood actor Robert De Niro and film producer Meir Teper, drawing inspiration from traditional Japanese inns known as ryokan. Nobu Hotels launched a Ryokan Retreat package in 2022 in partnership with Schubach Aviation that includes private jet transportation between its California properties Nobu Ryokan Malibu and Nobu Hotel Palo Alto. The package includes two nights at each property and an omakase dinner for two.

WHY IT'S INTERESTING

Luxury brands have always drawn some of their cachet from exclusivity. Now some luxury brands are ratcheting up that cachet with experiences that literally limit the number of people who can enjoy them.

79

REMOTE FINE DINING

Far-flung, intimate haute cuisine is enticing food aficionados to travel to the ends of the world.

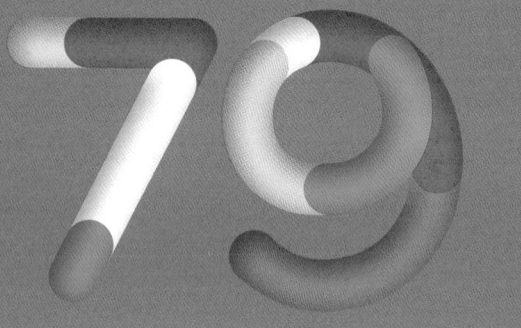

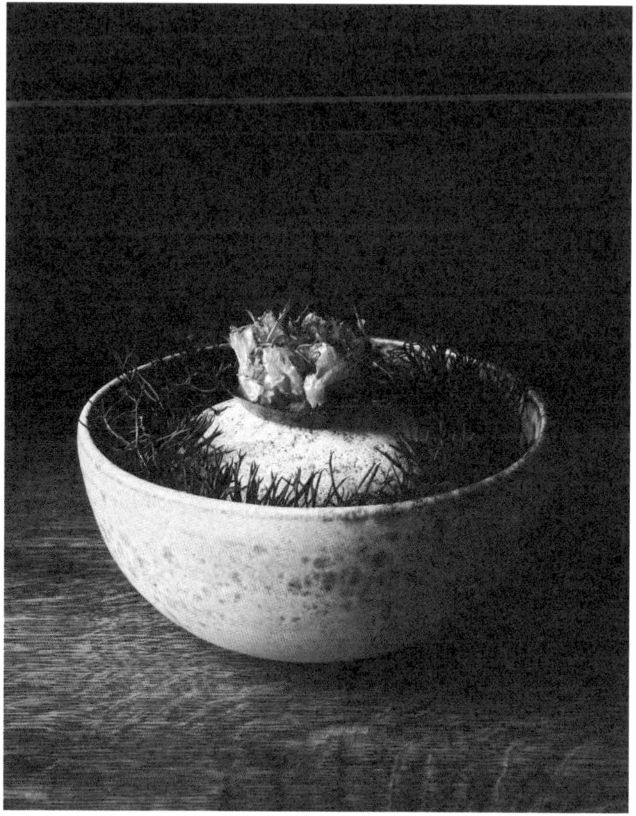

Koks, Ilimanaq, Greenland

Adventures for the palate start with the journey to the restaurant—getting there is part of the experience. Michelin-starred restaurant Koks relocated temporarily from its already remote Faroe Island location to Ilimanaq, a small village within Greenland's Arctic Circle, for summer 2022 and 2023. Feasting on the two-star menu requires an hour-long boat ride from the nearest town, Ilulissat. A September 2022 article by BBC reporter Adrienne Murray Nielsen likens the trip to "an odyssey" involving a boat ride that weaves through towers of icebergs, and describes the experience as "an epic food journey." The restaurant will return to the Faroe Islands in 2024 at a new home which is currently being built.

On the northwestern coast of Norway, spectacularly located among fjords, is fine-dining restaurant Kvitnes Gård, which opened at the end of 2021. The restaurant is reached via boat from nearby towns. All guests are required to stay the night for what the restaurant describes as "an experience—not a meal."

WHY IT'S INTERESTING

Fine-dining restaurants are not only elevating the menu but also framing the expedition to the restaurant as part of the wider experience. As luxury consumers seek out niche, limited, and unique experiences, expect more restaurants to pop up in less accessible parts of the world.

WUNDERMAN
THOMPSON   Koks, Ilimanaq, Greenland

80
RESIDENCE AT SEA

The next-gen digital nomad is taking to the sea—in style.

Cruise ship startup Storylines has announced its debut luxury residential cruise ship concept. Scheduled to set sail in 2025, the 18-deck MV Narrative will carry 1,000 residents around the world within its 547 condominiums, on an indefinite voyage that could last a lifetime. The ship offers 11 semi-customizable floorplans, several of which have already sold out, according to *Insider*, and interested buyers have various options: a 237-square-foot studio is selling for $1 million, and for $8 million, homebuyers can choose a 1,970-square-foot four-bedroom, two-floor home.

Each unit is fitted with storage units, closets, mounted TVs, a kitchen, and a bathroom. Residents who work remotely will also be able to lease private offices. The all-inclusive costs of these homes at sea will cover food, medical services, access to a pool and a marina, a wellness facility, and even a bowling alley. And, of course, access to international destinations every time the boat docks in countries such as Turkey, Greece, Italy, Montenegro, and more.

In October 2022, Ritz-Carlton launched a luxury yacht cruise costing a minimum of around $6,000 per week, hosted by its five-star hotel chain Evrima. The cruise treats guests to Michelin-star chefs, four pools, a champagne bar, a humidor room, a nightclub, and a spa on their voyage from Barcelona, Spain, to Nice in France.

WHY IT'S INTERESTING
Consumers taking up residence at sea are buying into an upscale evolution of nomadic lifestyles.

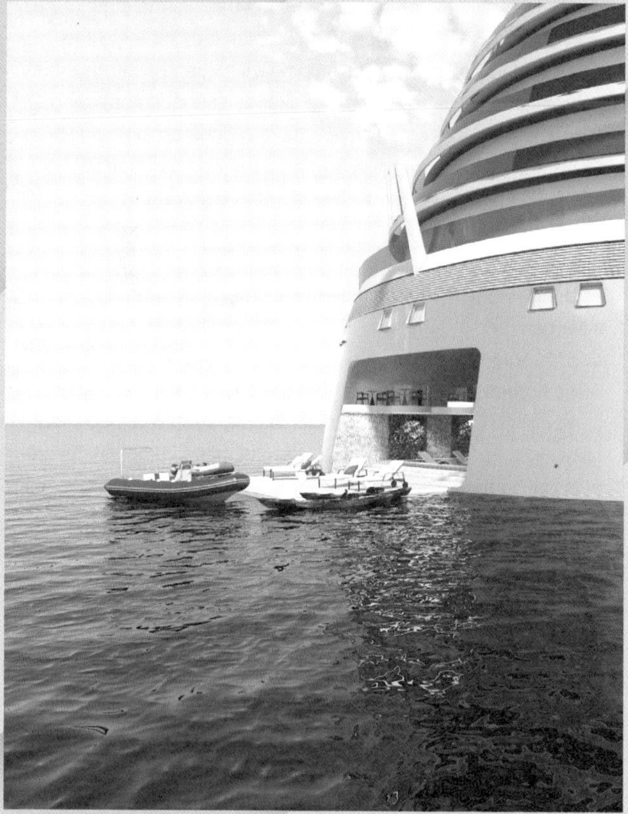

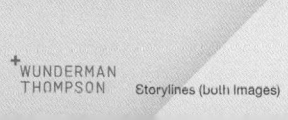

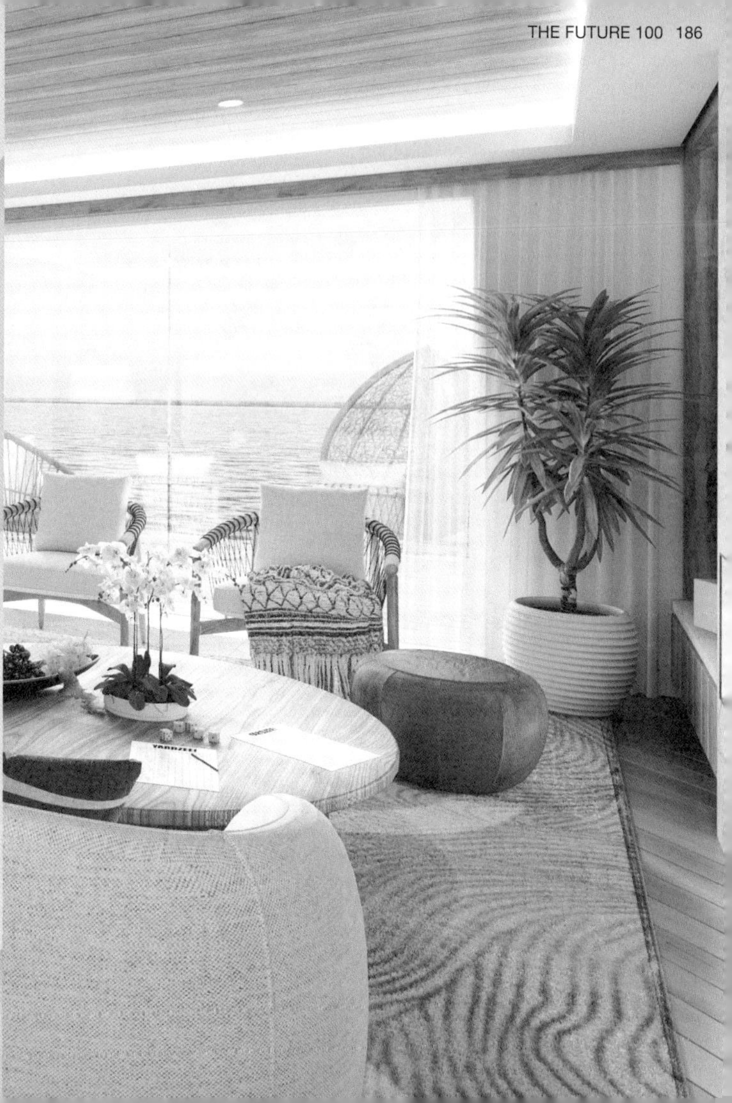

Storylines (both images)

HEALTH

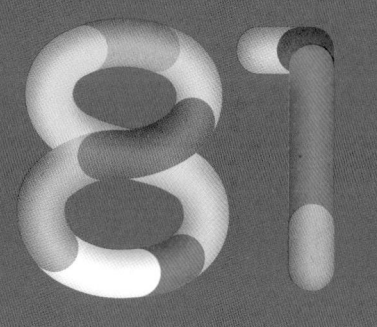

THE SUPERSELF

Self-care gets supercharged.

The way people are thinking about their health and wellbeing is evolving. "Coming out of the pandemic, people realize having this balance of life and appreciating physical and mental health is not something we should leave as a part-time pursuit," Gareth Roberts, the director of brand and operations support for Peninsula hotel group—which has observed a rise in wellness travel (see 84, Hospital-ity, page 188)—told the *Wall Street Journal*. Rather, health and wellbeing are becoming central considerations.

Selfridges is encouraging consumers to expand how they think about self-care and wellbeing. The retailer is repositioning itself as a provider of "feel-goodness," asking people to consider what it means to "live your best life." The activation, which was part of the brand's Superfutures theme for 2022, spans products, services, and content—from curated product selections to relaxing "sensory experiences" to podcasts and articles. It even includes what the brand calls a "new kind of retail therapy," connecting shoppers with confidence coaches, breathwork specialists, and sex therapists. "We're bringing to the fore the myriad ways Selfridges can help you become your Superself—through fitness, sustainability, beauty, food, creativity, and more," says Emma Kidd, the store's acting creative director.

WHY IT'S INTERESTING
The growing focus on emotional health that we tracked in "The Future 100: 2022" is expanding even more into an all-encompassing wellness lens. Caring for oneself now includes caring for physical health, mental health, and even environmental health—which, taken together, contribute to a new view of the Superself.

HOW TO DISCOVER YOUR SUPERSELF:

SUPERCHARGE FROM WITHIN

BIOHACKING TREATMENTS
BY DR VALI, COMING SOON

82

PSYCHOBIOTICS

Is gut health the latest path to mental wellbeing?

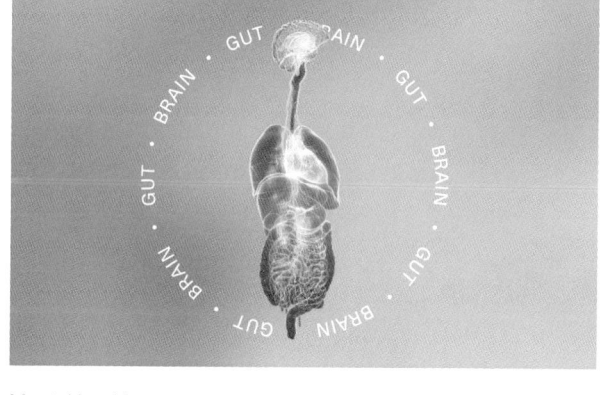

Mental health experts are harnessing the power of psychobiotics: probiotics that can yield specific benefits to the nervous system.

The award-winning probiotic and prebiotic supplement brand Seed Health launched a gut-brain development program with Axial Therapeutics in July 2022. Using research from the California Institute of Technology, the brand will link microbiome gut health to potential alleviation of anxiety, stress, and depression. Caltech was the first lab to uncover the relationship between intestinal microbes and neuropsychiatric conditions, and its research will be used to better understand and formulate potential microbiome treatments for mental and emotional health benefits.

Consumers are latching onto gut-mind benefits in their quest for emotional wellness. According to Research and Markets,

the global probiotics market grew from $39 billion in 2016 to $58 billion in 2021. Increasingly, supplements are marketed as boosting cognitive function, mood, and mental energy.

In August 2022, Bened Life, a US-based biomedical company, launched Neuralli, its first probiotic for brain health, formulated using its patented psychobiotic PS128. The company claims it can "help balance serotonin, dopamine, cortisol, and other molecules that affect mood, mind, and movement, while also helping regulate gastrointestinal tract health."

Cassandra Arendt, director of science communication at Bened Life, tells Wunderman Thompson Intelligence that Bened continues to see "an exponential increase in studies of the gut-brain axis in the scientific literature. This interest is now trickling down to the wider public." She also notes that as more "people are struggling with mental health issues, safer [treatments] with fewer side effects will always be in demand, and psychobiotics may meet that need for some people."

Also in August 2022, Thailand and Canada approved the registration of PS128, which claims to have "potential neurological and mental health benefits, such as improving sleep and reducing symptoms like those seen in anxiety, depression, autism, and Parkinson's disease."

WHY IT'S INTERESTING

As consumers look to improve their holistic health physically and emotionally, brands are leaning into the benefits gut health can have on mental wellbeing.

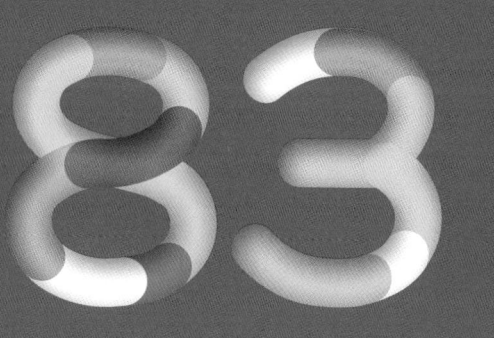

83
JOY WORKOUTS

Exercise designed for emotional uplift is helping people spark joy.

According to the World Health Organization, the pandemic triggered a 25% increase in anxiety and depression worldwide. As consumers embrace physical activity for its emotional benefits, fitness brands are rethinking their offerings to cater to emotional health.

Psychologist Kelly McGonigal unpacked the "joy workout" in a feature for the *New York Times*. The exercises—bounce, reach, sway, shake, jump for joy, and a move McGonigal calls "celebrate," which mimics tossing confetti—are selected from studies on movements that elicit positive emotions. "The Joy Workout is just one way to lift your spirits through movement," she wrote, noting that there are also plenty of other "science-backed ways to improve your mood with exercise."

Fitbit can now help wearers track and manage stress, linking physical and emotional health. The Sense 2, released in August 2022, features a new Body Response tracker that monitors heartbeat, skin temperature, and sweat levels. Whenever there's a shift in the wearer's temperature, for example, the Sense 2 flashes a notification to the wearer and prompts them to reflect on their mindset and situation.

The exercises—bounce, reach, sway, shake, jump for joy, and "celebrate," which mimics tossing confetti—are selected from studies on movements that elicit positive emotions.

"Fitness tracking reveals task-specific associations between memory, mental health, and physical activity," according to a study published by Dartmouth College researchers in August 2022. The report confirmed that, while effects on memory and mental health states vary depending on the physical exertion, "physical activity does provide a non-invasive means of manipulating cognitive performance and mental health." This could mean that "as strength training may be customized to target a specific muscle group, or to improve performance on a specific physical task, similar principles might also be applied to target specific improvements in cognitive fitness and mental health."

WHY IT'S INTERESTING

Fitness brands can aid consumers in their emotional and physical wellness simultaneously. Intent to feel good emotionally, not just physically, may indicate a change in the future of what we now call "fitness."

83

84

HOSPITAL-ITY

From IV drips to stem-cell therapies, the latest crop of wellness hotels merges healthcare and hospitality.

The global wellness tourism market is expected to exceed $1 trillion by 2030, growing at an annual rate of nearly 10% over the next eight years, according to a June 2022 report by Grand View Research. "The pandemic put a spotlight on our baseline health," Kane Sarhan, cofounder and chief creative officer of The Well, a health and wellness company based in Manhattan, told the *Wall Street Journal*.

Now luxury hotels are getting in on the growing market with new high-tech health services.

The Four Seasons Resort Maui at Wailea, Hawaii, recently partnered with Next Health, a Los Angeles-based preventive and diagnostic healthcare center. The new Next Health center offers Four Seasons guests a suite of health services including IV drips; an immune- and energy-boosting ozone treatment that fortifies the blood with oxygen; and stem-cell therapy, which goes for $12,000 per hour-long session. The new program also offers genetic biomarker testing. Guests can have their testing done in New York City or Los Angeles before taking off, and then meet with a Next Health provider once they've arrived in Hawaii to curate an itinerary based on their profile, which offers a hyper-personalized program for diet, activities, and health therapies.

In July 2022, medi-spa Lanserhof opened a new location in Germany that features high-end medical therapies like biorhythmic lighting in bedrooms; a dedicated on-site psychologist; and "mitochondrial training" CellGym sessions, which simulate oxygen deprivation. The medihotel also has MRI machines and CT scanners on site.

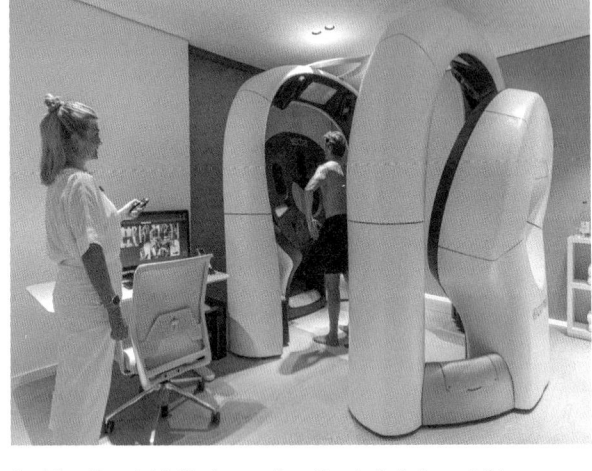

And the Ranch Malibu's new location in Italy has eight physicians on staff who conduct medical diagnostics for guests, including bloodwork.

"Wellness shouldn't be something you only address when you cross the threshold into the spa," Gareth Roberts, director of brand and operations support for the Peninsula hotel group, told the *Wall Street Journal*. "That outdated concept of 'Now you're in the world of wellness'? That's not authentic."

WHY IT'S INTERESTING

Health is an increasingly integral part of travel. The latest wellness retreats are bringing scientific therapies into the spa, for a new category of destination that's halfway between a hotel and a hospital—catering to travelers who prioritize health.

85
LYMPHATIC HEALTH

The newest focus for wellness is lymphatic.

Gua sha, a traditional Chinese medicine practice of scraping skin to encourage lymph flow, is being espoused by Western celebrities and showing up in luxury spas around the globe.

In gua sha, a tool is used to scrape lubricated skin to produce a light petechiae—sand-like red bruising indicating broken capillaries just under the skin. The goal is to promote the circulation of lymph, the colorless, watery liquid ferrying white blood cells to organs and carrying waste back, helping fight infections.

American actor and wellness guru Gwyneth Paltrow's Goop sells a heart-shaped rose quartz gua sha tool made by Kora Organics, a brand founded by supermodel Miranda Kerr. It comes with a diagram of the face showing how to scrape the tool in upward and outward strokes.

Equinox Hotel in New York's Hudson Yards, which promotes itself as a "temple to total regeneration," introduced lymphatic drainage treatments at its spa in August 2022. The Spa by Equinox partnered with Skin Science Solutions to introduce handheld lymphatic massage devices meant to drain, sculpt, and contour the body and face.

Lymphatic health is also increasingly on the repertoire of luxury spa treatments in Asia, alongside herbal scrubs and hot stone massages.

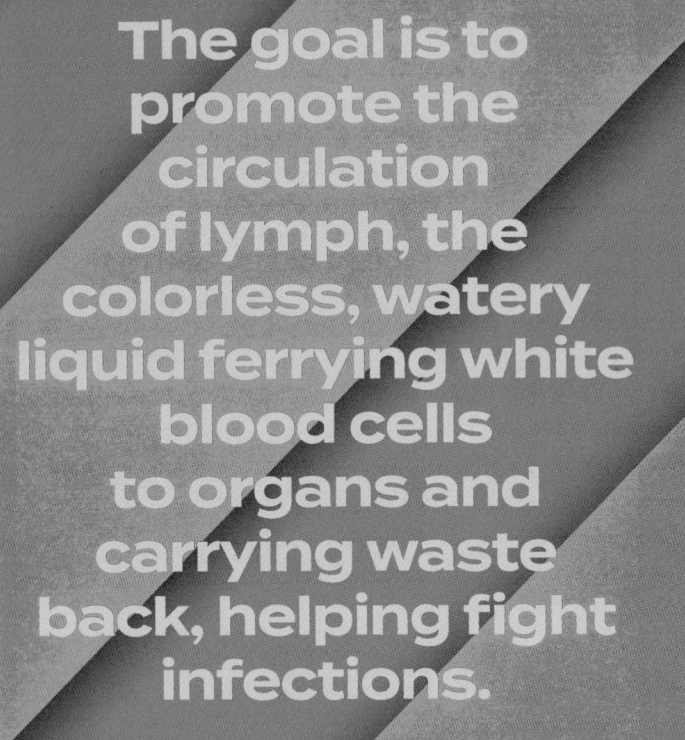

The goal is to promote the circulation of lymph, the colorless, watery liquid ferrying white blood cells to organs and carrying waste back, helping fight infections.

The Anantara Golden Triangle Elephant Camp and Resort in Chiang Rai, northern Thailand, offers a 60-minute gua sha facial treatment using plant extracts and traditional Thai ingredients as well as a 90-minute gua sha back detox massage in an open-air pavilion in a jungle setting.

The Como Shambhala Estate, a Singapore-owned luxury resort just outside Ubud in Bali, offers 60-minute and 75-minute manual lymphatic drainage sessions, described as a gentle massage aimed at carrying toxins and waste away from tissues.

WHY IT'S INTERESTING
Lymphatic health is the latest traditional Chinese medicine practice to be embraced by wellness brands, following acupuncture and reflexology, among others.

86

REVOLUTIONARY REST

A host of community influencers are advocating a slower approach to life.

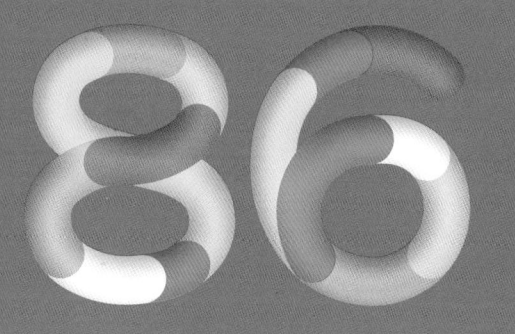

Tricia Hersey, the Nap Ministry © Charlie Watts and Tricia Hersey

A growing movement centers rest and recovery as a radical tool for marginalized communities to combat trauma, stress, and discrimination, promoting permission to take time for restoring selfcare.

The Nap Ministry is an organization that "examines the liberating power of naps," hosting collective napping and daydreaming events across the United States. Founder Tricia Hersey, aka the Nap Bishop, released *Rest as Resistance: A Manifesto* in October 2022. The book, like the organization, advocates rest as a form of self-care and a counter to grind culture; one that is vital for marginalized groups to sustain the fight against systemic issues.

Drawing upon similar inspiration, the Exhale wellness app launched in response to social unrest during the summer of 2020 to provide refuge for Black, Indigenous and Women of Color (BIWOC). The app, due to be relaunched in 2023, offers a safe space for guided meditations, affirmations, visualizations, and breathwork exercises that promote healing.

WUNDERMAN
THOMPSON   Exhale

> "To hear the simple and bold proclamation, 'You are doing too much. You can rest. You can just be. You can be,' is revolutionary."
>
> Tricia Hersey, founder, The Nap Ministry

The Mae House offers residential wellness stays to Black, Indigenous and People of Colour (BIPOC) families who might otherwise struggle to afford vacations, in a concept dubbed Rest as Residency. The luxury renovated farmhouse, 2.5 hours from New York City, welcomed its first guests in June 2022 and funds the program through a tiered pricing model.

While the movement for rest is led by marginalized communities, in an age of hyperproductivity, its message has resonance for anyone who could benefit from honing their rest ethic. As Hersey notes in her book, "To hear the simple and bold proclamation, 'You are doing too much. You can rest. You can just be. You can be,' is revolutionary. To believe it and continue to dream up ways to feel and find rest, care, and healing is liberation."

WHY IT'S INTERESTING

The reinterpretation of rest as a tool of resistance adds another layer of nuance to the concept of holistic wellness. Brands can promote permission to rest, helping to shape a healthy pivot away from grind culture.

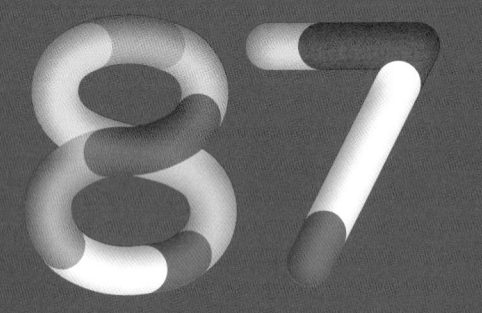

MENOPAUSE RETREATS

From HRT education to nutritional advice, retreats designed specifically for the menopause journey are on the rise.

Amilla Maldives debuted its Menopause Retreat in summer 2022. The five-day program includes talks on balancing hormones, breathwork, and tree-hugging therapy. Addressing the potential challenges of this natural lifestage, Amilla's women-only retreat aims to "educate, empower, and inspire new ways of living."

Italian wellness resort Preidlhof in South Tyrol offers a six-day menopause sanctuary that blends medical health sessions with ancient healing, and in Australia, the Great Ocean Road Resort has lined up five menopause retreats throughout 2023.

Women attending menopause-specific retreats have benefited from its targeted package. "You have given me my spark back," "thank you for helping me sleep," and "I feel alive again" are some of the comments received by UK-based Menoheaven from visitors who attended its three-day retreat. Situated by the sea in Sussex, Menoheaven started in 2017 in response to a lack of attention for people navigating the stages before and during the menopause. "It didn't exist in the United Kingdom at this time," Tania Smith, cofounder of Menoheaven, tells Wunderman Thompson Intelligence. "Our retreats give women the chance to put themselves first and to take a literal 'pause,' so they can focus on themselves, learn from experts, share and hear other experiences, and reflect on the changes—if any—they need to make in their lives."

Menoheaven offers one-on-one sessions that cover everything from hormone replacement therapy to spiritual healing. "Nurturing the mental, spiritual, and physical at challenging times is a winning combination, and we've found it has worked well with women in perimenopause and menopause," says Smith. Since opening, Menoheaven has begun welcoming more women in perimenopause, preparing for the next stage.

WHY IT'S INTERESTING

The global menopause market is expected to reach $24.4 billion by 2030, according to a November 2022 study by Grand View Research. Hotels and resorts are responding by expanding their services to cater for this underserved life stage.

Wait, Pause! Women's Retreat

Above: Amilla Maldives Menopause Retreat
Right: Menoheaven

Across the United States, United Kingdom, and China, 56% of people report feeling mentally healthier thanks to technology, according to research from Wunderman Thompson Intelligence, and 81% say they switch on digitally to unwind.

Alo yoga unveiled an immersive yoga and meditation experience on Roblox in February 2022 to promote wellbeing. The virtual Alo Sanctuary, designed as "a place of retreat and healing," includes guided meditations, daily on-demand yoga, and a sound-bath inspired soundtrack.

"We've heard many powerful stories about how Roblox has served as a healing platform and a central lifeline for our community members' wellbeing," said Christina Wootton, VP of global brand partnerships at Roblox. "Now our community has a space to practice mindfulness and learn about the importance of meditation directly from top wellness experts."

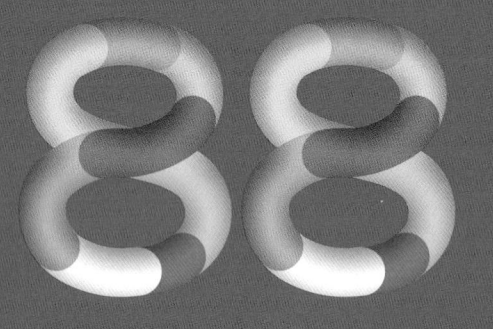

88
META-MINDFULNESS

The metaverse is getting mindful to help humans and avatars alike unwind.

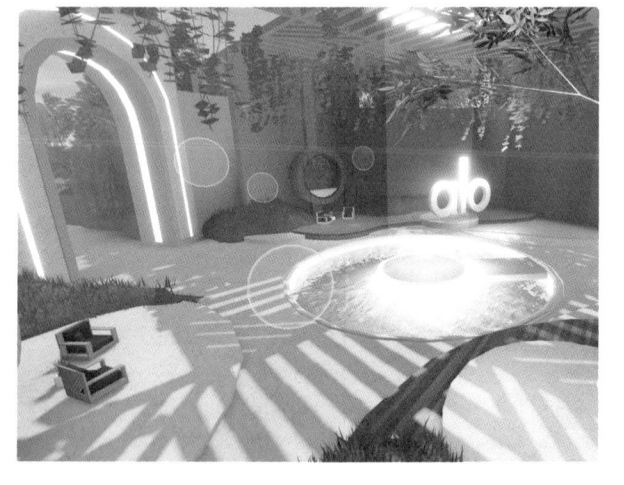

Tripp is also working to create a mindful metaverse. It leverages virtual reality technology to "hack mindfulness" and "hack other moods to give you more agency over how you feel," Tripp CEO and cofounder Nanea Reeves tells Wunderman Thompson Intelligence. In June 2022, the company raised over $11 million to boost its virtual meditation offerings, with investments from Amazon, Qualcomm, and Niantic.

WHY IT'S INTERESTING

The metaverse and mindfulness aren't mutually exclusive. People are bringing their health and wellbeing habits with them into the metaverse, and are looking for brands to help them cultivate their metamindfulness practices.

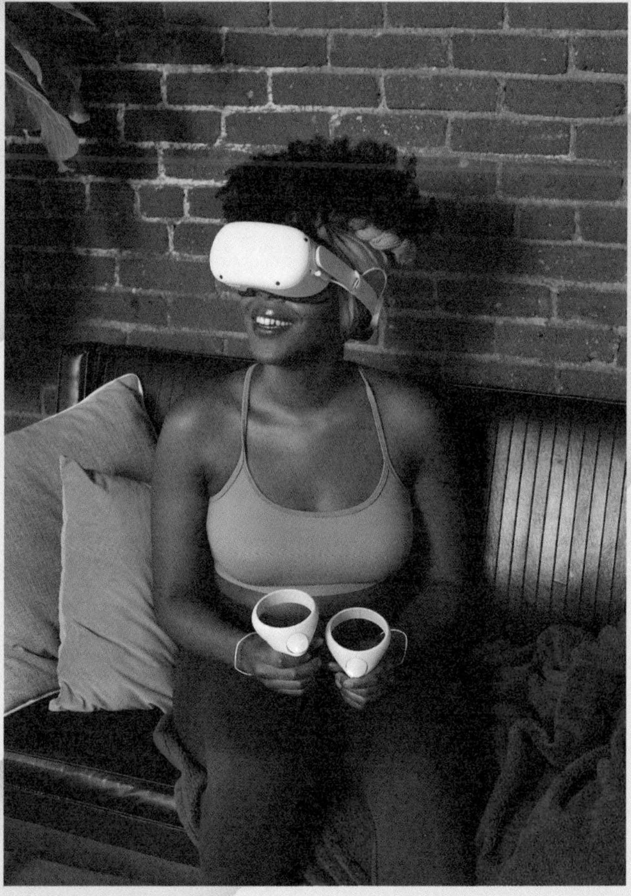

Left: Alo Sanctuary, Alo yoga
Right: Tripp

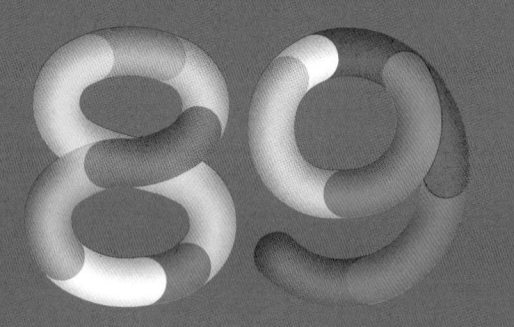

89

CULTURAL PRESCRIPTIONS

Physicians are prescribing cultural visits to museums, galleries, and other venues to help patients manage their mental wellbeing.

A growing body of research underlines the therapeutic value of culture for patients with mental health conditions and chronic pain.

In Brussels, the Brugmann University Hospital has launched a six-month pilot project that allows doctors to prescribe free trips to one of five participating cultural institutions for patients with depression, anxiety, and other mental health conditions. Patients might explore the city's historic sewer system, or browse costumes created for the city's cheeky Mannekin Pis statue at the dedicated GardeRobe museum.

The aim, as Dr Johan Newell, psychiatrist at Brugmann University Hospital, tells Wunderman Thompson Intelligence, is to help patients reconnect with the world. "Visiting art is a gateway for connecting with our inner emotional world. It helps us to slow down and be present in the moment. It's a way to help people suffering from mental disorders to find a meaningful purpose to go outside and reclaim a place in active society."

The Massachusetts-based CultureRx program funded by the Mass Cultural Council also promotes patient engagement with arts, science, and culture. In June 2022, the initiative reported positive results from a three-year pilot, and now hopes to expand its provider partnerships in 2023. The Greek Ministry of Culture is funding a program that supports arts institutions like the National Museum of Contemporary Art and the Athens State Orchestra to develop innovative cultural prescription services for citizens.

WHY IT'S INTERESTING

The borders of wellness continue to expand and blur as people develop a deeper understanding of the health value of cultural activities. Culture is now more than mere leisure, offering moments of restorative wellness and a way to engage meaningfully with the world. Just what the doctor ordered.

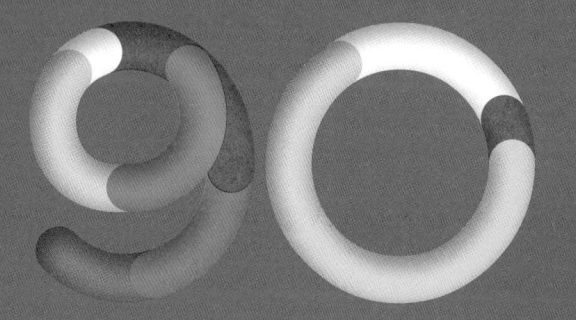

90

NUTRITIONAL BODYCARE

The largest organ of the body—the skin—is getting a complete nutritional boost.

+WUNDERMAN THOMPSON Iota beauty

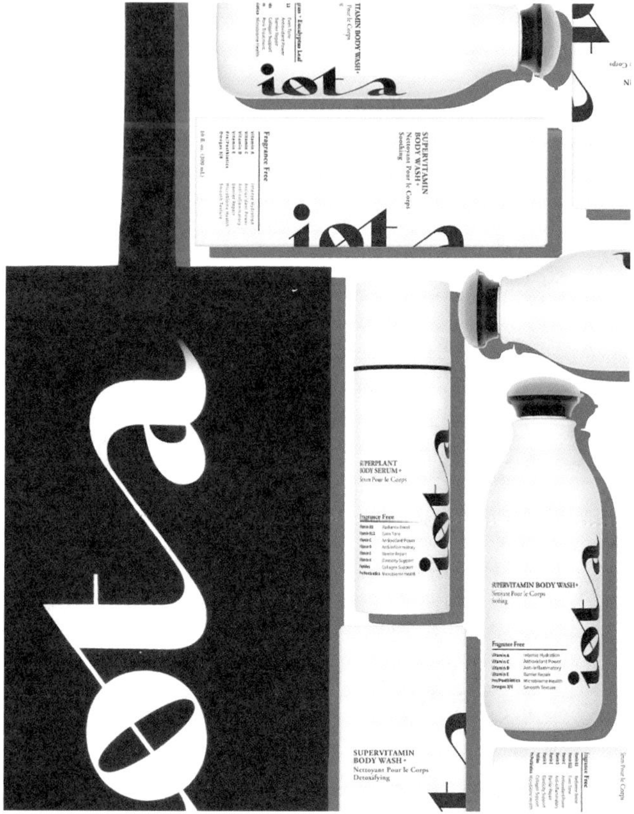

"Much like the way we approach our diet in diversifying our plate with nutrients, we should take a similar, balanced approach to skincare."

Monique Meneses,
cofounder, Iota

"Skin health *is* health," Monique Meneses, cofounder of Iota, tells Wunderman Thompson Intelligence. "Just like our gut microbiome, our skin microbiome also impacts the whole body." New-York based Iota launched at the end of September 2022 as "the first nutritional bodycare brand" focusing on the skin from the neck down. Iota products include the Supervitamin Body Wash+ and Superplant Body Serum+, which combines 24 essential nutrients to boost skin health with microbiome balancing properties. Meneses likens Iota's offering to a nutritious meal for our skin. "Much like the way we approach our diet in diversifying our plate with nutrients, we should take a similar, balanced approach to skincare."

According to the American Academy of Dermatology, the most common skin condition is acne, which affects up to 50 million Americans yearly. One in 10 people develop atopic dermatitis in their lifetime, and 16 million Americans are affected by rosacea. Iota is dedicated to raising awareness around skin health and tackling skin concerns with its products. "Recent studies have linked poor skin health with broader risks like inflammatory and autoimmune diseases, heart health, and allergies," explains Meneses. "Iota was crafted specifically with comprehensive health in mind."

Advanced Nutrition Programme also focuses on optimizing skin health, with supplements that target specific skin concerns. The brand's Skin Vitality multivitamin contains 28 nutrients to nourish the skin.

WHY IT'S INTERESTING
The year of bodycare has arrived. Facial skincare offerings are already abundant, and now brands are now homing in on skin from the neck down to support overall health.

91

WORK

100

91

INCLUSIVE-PRENEURS

Entrepreneurs from underserved communities are innovating for themselves.

WUNDERMAN THOMPSON

Fay Reid, founder of 9 to 5 Menopause

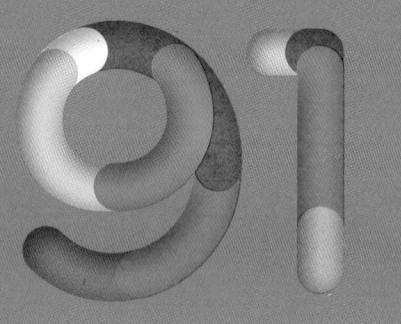

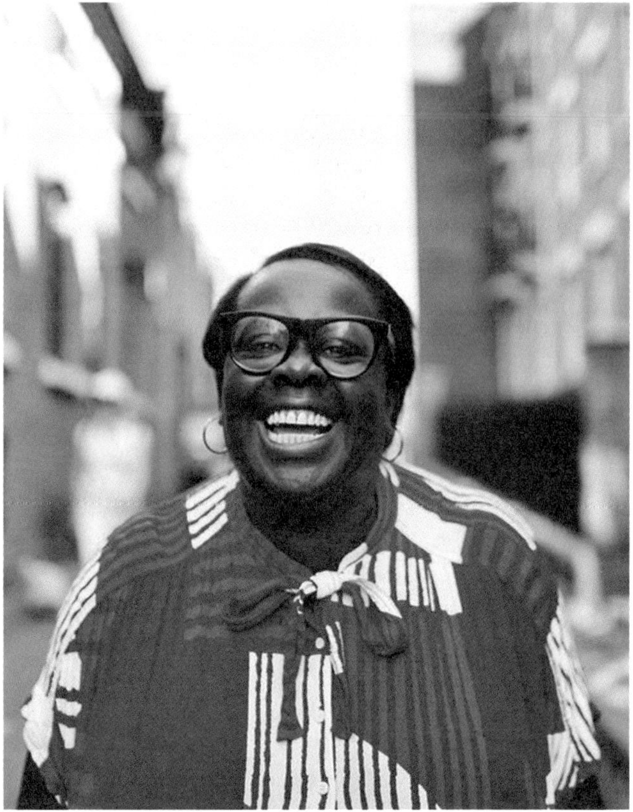

Underserved communities are driving a wave of inclusive entrepreneurship, devising products and services that address the unmet needs of their communities.

Frustrated by the logistical challenges disabled fans face when attending sporting events, Victor Ocando founded Adapt The Game to normalize spectator enjoyment for all. Ocando, who was born with cerebral palsy that limits his mobility and speech, is using his US-based startup to develop an app that will allow users from the disabled community to browse specified seat accessibility details and buy suitable tickets. Its ultimate aim is to improve the game-day experience for disabled sports supporters, from football to soccer and baseball.

Struck by a lack of provision, Londoner Fay Reid launched her 9 to 5 Menopause project to offer working women of all ethnicities education, tips, and resources on the menopause. "I started having symptoms at the age of 46 but the people who were talking about menopause were white, affluent women who didn't have a job," Reid tells Wunderman Thompson Intelligence. "They recommended private clinics, nutritionists, and yoga. That is not my life, I've got a job to go to. So I started 9 to 5 Menopause, because there were no women in the workplace talking about menopause." Reid started 9 to 5 Menopause as a social media platform to share her personal experiences, and now works closely with British businesses, educating them on better policy and provision.

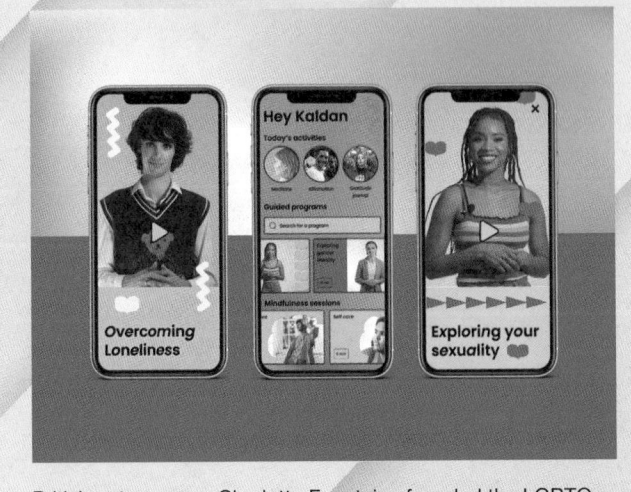

British entrepreneur Charlotte Fountaine founded the LGBTQ+ therapy app Kalda after growing tired of the one-size-fits-all approach to mental wellbeing. For people in the LGBTQ+ community, who often suffer disproportionately, exploring mental health issues in a heteronormative environment can be oppressive. Kalda, which launched in 2022, is a self-guided tool specifically designed by LGBTQ+ therapists, offering weekly group therapy and daily peer-to-peer support.

WHY IT'S INTERESTING

Inclusivepreneurs are shaping a new generation of businesses, designing with and for the unmet needs of their own communities. Companies and brands can offer support by collaborating with them, adding them to supplier rosters, or investing in their businesses.

VIRTUAL CEOS

**Will the boardroom of the future be
filled with virtual leaders?**

Artificial intelligence (AI) is now a vital tool for companies as they seek
to improve efficiency and automate tasks that technology can do better, quicker, and more cheaply than humans. Traditionally this AI operates
in the background, hidden from public view, but forward-thinking companies are starting to highlight its potential by giving virtual employees plum roles within leadership teams.

Chinese gaming company NetDragon Websoft, which operates multiplayer online games and apps, has appointed an AI-powered virtual humanoid robot called Ms Tang Yu as the CEO of its subsidiary company, Fujian NetDragon Websoft. Seen as a milestone as NetDragon establishes itself as a metaverse organization, the move aims to pioneer AI's ability to transform corporate management. The virtual CEO will be tasked with streamlining the company's processes, enhancing the quality of its outputs, and improving the speed of execution. Tang Yu will also operate as a real-time data hub and analytical tool to support daily decision-making and risk management operations.

Similarly, Web3-focused luxury rum brand Dictador has unveiled a "human-like robot, incorporating AI" called Mika as its CEO. The robot, created by Hanson Robotics, will serve as a board member and be responsible for running the brand's Arthouse Spirits DAO (decentralized autonomous organization) project, as well as communicating with the DAO community

Virtual leadership "will change the world as we know it, forever."

Marek Szoldrowski, president, Dictador Europe

on Dictador's behalf. Having previously launched rum NFTs and created the DAO community, the brand sees this as the logical next step as it embraces the possibilities of technology. President of Dictador Europe Marek Szoldrowski said the innovation "will change the world as we know it, forever."

WHY IT'S INTERESTING

We first tracked the rise of the digital workforce in 2018, when companies were introducing avatar spokespeople or concierges to balance the human and digital touch, enhancing both the working environment and the customer experience. As the metaverse workforce continues to take shape, how will it impact leadership and the C-suite?

93

REWIREMENT

Retirement is out. Rewirement is in.

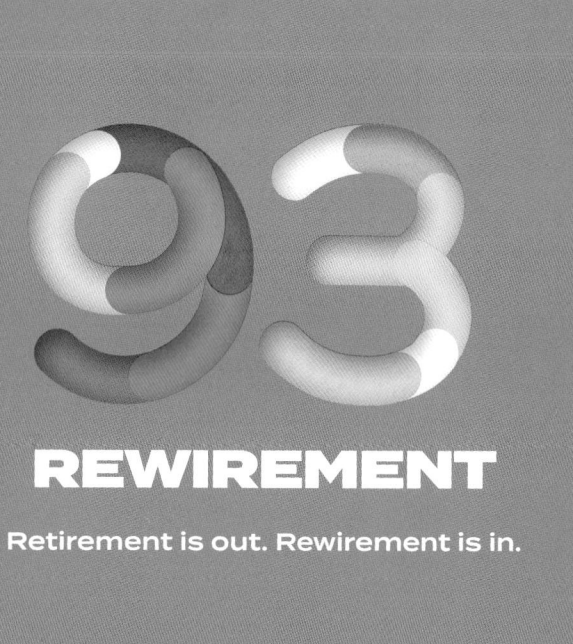

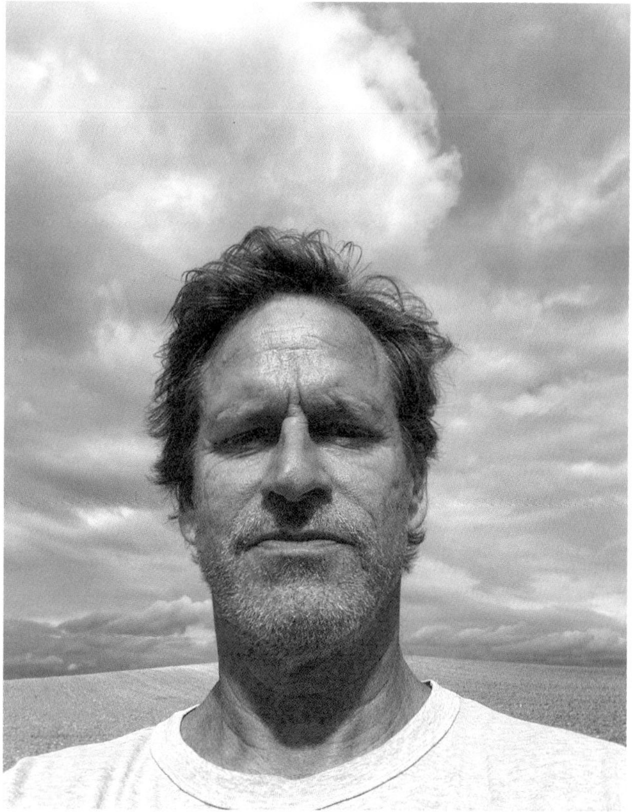

WUNDERMAN THOMPSON Chris Welsch

In August 2022, tennis superstar Serena Williams declared she was stepping away from the sport to focus on her family and other business ventures.

"I have never liked the word retirement. It doesn't feel like a modern word to me," Williams told *Vogue* in a cover story about her motivations. "Maybe the best word to describe what I'm up to is evolution. I'm here to tell you that I'm evolving away from tennis, toward other things that are important to me."

Williams isn't the only one shunning traditional retirement. For a few years now, the word "rewirement" has been used by financial planners who work with those looking to retire. Now it's becoming a more expansive term that encompasses parts of people's lives beyond the financial.

"I heard the term rewirement from a friend and of course I pounced on it, because retirement just sounds so stodgy," Jackie Crosby, who retired in 2021 after an illustrious career as a reporter for the *Minneapolis Star Tribune*, tells Wunderman Thompson Intelligence. The two-time Pulitzer winner now splits her time playing bass guitar in three bands, including one called Chemistry Set. She's relishing the freedom of being her own boss for the first time in decades, and spending time with people she cares about instead of constantly rushing back for a newspaper deadline.

In France, Chris Welsch, a semi-retired photographer and editor, uprooted his life in Paris to move to a countryside home in Burgundy. COVID-19 was one galvanizing factor. "I don't want to spend the rest of my life in a small Paris apartment and grow old

in a place where I can't see a tree out the window," he tells Wunderman Thompson Intelligence. "Now I hope to get more and more involved in the community here in Burgundy where I live."

Nor does rewiring mean winding down work. Welsch recently took a full-time job with Microsoft Communications in Europe, traveling around the continent to write about the impact of technology on people and the planet.

WHY IT'S INTERESTING
Post-pandemic, life and work are taking on a whole new meaning, particularly in later decades. Rewirees are reassessing their priorities, rediscovering themselves, and dedicating time to their passions and their families.

94
EQUITY BENEFITS

Inclusive companies are going beyond traditional benefits to improve the lives of all their employees, especially those who have been traditionally marginalized.

Employers who want to truly lead when it comes to diversity, equity, and inclusion are looking beyond one-size-fits-all benefits, aspiring to understand and improve the lives of their employees from marginalized backgrounds. By acknowledging and addressing existing disadvantages, employers are working to reach a more equal and inclusive workplace for all.

Recognizing the specific healthcare needs of diverse groups is one way companies are seeking to close the equity gap. In China, Alibaba benefits include healthcare checkups for employees and their children, and even employees' parents— an acknowledgment of the high medical costs associated with caring for ageing family members.

In Argentina, ecommerce company Mercado Libre is helping to fund gender reassignment surgeries for trans workers. PayPal's free UK menopause scheme is separate from its health insurance program, allowing more employees to participate without having to pay for insurance. In the United States, companies including Amazon, Bank of America, and BuzzFeed are helping their employees with reproductive health by creating programs to pay out-of-state travel costs for abortions.

Aiming to improve health outcomes and address racial inequality in maternal care, Walmart announced it would begin offering doula support for its associates in several states in June 2022. After launching the initiative in Georgia, Walmart

stated it chose to extend coverage to Louisiana, Indiana, and Illinois because of the potential for instant impact for employees living there. The company said that in Louisiana, the mortality rate is five times higher for Black mothers than it is for white mothers and that in Indiana, 33 counties don't have OB-GYN services. Coming from local communities themselves, doulas have been shown to positively impact the outcome of pregnancies, in both the health of the mother and child, as they bring a level of cultural understanding that can be lacking in traditional medical settings.

WHY IT'S INTERESTING

By considering the unique needs of those from traditionally marginalized backgrounds, companies are reflecting the broadening definition of health and wellbeing, as well as further humanizing the workplace.

94

Walmart announced it would begin offering doula support for its associates in several states in June 2022.

THE FIVE-STAR OFFICE

In a sustained bid to draw employees back to the office, businesses are adopting ideas from the hospitality sector.

WUNDERMAN THOMPSON   Amazon HQ2

A 25-meter swimming pool, a 200-meter rooftop running trail, and a massage room are just a few of the perks reminiscent of upscale hotel stays at Google's London Kings Cross development. The company's ambitious headquarters construction, nicknamed "the landscraper" due to its colossal square footage, is expected to benefit both Googlers and locals, who will have access to some of the facilities too. Completion is set for 2024.

Tech giant Amazon is currently developing its second headquarters (HQ2) in Virginia, in the United States. The spiral-shaped office, called The Helix, will include an outdoor hiking trail winding up and around the exterior architecture, which will be swathed in plants gathered from the local Blue Ridge Mountains. For Amazon's office workers, immersion in nature extends beyond the exterior, with a forest plaza and cascading water feature taking biophilic design to the extreme.

At London agency Ask Us For Ideas, a dimly lit subterranean space is a world away from the fluorescent-lit offices workers have become accustomed to. "The mood is calmer, moodier, and more introspective," Hugh Scott Moncrieff, director of Cake Architecture, the studio behind the 2022 design, tells Wunderman Thompson Intelligence. Hardwood flooring, shag rugs, and mid-century armchairs adorn the space, playing on the constraints of what an office can be and encouraging the use of the space for events beyond work. "They host one-on-one sessions there, breathing and yoga classes, as well as evening lectures and cocktail parties," says Moncrieff.

World-class service is also being brought into the corporate environment. L'Oréal's second US headquarters, opened in Los Angeles in August 2022, includes a concierge service for employees. At a charge of $5 per hour, the office concierge runs errands, from filling up workers' gas tanks to collecting their laundry. The service gives workers relief from everyday chores, freeing up their time and adding an extra perk to working from the office.

WHY IT'S INTERESTING
The next generation of workspaces gets a five-star upgrade, catering to a class of workers that now values the comforts of working from home. For businesses, the race is on to make the office more inviting.

+ WUNDERMAN THOMPSON   The Soho office of Ask Us For Ideas

The Soho office of Ask Us For Ideas

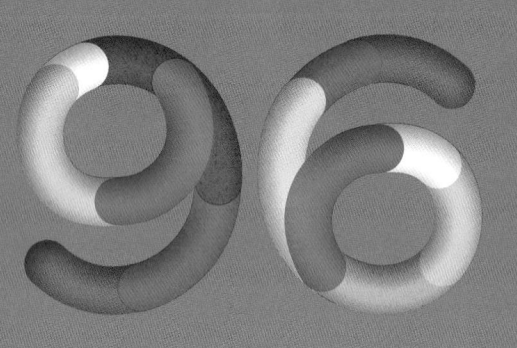

NON-LINEAR WORK

Asynchronous work—keeping different hours to colleagues—is here to stay.

During the pandemic, much was said about how being constantly connected led to burnout for many remote workers, who found it difficult to switch off. But it also showed that asynchronous work can produce results that are as good, and even better, than the traditional nine-to-five workday.

Parents of young children could zip out for a basketball match or cook a meal in between working, and maybe do emails after dinner. Other remote workers could fit in a run or a yoga class in the time it usually took them to commute to work.

"Asynchronous work allows people to save commuting time, get admin tasks done during low productivity hours, fit in more exercise, and save money having homecooked meals," Laura Giurge, assistant professor of behavioral science at the London School of Economics and Political Science, told the BBC.

Now a workforce used to this flexibility is demanding it even after the pandemic. Employee surveys are finding many want a hybrid work option, with a combination of a few days a week in the office interspersed with a few at home.

Asynchronous work can produce results that are as good, and even better, than the traditional nine-to-five workday.

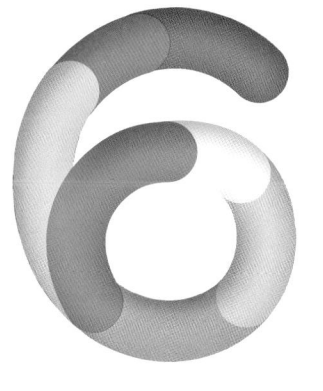

A slew of asynchronous work tools and platforms is flooding the market. Slack and Microsoft have incorporated short video clip messages in their products following the example of startup Loom—which makes it easier to send videos through email. Microsoft, whose Teams platform already allows remote teams to work collaboratively, is launching a beta version of Places, an app that allows tracking of hybrid teams.

Another app, Flown, offers "digital body doubling," which mimics anything from another person being present to being part of a "flock" of remote workers—all so that remote workers stay on task and accountable.

WHY IT'S IMPORTANT
Nonlinear work is here to stay and employers and employees are both getting used to it, drawing on new tech platforms and apps to overcome the downsides while enhancing the benefits.

Amid a looming financial crisis and a volatile stock market, many former workers are coming out of retirement and heading back to the office. The number of British people aged 65 or over entering the workforce rose by 173,000 in the first quarter of 2022, according to figures from the UK's Centre for Ageing Better. And a May 2022 report from AARP, citing data from Indeed, found that 1.7 million Americans who retired a year earlier had returned to the workforce.

Kim Chaplain, a specialist adviser for work at the UK's Centre for Ageing Better, told the *Guardian* that the organization "suspects the rising cost of living is playing a role." The *Guardian* profiled Bernadette Hempstead of Suffolk, England, who receives a small private pension and a state pension as a retired human resource employee. However, those two sources of income were not enough to cover her living expenses. "As things get more expensive, it became impossible," said Hempstead.

Others are returning in search of social interaction. "We have a real serious issue in this country of senior loneliness and depression. The pandemic really exacerbated that," Andrew Meadows, senior vice president at Ubiquity Retirement + Savings, told AARP. "Many seniors were forced to stay at home, and now they are thinking of entering the workforce again for social interactions."

WHY IT'S INTERESTING

Older generations are redefining traditional later-in-life stages, eschewing retirement in favor of employment—whether out of economic necessity or in search of social engagement.

97

UNRETIREMENT

A generation of retirees are heading back to work in search of social interaction and financial stability.

98

SUPER-COMMUTERS

A new breed of commuter is emerging—one who spends the week working in the city and the weekends at home in the suburbs.

Out-of-city commuters are traveling back into town as in-office mandates commence, and hotels are offering specialized deals to cater to these mid-week crowds.

Supercommuters—a term coined by the *New York Times*—are paying for accommodation deals to keep their city commutes comfortable while maintaining their suburban lifestyle.

In the United Kingdom, the Accor Group, whose hotels include the Savoy and the Pullman London St Pancras, has developed a Commute and Stay promotion. It offers two discounted midweek nights, a flexible cancellation policy, and scheduling

assistance for work and client gatherings.

Marriott launched a Day Pass program in early 2022, with hotels offering end-of-day check-out options and coworking spaces. The program, which is currently dialed back, offered flights across Europe and the United Kingdom from the adjacent airport to aid commuters who have moved away from the city but need to return regularly for work.

The Hoxton in Chicago offers a Work Stay Play package for commuters who subscribe to a monthly flat rate. Membership includes access to the hotel's coworking space, perks for work and pleasure, and one stay per month at any location. The general manager encourages visitors "to take full advantage of those workcations."

In 2022, several major companies mandated a return to the office for their employees. In November, Elon Musk made clear he wanted Twitter staff back in the office for at least 40 hours a week. Apple and Google implemented policies requiring workers to return for at least one to three days a week beginning in April, Meta required employees to return to the office in March, and Microsoft will ask employees to return to a hybrid model that would require employees to return to part-time in-person work.

WHY IT'S INTERESTING

As work conditions continue to evolve, supercommuters are embracing long-term commutes and subscribed hotel stays in order to maintain a comfortable distance from city life while showing up for in-office duties.

WUNDERMAN
THOMPSON   The Savoy

WORKPLACE WELLNESS

Companies are going beyond generic wellness programs to attract and retain talent.

Employers are thinking more creatively about workplace wellness programs as the need to prioritize employee mental health rises up the agenda. According to the World Health Organization, 12 billion working days are lost each year due to employee depression and anxiety, at a cost of $1 trillion to the global economy. Economic turmoil and a growing skills gap mean companies around the world are having to work harder to take care of their staff physically and mentally.

While many companies now offer off-the-shelf mental wellbeing programs, others are looking to actual time off as a solution. Hoping to prevent burnout, companies such as PwC, LinkedIn, and WPP shut their offices for company-wide mental health days, offering employees one or two days off. In September 2022, Indian ecommerce platform Meesho went even further, announcing a whopping 11-day break for its employees for the second consecutive year.

Stress caused by the cost-of-living crisis adds more pressure on employee mental wellbeing. According to 2022 research from MetLife UK, 64% of workers feel that their financial situation has made them stressed, anxious, or depressed and this can lead to a loss of productivity. "We used to think about financial wellbeing and wellbeing separately but now we have to see it more holistically," Steve Watson, head of proposition at UK-based workplace savings provider Cushon, told the *Financial Times*.

Honest Burgers, a UK-based fast casual restaurant chain, is offering employees access to Wagestream, a financial wellbeing app that includes access to financial advisors. The initiative was shortlisted for Best Financial Wellbeing Strategy for a Small Employer at the Employee Benefits Awards 2022. A recent RAND Europe study found that mental health improved for those taking up financial literacy employer schemes like this.

WHY IT'S INTERESTING

According to research by Mercer Marsh Benefits, the most valuable benefits businesses can give focus on improving employee mental health. With basic mental wellbeing initiatives becoming a standard expectation, employers are rewriting the rule book to attract and retain staff.

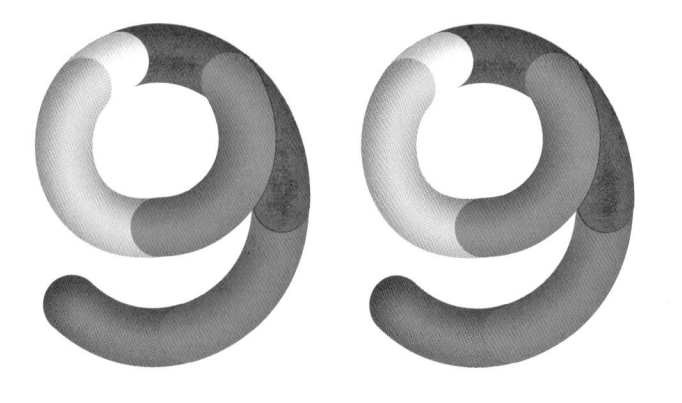

"We used to think about financial wellbeing and wellbeing separately but now we have to see it more holistically."

Steve Watson, head of proposition, Cushon

GENERATION FLEX

Employee expectations are rising. Despite economic woes, could the balance of power be tipping in their favor?

"The war for talent is over. Talent won." So said Tim Ryan, US chair and senior partner of the global consulting firm PwC, speaking at the CNBC Work Summit in October 2022. Employees, said Ryan, are now insisting on choice and flexibility in how they get work done.

Chris Hyams, CEO of Indeed, also notes the rise of a more demanding worker. In an August 2022 interview with *Fortune*, Hyams pointed to "a powerful new demand for work-life balance" as a sign that the workplace social contract is changing. Underlining this shift, workers are flexing their muscles.

Case in point is the back-to-the-office push, which is proving to be an ongoing negotiation. *Financial Times* analysis of Google phone-tracking data suggests that, as at mid-October 2022, trips to workplaces in the world's seven largest economies are all tracking well below pre-pandemic levels.

In the United States, despite reported declines in job quit rates, McKinsey cited evidence that senior women are switching jobs at the highest rates ever seen, outpacing their male counterparts. Its "Women in the Workplace 2022" report in partnership with Leanin.Org finds that women are walking away to better opportunities.

Finally, as industrial unrest rages in many countries, we are seeing a return to unionization, most notably at US companies such as Apple, Amazon, Chipotle, and Starbucks. While some companies push back, others see value in listening. Microsoft

"The war for talent is over. Talent won."

Tim Ryan, US chair and senior partner, PwC

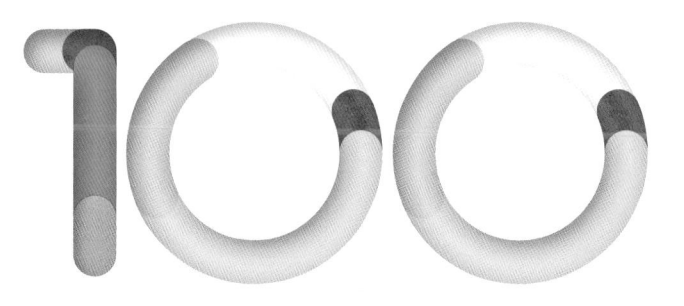

announced in June 2022 that it would formally recognize the right of workers to form and join a union.

While some economists predict that the power pendulum will swing back to employers as soon as recession bites, PwC's Ryan respectfully disagrees: "Anyone who thinks the power dynamic is going to go back, honestly and humbly, I think they are making a mistake."

WHY IT'S INTERESTING

As economies get tighter, companies should not be complacent when it comes to talent. Progressive companies will listen to their workforce's concerns, focusing on giving their employees the sense of control and flexibility they seek.

ABOUT WUNDERMAN THOMPSON INTELLIGENCE

Wunderman Thompson Intelligence is Wunderman Thompson's futurism, research and innovation unit. It charts emerging and future global trends, consumer change, and innovation patterns—translating these into insight for brands. It offers a suite of consultancy services, including bespoke research, presentations, co-branded reports and workshops. It is also active in innovation, partnering with brands to activate future trends within their framework and execute new products and concepts. The division is led by Emma Chiu and Marie Stafford, Global Directors of Wunderman Thompson Intelligence.

For more information visit:

wundermanthompson.com/expertise/intelligence

About The Future 100

Wunderman Thompson Intelligence's annual forecast presents a snapshot of the year ahead and identifies the most compelling trends to keep on the radar. The report charts 100 trends across 10 sectors, spanning culture, tech and innovation, travel and hospitality, brands and marketing, food and drink, beauty, retail and commerce, luxury, health, and work.

CONTACT

Emma Chiu
emma.chiu@wundermanthompson.com

Marie Stafford
marie.stafford@wundermanthompson.com

Wunderman Thompson Taipei
wt.taipei@wundermanthompson.com

COVER

Planet City. Courtesy of Liam Young

FONTS USED

Termina; Helvetica Neue (TT)

WUNDERMAN
THOMPSON